T0418447

The Poesis of Peace

Exploring the relations between the concepts of peace and violence with aesthetics, nature, the body, and environmental issues, *The Poesis of Peace* applies a multi-disciplinary approach to case studies in both Western and non-Western contexts including Islam, Chinese philosophy, Buddhist and Hindu traditions. Established and renowned theologians and philosophers, such as Kevin Hart, Eduardo Mendieta, and Clemens Sedmak, as well as upcoming and talented young academics look at peace and non-violence through the lens of recent scholarly advances on the subject achieved in the fields of theology, philosophy, political theory, and environmentalism.

Klaus-Gerd Giesen is Professor of Political Science at the Université d'Auvergne in Clermont-Ferrand, France. He specializes in international relations and political philosophy. More information can be found on his website: www.giesen.fr.

Carool Kersten is Senior Lecturer in the Study of Islam and the Muslim World at King's College London, UK. He is the author and editor of several books on contemporary Islam, including *Islam in Indonesia: The Contest for Society, Ideas and Values* (2015), *Alternative Islamic Discourses and Religious Authority* (2013), *Demystifying the Caliphate* (2013), and *Cosmopolitans and Heretics* (2011).

Lenart Škof is Professor of Philosophy and Head of the Institute for Philosophical Studies at the Science and Research Centre Koper, Slovenia, and Professor at Alma Mater Europaea, Maribor, Slovenia. He is also Visiting Professor of Religion at the Faculty of Theology, University of Ljubljana, Slovenia. He recently co-edited *Breathing with Luce Irigaray* (2013) and is an author of several books, among them *Pragmatist Variations on Ethical and Intercultural Life* (2012) and *Breath of Proximity: Intersubjectivity, Ethics and Peace* (2015). He is President of the Slovenian Society for Comparative Religion. More information can be found at: http://upr-si.academia.edu/LenartŠkof.

The Poesis of Peace

Narratives, Cultures, and Philosophies

**Edited by Klaus-Gerd Giesen,
Carool Kersten, and Lenart Škof**

Routledge
Taylor & Francis Group

LONDON AND NEW YORK

First published 2017
by Routledge
2 Park Square, Milton Park, Abingdon, Oxon OX14 4RN

and by Routledge
711 Third Avenue, New York, NY 10017

Routledge is an imprint of the Taylor & Francis Group, an informa business

British Library Cataloguing-in-Publication Data
A catalogue record for this book is available from the British Library

Library of Congress Cataloging-in-Publication Data
A catalog record for this title has been requested

ISBN: 978-1-4724-7022-5 (hbk)
ISBN: 978-1-315-55461-7 (ebk)

Typeset in Times New Roman PS
by diacriTech, Chennai

Contents

Contributors

Petri Berndtson is a PhD student in philosophy at University of Jyväskylä, Finland. His main research interests and expertise lie in the experiential phenomenon of breathing, phenomenology (especially Merleau-Ponty), embodiment, the elemental poetics of air (Bachelard), and contemplative studies. Berndtson used to be a full-time lecturer of philosophy at Lahti University of Applied Sciences, Finland. He has also invented a method called Philosophical Breathwork which is a philosophico-experiential way of working with breathing. More information can be found at his websites: www.philosophicalbreathwork.com and jyu. academia.edu/PetriBerndtson.

Pauline von Bonsdorff has been Professor of Art Education at the University of Jyväskylä, Finland, since 2002. She has published widely on environmental aesthetics, theory and philosophy of art (especially architecture), phenomenological aesthetics, art education, and the aesthetics of childhood.

Victor Forte, MS, PhD, is an Associate Professor of Religious Studies and Director of Asian Studies at Albright College in Reading, PA, USA. He received an MS in Environmental Science from Drexel University, and a PhD in Religion from Temple University in Philadelphia, PA. Dr Forte teaches courses on Buddhist studies, Asian religions, Asian film and culture, and religion and the environment. His main research interests are in Buddhist ethics, comparative philosophy, and interreligious dialogue, and he has published articles in these fields, including, 'Early Buddhist Inclusion of Intentionality in the Laws of Causation', 'The Ethics of Attainment: The Meaning of the Ethical in Dōgen and Derrida', 'Finding Peace in the Simile of the Saw', and 'Reflections on the Ethical Meaning of Shinran's True Entrusting'.

Klaus-Gerd Giesen is Professor of Political Science at the Université d'Auvergne in Clermont-Ferrand, France. He specializes in international relations and political philosophy. More information can be found at his website: www.giesen.fr.

Owen Gurrey is currently studying for a PhD in Literature at the University of Sheffield. His interests include post-structuralism and psychoanalysis, the history of language philosophy, contemporary British and European poetry, and theories of spectatorship and observation – specifically the evolution of cinema and photography and its effects on the nature of narrative. His PhD is a study of a number of contemporary 'northern' British poets and concerns the disinheritance of post-industrialism and material culture in the creation of a new poetic register that is in one sense neo-Romantic yet concerned with eco-criticism and the aesthetics of the environment. Gurrey also works as a musician and recording artist. He lives in York, UK.

Kevin Hart holds the Edwin B. Kyle Chair of Christian Thought in the Department of Religious Studies at the University of Virginia, where he also holds professorships in the Department of English and the Department of French. His recent scholarly works include an edition of Jean-Luc Marion's *The Essential Writings* (2013), *Kingdoms of God* (2014), and *Poetry and Revelation* (2017). His most recent collections of poetry are *Morning Knowledge* (2011) and *Wild Track: New and Selected Poems* (2015). He is currently completing two new scholarly books, *Contemplation* and *Blanchot Encore*, and has completed a new book of poems, *Barefoot*.

Paul Haught is Vice President for Academics and Student Life at Christian Brothers University in Memphis, Tennessee. His main area of research is environmental ethics, primarily from within a virtue theoretical framework. His publications have also addressed environmental justice, narrative, and place.

Emily A. Holmes is Associate Professor in the Department of Religion and Philosophy at Christian Brothers University in Memphis, TN. She is the author of *Flesh Made Word: Medieval Women Mystics, Writing, and the Incarnation* (2013) and the co-editor of *Women, Writing, Theology: Transforming a Tradition of Exclusion* (2011) and *Breathing with Luce Irigaray* (2013). Her teaching and research interests include women's writing practices, feminist theology, the spirituality and ethics of eating, and the theology of food.

Carool Kersten is Senior Lecturer in the Study of Islam and the Muslim World at King's College London, UK. He is the author and editor of several books on contemporary Islam, including *Islam in Indonesia: The Contest for Society, Ideas and Values* (2015), *Alternative Islamic Discourses and Religious Authority* (2013), *Demystifying the Caliphate* (2013), and *Cosmopolitans and Heretics* (2011).

Tina Košir is a PhD candidate in Philosophy at the Faculty of Arts, University of Ljubljana, Slovenia. Her PhD research consists of examining correspondences between ontology and aesthetics in non-dual Kashmir Śaivism, especially in the works of Utpaladeva and Abhinavagupta. Her methodological approach is not only to analyse the concepts and ideas in their historical context, but also to consider them as valuable perspectives that can and should be consulted in contemporary debates.

Eduardo Mendieta is Professor of Philosophy at Penn State University. He is the author of *The Adventures of Transcendental Philosophy* (2002) and

Global Fragments: Globalizations, Latinamericanisms, and Critical Theory (2007). He is also co-editor with Jonathan VanAntwerpen of *The Power of Religion in the Public Sphere* (2011), with Craig Calhoun and Jonathan VanAntwerpen of *Habermas and Religion* (2013), and with Stuart Elden of *Reading Kant's Geography* (2011). He recently finished a book titled *The Philosophical Animal,* which will be published by SUNY Press in 2016.

Helena Motoh is an Associate Professor at the Faculty of Humanities and Senior Research Associate at the Scientific and Research Centre, University of Primorska, Slovenia. She has completed a two-course study in philosophy-A and Sinology-B at the Faculty of Arts and as a Junior Researcher at the Department of Philosophy, Faculty of Arts. She received her PhD degree in 2006 for her thesis titled 'Reception of the Chinese Philosophy Ideas in the Modern European Philosophy of the 18th Century'. During her doctoral study she was a visiting researcher at the University of Nanjing, China, in 2005. She is the author of a scientific monograph titled *Tickling the Ears and the Chinese Influence: The Reception of Chinese Philosophy Ideas in Modern European Philosophy*, which was published by Založba Sophia in 2007, and co-author of a scientific monograph *Žižek and His Contemporaries*, published by Bloomsbury (2014). Her research results are regularly published in scientific journals and other publications in Slovenia and abroad.

Clemens Sedmak is FD Maurice Professor for Moral Theology and Social Theology at King's College London. He has been Visiting Professor at the Jomo Kenyatta University in Nairobi, Ateneo de Manila University in the Philippines, the University of Notre Dame in Indiana, and the Universidad Iberoamericana in Mexico City. He is married with three children.

Lenart Škof is Professor of Philosophy and Head of the Institute for Philosophical Studies at the Science and Research Centre, Slovenia, and Professor at Alma Mater Europaea, Slovenia. He is also Visiting Professor of Religion at the Faculty of Theology, University of Ljubljana, Slovenia. Lenart Škof has received a KAAD grant (Universität Tübingen), a Fulbright grant (Stanford University, academic host: Richard Rorty) and a Humboldt fellowship for experienced researchers (Max Weber Kolleg, Universität Erfurt, academic host: Hans Joas). His main research interests lie in ethics, new cosmology, comparative religion, intercultural and Indian philosophy (he translated Yajurvedic Upanishads from the Sanskrit), the philosophy of American pragmatism and the philosophy of Luce Irigaray. He recently co-edited *Breathing with Luce Irigaray* (2013) and is an author of several books, among them *Pragmatist Variations on Ethical and Intercultural Life* (2012) and *Breath of Proximity: Intersubjectivity, Ethics and Peace* (2015). He is President of Slovenian Society for Comparative Religion. More information can be found at: http://upr-si.academia.edu/LenartŠkof.

Editors' Introduction

Poesis of Peace: Narratives, Cultures, and Philosophies

Klaus-Gerd Giesen, Carool Kersten, and Lenart Škof

Peace is a far from unequivocal expression. Although one may say that the various meanings of the concept of peace were somehow always present, its links in modern European thinking with war and the natural rights doctrine have several limited the concept's semantic reach: 'peace' became ultimately equivalent to the absence of (inter-state) war. Nowadays, this is not to be taken for granted anymore. The word 'peace' may be applied not only to political or moral issues, but also to culture, gender, environment, education, or social recognition, to mention but a few. The sort of unifying substratum once given by the material background of the concept is now largely considered to be just one among many other conceptualisations of peace.

Too often still, peace studies remain confined to fields like security studies, political theory, and international relations, where they are generally conceived in terms of non-violent conflict resolution or management. Even in those instances where a spiritual dimension is introduced, the immediate goals continue to be defined in political and situationally specific terms. This has been the case with Gandhi's struggle for Indian independence, Martin Luther King's civil rights campaign in the United States, and Desmond Tutu's truth and reconciliation commission which sought to heal the wound of Apartheid in South Africa.

A book on *The Poesis of Peace* cannot and shall not avoid trying to unfold the many more multiple meanings of peace in the present time. At the same time, the complexity of the present state of affairs can only be understood if the different approaches that have led to a more multifarious use of the term 'peace' are properly explained. However, it would be misleading to think that such an inquiry should have the purpose of defining or redefining peace. In our view such a procedure would miss the point, since we assume that its present uses are not arbitrarily fixed, but the outcome of a political and ideological 'struggle for definitions'. Indeed, we believe that what is actually understood by peace represents one of the main categories of the period of transition in which we live. That is also the reason why we chose to consider peace in relation to its religious, artistic and philosophical roots, that is to say, primarily as the object of a struggle to suppress or to diminish it, as a political aim of (broadly defined) social and political movements over the last decades. That is why we have chosen to use *poïesis* (ποίησις) as a common ground. Originally, the word means 'to make'. Indeed, peace is constantly to be made. Neither technical production nor creation in the romantic sense, *poïetic* work reconciles thought with matter and time, and the person with the world.

Throughout history, sages, philosophers, artists and theologians have searched for the proper measure to secure what in a most intimate sense could be described as 'peace'. In search for this measure, and for a proper self-affection which could enable and host its enigmatic revelation, sometimes they were close to silence; in other cases they were actively pursuing a ground for its foundation for peace as a panacea for the human condition in all its fragility and precariousness. Formulated in the languages or discourses of Being, different hierarchies, or varied (but essentially identical) Gods, theological and philosophical deliberations have not infrequently derailed into dissent, conflict, even war.

*

The contributions brought together in the present volume have in common that they seek to critically assess the phenomenon of peace and its recent evolution, in ways that depart from the often convenient rationalisations. Originally presented at a conference organized by Lenart Škof in May 2015 in Gozd Martuljek, in the Slovenian Alps, all selected papers have been rewritten and edited for inclusion as chapters in the present collection. The contributors hail from a wide range of countries and academic cultures. It was felt by the editors that widening the academic horizon was equally important as recruiting authors from a varied geographical background. With this collection of papers, we would like to enliven the debate, drawing on different discourses, as present in philosophies of the ancient world, modern and contemporary thinking, as well as the poetry of peace to reanimate a new poesis of peace for the present age of insecurity and fear. Peace seems to be lost – at least on the surface, with media coverage of the many threats and dangers we all are facing in an increasingly insecure and unstable world. World history shows the recurrence of epochs saturated with the fear for elementary dangers (such as natural catastrophes and disasters) as well as for many and varied social or political upheavals and wars.

With this backdrop, the primary objective of this book is to offer a selection of studies in the form of short essays that serve to prod new tracks for reflection. To this effect, it is important to identify the transformation of contemporary peace in spatial and temporal terms. As much as war and violence, peace has become diffused and can only rarely be localized in advance, its spatial as well as temporal beginnings indeterminate. What really is peace? How is it to be imagined, conceived or constructed? Presented in three different parts, the papers collected in this book offer different approaches to peacemaking and to conceiving a future, non-violent culture of peace: 'Peacemaking and Narratives of Peace', 'Intercultural Approaches to Peace and Non-Violence', and 'Poetic Dwellings and Landscapes of Peace'.

Part I – Peacemaking and Narratives of Peace

In his chapter, Mendieta offers an innovative and insightful reading of Homer's *Iliad*. The author argues that the *Iliad* is not only one of the greatest poems of all times, but also a great poem to peace – and the poesis of peace – that understands peace not simply as the absence of war, but as the creation of a just order. This thesis is approached through a careful re-reading of three pivotal scenes in the *Iliad*: Hector's meeting with his wife before he goes off to die at the hands of Achilles; the description of Achilles' Shield; and Priam and Achilles' encounter towards the end of the narrative of the poem. Mendieta's intention in this chapter is to claim that both war and peace start in the minds of men (in his paraphrase of Sir Henry Maine) and that it is our task to imagine and invent peace – as we can obviously always imagine and invent various hostilities as acts of our aggression or even war. Mendieta relates peace in the *Iliad* to some of the most subtle layers of human existence – for example, in exchanging armours (between Glaucus and Diomedes) he shows the act of a vow of peace as an expression of a more primeval human condition – a gesture of being partially naked and thus exposing our flesh to the possible deadly violence of weapons. He reads a dialogue between Hector and his wife Andromache as a quintessence of all laws of intimacy that every war brutally destroys. For Mendieta these narratives of Homer are in fact symbols for freedom, equality (also between man and woman) on one, and proximity and vulnerability on the other side. Mendieta beautifully develops his argument based on familial (Hector and Andromache) or filial (Priam and Achilles) genealogies, which only can guarantee focus on individuals with their vulnerability, and desire to imagine and invent peace for future generations. This is in the forefront of Mendieta's interpretation of an imaginary as depicted on Achilles' shield: two cities – the city of peace vs. the city of war. Later in his chapter, by discussing legal and political consequences of this move, Mendieta refers to Ernst Bloch and his dichotomy between natural law theories and social utopias as being the most powerful 'weapon' we have invented so far against human degradation and human suffering. Homer in Mendieta's insightful reading thus helps us design and invent models of peaceful coexistence and invest our lives with a deep sense of peace.

Clemens Sedmak approaches the question of peaceful coexistence from an ethical point of view. He develops an understanding of peace involving a culture of peacefulness defined as a resource to cope with human vulnerability in social situations. The core of this chapter is in the development of his concept of 'a wound of knowledge'. For that purpose Sedmak starts with a story of Issa Grace (2013–2014), a tiny baby, affected by fatal health conditions from her birth. Sedmak shows that the story of this baby, surrounded by a number of people, helping and assisting her in her only year of life, demonstrates our ethical capacity to become ethical persons – which Sedmak relates to the theological notion of *the pedagogy of the weak*. For Sedmak, Issa herself was a true lesson for everyone in the mystery of love, but before all a teacher for her parents, and everyone close to her. From this story Sedmak then develops his theory of peacefulness and peace building as states of humbleness, of knowing the languages of love and care, but, most importantly, knowing our vulnerability. Vulnerability, for Sedmak, is basically being susceptible to harm, misuse etc. It is also the knowledge of our fragility – we are never in full control of our lives. In its four dimensions (capacity to be wounded, contingency of the world, fragility and fallibility) it is the place where our most intimate knowledge about shared existence dwells, an inner place or hidden reservoir of peacefulness, and also a place where –based on our experiential and pragmatic notions – also claims for justice can originate.

Pauline Sofie von Bonsdorff thinks about peace from the point of view of her personal and aesthetic experiences of interspecies proximity. In her chapter she describes aesthetic imagination as a thinking that is open to, reciprocal with and touched by the world – as an opposite of control, dominance, or aggression. For von Bonsdorff it is precisely our communication with animals that calls for new aesthetic imagination, i.e. our thinking with nature and through her. Following Michel Serres' claim that humans are presently at war with nature, von Bonsdorff argues that it is precisely this lack of awareness (respect) and proximity (closeness) to nature that causes fundamentally flawed relationships of ourselves with non-human species and environments. Analogously to Sedmak and his call to awareness of our vulnerability, she calls for a new category – 'animate peace' – as a reminder of what we have in common with our animal companions on the Earth. For von Bonsdorff, it is in our relations with domestic animals that we experience that they are even more sensitive than we are. The chapter's beautiful and sensitive narratives of the author's domestic horses and cats show the fundamental intersubjective and inter-species structure of her ethical intuitions: she carefully develops a phenomenology of the between-us with domestic animals only to encourage us to think of peace also in terms of our touching and being touched. These practices always already embody the very ideals of peacemaking, and it is through the imagining of peaceful relations in our everyday practices that we are finally also directed to our self-education peace; for von Bonsdorff, nothing is more important to the imagining of peace as our trust, benevolence and non-violence.

Petri Berndtson is a philosopher devoted to an idiosyncratic philosophical theory of peaceful coexistence based on certain 'esoteric' teachings of Merleau-Ponty. In this chapter Berndtson develops an argument that peace can only be thought of as based on a preliminary philosophical phenomenon called *the primordial respiratory peace*. Merleau-Ponty has indicated that there is a pact between an individual and the world; he has also argued that even before I am aware of this pact, there is a subject beneath me, existing as a body-subject. Read together with another passage of Merleau-Ponty on a newborn as a being existing within a primordial situation of *respiratory* body, Berndtson takes the starting point towards an original interpretation of the French phenomenologist. The author argues that peace (etymologically related to pact or *Pactum* in Latin) is proof of our primordial existential situation of being in harmonious agreement with the world. Antedating our experience, the temporality of this move is paradoxical, yet it establishes the primordial, perhaps hidden and esoteric *community of conspirators* (conspiracy understood as an act of breathing together, i.e. in a communal manner), which to Berndtson is the most universal community and which is also close to von Bonsdorff and her ideal of animate peace. In this sense, respiration/breathing and – according to Merlau-Ponty – the immense external lung bring peace to our bodies, and our Selves.

Lenart Škof's chapter is inspired by Irigaray's reading of *Antigone*. At the beginning it wishes to offer a new cosmologico-ethical interpretation of *Antigone*. His analysis is guided by Antigone's famous words 'My nature is to join in love, not hate'. In this, he follows Irigaray, who is thinking in the close vicinity of the cosmic laws and ancient orders of femininity (Erinyes and unwritten laws). The chapter shows that Antigone's act is an ultimate litany for the dead, but her faith is a radical faith for the living, offering an ethics for life. In the second part, an innovative comparison is carried out – between Antigone and Sāvitrī from the *Mahabharata*. Princess Sāvitrī represents all three genealogical orders found in Irigaray's reading of Antigone: sexual, cosmic and generational. The highest ethical demands of both Antigone and Sāvitrī are thus represented as signs of an absolute hospitality, a place we can secure first in ourselves for others – both deceased and living beings – in ethical as well as in political contexts. Škof shows that universally, no duty can be higher than our deepest cosmo-ethical faith and bodily sensibility to the other in pain. Antigone's and Sāvitrī's ethical acts are thus interpreted as ultimate signs for a peaceful community-to-come, a future event of peace.

Part II – Intercultural Approaches to Peace and Non-Violence

Carool Kersten's contribution is positioned on the interstices of philosophy, religion and literature and looks at the ways in which two intellectuals from Iran try to transcend or subvert the dichotomy between the West and Islam. He seeks to identify parallels, convergences and contrasts between the intellectual histories written by Ali Mirsepassi and Hamid Dabashi of the collapse of the Islam vs. the West binary in an increasingly globalising world. As a social scientist Mirsepassi has concerned himself with identifying 'non-Islamic' elements in the 'philosophies of despair' manifested in both Persian nativism emerging in the 1930s and the Islamist ideology underpinning the eventual establishment of the Islamic Republic of Iran in 1979. Both strands are traced to the inherently violent totalitarianism of Jacobin Enlightenment and Heidegger's search for cultural-religious authenticity. For an alternative 'philosophy of hope', Mirsepassi turns to the anti-foundationalism and pragmatic appreciation of everyday experiences of Dewey's 'Conceptual Pluralism' and the British Enlightenment as points of departure for realizing human freedom and deliberative democracy. With a dual academic background in the history of Islam and sociology of knowledge, the cultural critic Hamid Dabashi has transformed his work on Shi'a Islam as a 'religion of protest' and his earlier formulation of an Islamic liberation theology into a 'hermeneutics of alterity', which is presented as a counterpoint to the 'metaphysics of identity' underlying the false binary of 'the West' vs. 'the Rest'. Whereas books like *Theology of Discontent* and *Post-Orientalism* reject the violent teleologies of the French Revolution, Bolshevism and Islamism, his *Being Muslim in the World* proposes an alternative, decentred, post-colonial, post-Orientalist and post-Western world, where Arendt, Gadamer and Bakhtin loom over what Dabashi calls a new 'geography of liberation' and a restored 'worldly cosmopolitanism' previously articulated through Muslim literary humanism and presently found in the notion of *pensiero debole* or 'weak thought', developed by the Italian philosopher Gianni Vattimo.

In his chapter, Klaus-Gerd Giesen examines the philosophy of non-violence in the work of the French writer Lanza del Vasto. The latter had been Gandhi's first disciple in the Western world. The originality of his thought lies in the attempt to formally introduce Gandhi's *ahimsa* concept into Catholicism. The author demonstrates that such an 'import' of a non-violent approach into Catholicism remains a rather difficult task. Lanza del Vasto overcame the difficulty by 'perverting' the Catholic Church's official just war doctrine, i.e. by transforming it into a doctrine of just and non-violent conflict. It is argued that Lanza del Vasto uses, indeed, most just war norms of *jus in bello* and *jus ad bellum*, and adds even a Kantian *jus post bellum*, while rejecting some other criteria. However, Giesen emphasizes that Lanza del Vasto's 'casuistry' expels, so to speak, all violence from it. Each norm is closely examined. All together, Lanza del Vasto seems much closer to Kant's philosophy of war and peace than to classical just war theorists such as Aquinas or Vitoria. In any case, his pacifism stands for a true and important renewal in Christian thought on war and peace, and opens the door to more radical approaches.

Helena Motoh's chapter invites us to reflect upon the Classical Chinese elaboration on a peaceful coexistence. The term *an* ('peace') is invoked first as a pictogram defining 'roof' and 'woman' as its constituent parts. Motoh elaborates on the possible meaning of this ancient pictogram which can then be used to discuss the classical Chinese understanding of peace. One of the classical usages and translations of *an* as 'home' proves to be very close to Heidegger's ontological elaboration on 'hearth' and 'dwelling'. But the core of Motoh's interpretation revolves around the problem of translating a term, its semantic overlappings, and thus the question of comparison between Western and Chinese understandings of peace. According to the definition of peace during the *Shi ming* Dynasty we have three elements inaugurating the thinking of peace: quietude, stillness and comfort. Peace as a *place* of our dwelling (as understood in the *Book of Changes*) again invites us to think of our search for virtue, which corresponds with our search of peace. To dwell in peace, to be at home is what Motoh finally understands as our most intimate comfort, both being in a place as well as having our own place, which could lead us to some of the contemporary political usages – not only in the state of war, but also as related to the endangered and radically interrupted dwelling of the multitudes of migrants and refugees who thus cannot find peace.

In his chapter Victor Forte discusses the early Buddhist cultivation of peace. His interest lies in questions related to Buddhist monastic practitioners and the poesis of peace that their lives reflect and communicate in the world. Within Pāli texts wholesome states of mind (*kusala*) certainly are of greatest relevance to the topic of peace. Already *Dhammapada* brings early Buddhist teaching on avoiding evil and negative karma. After elaborating on these states, Forte is primarily interested in a Buddhist text widely ignored by Western interpreters of the Pāli Canon, namely the Sutra of *Kakacūpama Sutta*. In this discourse a *bhikkhu* (Buddhist monk) is admonished by the Buddha for being angry when his fellow *bhikkhunīs* (Buddhist nuns) are being insulted etc. This situation opens very difficult ethical questions regarding various responses towards evil deeds not only by *bhikkhu(nī)s* but generally by any ethical subject. According to the Buddha and his radical teaching of non-violence, Buddhists are *not* allowed to defend victims, but – instead – should concentrate on wholesome states of mind – regardless of the circumstances even in case of having one's limbs savagely severed one by one by the saw, as explained in the *Kakacūpama Sutta*. However extreme and counterintuitive this thought may be to us, who have not decided to live as renouncers of the world, and who therefore want to keep our personal relations intact and defend our loved ones against harm, it nevertheless represents the essence of the Buddhist teachings on non-violence and peace. To resolve this question Forte refers to the notion of *internal consequentialism*, which distinguishes Buddhist ethics (being in this account a *sui generis* ethical system) from the well-known Western ethical categories (such as utilitarianism). In Forte's interpretation, ultimately peace is attained only when renouncers of the world are skilled producers of the values and ideals of loving, kindness and compassion, as described in the *Kakacūpama Sutta* and when they, as 'peace incarnated', are able to walk among us.

Tina Košir engages with the thought of Abhinavagupta (ca. 950–1020), a thinker who arguably ranks amongst the greatest minds in Indian intellectual history, both for his contributions to the fields of poetics and Kashmiri philosophy of non-dual Śaivism. In his work *Śāntarasaprakaraṇa*, Abhinavagupta argues vigorously in favour of *śānta* (peace, tranquillity) as *rasa,* establishing it as the fundamental component of the aesthetic experience. In his view, the sole basis of *śānta rasa* is the Self, which is ultimately the basis of all emotive states. Hence all *rasas* originate and culminate in *śānta rasa*. In non-dual Kashmiri Śaivism, in its ultimate sense the Self is the ubiquitous absolute Consciousness, as a fundamental ontological principle as well as the epistemological base of any cognition. Its nature is peace, not only intuited as a transcendental concept but also palpably felt as *rasa*. It is a notion of peace at once metaphysical and aesthetic. At the end of her chapter, Tina Košir takes Abhinavagupta's *śānta rasa* out of its original context and discusses its relevance for contemporary narratives of peace. Here she comes close to Victor Forte's elaborations for it is compassion that arises from experiencing *śānta rasa* which is – analogous to the Buddhist ethics – transmitted to the world of intersubjective relations.

Part III – Poetic Dwellings and Landscapes of Peace

Kevin Hart has offered a lengthy meditation on the reading and interpretation of Hölderlin's oeuvre by the French philosopher and literary critic Maurice Blanchot (1907–2003). A close friend of both Emmanuel Lévinas and Georges

Bataille, Blanchot remains an enigmatic figure in twentieth-century French thinking, but has nevertheless exercised considerable influence on poststructuralists, such as Jacques Derrida. Given these connections and their shared interest in the poet, it is not surprising that Martin Heidegger is also a close intellectual companion of Blanchot in his journey through the work of Hölderlin. However, as Hart explains, Blanchot has also other fellow travellers, including Stéphane Mallarmé, René Char and Karl Jaspers. The resulting quartet features in 'the four occasions that Blanchot writes at length about Hölderlin'. Central to Blanchot's engagement is his rejection of unity in a poem and – as a consequence – his dismissal of a 'wholeness' to a poet's oeuvre, as well as a tendency to focus on the relation between poetry and philosophy and religion respectively rather than a concern for aesthetics. In spite of these disavowals and of being a radical atheist himself, Blanchot makes one big claim about Hölderlin's poems: they all involve the sacred and the holy. For that reason, in his writings about Hölderlin, Blanchot employs a religious vocabulary that draws on the lexicons of Paganism, Judaism and Christianity. Hart's *précis* connects a great many quotes from Hölderlin with digressions into the work of writers of the Greek Tragedies and Hellenic philosophy, Latin-Roman poetry, and Christology, while putting Blanchot in conversation with Heidegger in order to point out the similarities and many contrasts between the two. According to Hart, the key issue for Blanchot's Hölderlin is tragic sacrifice, not in the aesthetical or ethical sense found with Aristotle or Hegel, but as a religious notion. Although no orthodox Christian, Hölderlin is seen by Blanchot as a poet whose idea of the sacred centres on tragic sacrifice. It also makes the poet into an interstitial figure 'between mortals and gods, between the old gods and the new gods, maintaining "the extreme limit of suffering"'. This brings Hart's essay full circle to the shattering of Hölderlin's manifold profiles which find their parallel in the break-up of the 'unity and wholeness that religion has traditionally offered'. It also leaves the reader pondering how such 'endless contestation with no redemption', associated with an understanding of the sacred as existing without religion, can be squared with a poesis of peace.

Owen Alan Gurrey's exploration of literary landscapes pushes the poesis of peace not just into poetry and poetics; it also constitutes an edgy venture into the grittiness of what he calls 'the edgelands' on the peripheries of human habitation, the liminal spaces that are neither urban nor rural, let alone unspoilt nature. Taking his cue from the paleolithic human in Glyn Maxwell's *On Poetry*, a motif resonating with the writings of Peter Matthiessen and Bruce Chatwin, Gurrey's essay closely follows the trajectory of Paul Farley's poems, which offer a wilderness topography that is very different than, say, Gary Snyder's 'practice of the wild'. He also uses the birds in Ted Hughes' poem *Crow* to introduce ornithologists and other birdwatchers as those 'who have got to know the edgelands better than most'. Dumpsites, rubbish tips and scrapyards are introduced to jolt readers out of their habit of romanticising the condition of primordial man; aesthetic preferences are contrasted with the pragmatic gaze with which paleolithic humans viewed their surroundings. It offers the prospect of a 'new theory of wilderness' which will help contemporary humanity in redefining their relationship with the in-between places of the urban edgelands. Once 'their power as signifiers of new kinds of compounded territories' is recognised, edgelands provide a re-connective thesis out of which a poetry 'in praise of strong neglect' can help us make peace again with dramatically transformed landscapes, agriculture and nature.

In her chapter Emily A. Holmes examines the correlation between gardening and a sense of peace. She addresses the possibility of community-based agriculture as a practice of peace and active non-violence. Her text definitely is a sharp critique of the violence, commodification and militarization of conventional agriculture. However, Holmes at the same time cautions against the dangers of idealizing or romanticizing community-based forms of agriculture. Rather than seeing community-based forms of agriculture as a retreat from conflict, or an antidote to violence, or as an oasis of peace in the midst of destruction, she argues that they can create peace only insofar as they provide opportunities to address conflict within human communities, as well as the violence between human and other species. According to her, growing food communally requires dedicated and intentional spiritual practice, the kind of self-awareness and self-discipline described by Martin Luther King in his philosophy of non-violence.

Finally, Paul Haught interrogates the influence of the concept of anthropogenic climate change on aesthetic appreciation. He finds that since climate change's disruptive effects are profound, they influence human aesthetic experiences of the natural world, especially of particular places. Indeed, Haught empathizes that it is clearly possible for people to aesthetically appreciate landscapes, rivers, forests, plants, and insects without knowing much about what they are sensing. However, when those objects are experienced as or as part of places, the human being possesses a less naïve perspective. That is because a place is a *somewhere* to which human individuals and communities can have a special commitment: places imply care. Therefore, climate change amplifies the aesthetically normative features of places. At the end of his contribution, Haught differentiates places by different types to call attention to the normative pressures that they put on aesthetic appreciation by creating expectations for aesthetic experiences. According to him, these expectations occur sometimes as a result of human design; others are derived from the non-anthropogenic features of those places. With respect to the latter, the climate change concept may be strongly implicated in an awareness of vulnerability to loss of aesthetic value.

*

In conclusion then, this volume looks at peace and non-violence through the lens of recent scholarly advances made in the fields of theology, philosophy, political theory, literary criticism, aesthetics, and environmentalism. This multidisciplinary approach is applied to case studies in both Western and non-Western contexts.

By looking at narratives in different cultures and landscapes, the book introduces and establishes a new notion called 'the poesis of peace', conceived as a process of establishing a new culture of aesthetics and thinking of peace in various intercultural as well as interpersonal, social and political contexts, thus offering a deeper philosophical contemplation of the notions of peacemaking and non-violence than found in the more applied fields of international relations, political science and practical theology.

Part I

Peacemaking and Narratives of Peace

1 Peace Is Not the Absence of War

The Vernaculars of the *Humanum*

Eduardo Mendieta

Introduction

Sir Michael Howard, the great military historian, professor of military and naval history at Yale and former Regius professor of history at Oxford, begins his book, *The Invention of Peace: Reflections on War and International Order*, with the same words that make up the epigraph of the entire work: 'War appears to be as old as mankind, but peace is a modern invention'. Sir Henry Maine, the nineteenth-century comparative jurist and historian of law, wrote these words. Howard devotes the rest of the book to offering a synoptic overview of the development of the legal institutions that have sought to limit war. Howard makes the important point, correcting what Sir Henry Maine had claimed, that war 'starts in the minds of men, but so does peace'.[1] War, Howard also notes, gave birth to the state, as the state was the indispensable administrative system that allowed princes to wage war over great distances and over long periods of time. Peace, like war, is imagined in the minds of humans. So, both are in fact results of poesis. In this sense they are imbricated. War is also the result of the imagination. To give ourselves the license to kill another human, nay to convince ourselves that we must, requires an education of the imagination and the training of the body, as well. War is also the anatomopolitics of the body, to use Michel Foucault's language, another great philosopher of war. A certain kind of lack of imagination may lead to war, but a certain kind of educated imagination can also lead to war, in fact, make it necessary.[2] But peace is born from an imagination that insists on what Susan Sontag called 'necessary concessions and new arrangements. The necessary abatement of stereotypes. The necessary persistence of dialogue'.[3] The poesis of peace is precisely the necessity of imagining a world in which we have to make concessions and arrangements, and engage in open ended dialogue, for which we will need words, and for which our old words, our calcified conventions, are impediments and not facilitators.

There is another phrase that seems to echo those of Sir Henry Maine, and that is T.W. Adorno's often quoted remark from *Negative Dialectics*. In the section titled 'Universal History', Adorno writes: 'No universal history leads from savagery to humanitarianism, but there is one leading from the slingshot to the megaton bomb. It ends in the menace which organized mankind poses to organized men, in the epitome of discontinuity'.[4] Adorno seems to be claiming that war has been a continuous presence in the history of the human species, while peace seems to be both precarious and infrequent. Adorno is also implying that there are two rationalities with their corresponding history: on one side, there is the instrumental rationality that has allowed us to invent ever more sophisticated weapons of destruction and mass killing, with its history of relentless progress; on the other, we have the practical or moral rationality, advancing by fits and starts, hesitatingly, without a necessary telos. Humanitarianism, perhaps embodied in the form of human rights and an ethics of compassion, is not a result of universal history, something fated to happen or come about. Adorno is urging us to recognize that our humanitarian institutions have been wrested from history, despite history, against instrumental reason, and despite instrumental reason. But, Adorno also notes that it is universal history that leads from the slingshot to the megaton bomb that has turned 'organized mankind' into a total menace to 'organized humans'. Organized mankind may stand for the species organized into armed states. Mankind is the species, which driven by its species' imperative to survive must deploy its instrumental reason against nature and against its own nature to survive. But the species is now a menace to 'organized humans', i.e. individuals pursuing their individual ethical plans. Here Adorno is critiquing Kant, who thought that the human species alone progresses morally, and individuals are cannon fodder for the project of nature. Kant, interestingly, asked in his anthropology and his essay against Moses Mendelssohn, whether we ought to consider humanity at all 'likable' or 'despicable', whether we are justified in being misanthropic? Kant's answer is that the moral perfectibility of humanity, driven by our 'unsocial sociability', has rendered us sublime. But this moral sublimity belongs to the dignity of the humanity in me that can apply the moral law. This sublimity belongs not to me, as an individual, but to me insofar as I have the dignity of the moral legislator. This dignity belongs to the species. In contrast, Adorno is saying that it is organized *Menschheit* that is a terrifying menace to individual humans, *Menschen*, organized in their ethical communities. Adorno's answer to Kant seems to be that in fact, humanity as a species is indeed despicable and unlikable.[5]

When Adorno wrote *Negative Dialectics*, between 1959 and 1966, we were living through the height of MAD, mutually assured destruction. Humanity itself had become its own worst nemesis, for we were ready to obliterate the planet. But, I am particularly interested in the sentence that closes my Adorno quote: 'It ends in the menace which organized mankind poses to organized men, in the epitome of discontinuity'. What is the 'epitome of discontinuity' here? I think Adorno meant that something like peace is not a necessary result of some providence of god or telos of nature. There is no link between technological and material progress and moral enlightenment. Humanitarianism is a leap into the void of contingency and the revocability of moral progress. In this sense, we could say that Sir Henry James, Howard and Adorno are on the same page: war, as an expression of our will to survive, has a continuous history that peace does not have. Peace is an invention drawn not from dominating nature, but wrest from our moral imagination.

Peace is not something that is preserved by holding in abeyance war, but it is something that is attained beyond war, beyond nature, beyond the technical and instrumental capabilities of humanity. But to attain peace, we must invent it.

Agreeing with Sir Henry James and Michael Howard to a certain extent, while also siding with Adorno, I will develop in this chapter the thesis that peace is an invention, but not a new one, and that the invention of peace has been the product of relentless and courageous acts of poesis. I will argue, more specifically, that the poesis of peace, the invention of peace, is the result of the poetry of thinking that links memory and hope, remembrance and utopia, through the embrace of a vulnerable body, which suffers the sorrows of loss and yearns for a better future. Appealing to Ernst Bloch, I will develop the argument that the project of 'perpetual peace' offers the synthesis of social utopias and natural law theories. For the moment let me anticipate by quoting Bloch, from his seminal text *Natural Law and Human Dignity*: 'Social utopian thought directed its efforts toward human happiness, natural law was directed towards human dignity. Social utopias depicted relations in which *toil* and *burden* ceased, natural law constructed relations in which *degradation* and *insult* ceased'.[6] Where degradation and insult has ceased, even made illegal, and where punishing toil and burden have been abolished, this has happened because peace has been attained. This is what Isaiah 32:17 meant, where it is written that 'peace is the work of justice'. Justice is the pursuit of both happiness and dignity. Peace is the name for this marriage of dignity and joyful happiness, or what Aristotle called *arête and eudaimonia*. Peace is precisely this pursuit of human excellence with the complete blossoming of our human potential.

In order to develop this argument I will take us through an unusual detour. I want to do a close reading of four passages in Homer's *Iliad* that I argue reveal this to be the greatest book about war, but also be the greatest poem to peace. I will conclude in a third section by developing what I will call the legal orthopedia of peace, the poesis of peace through law.

On Homer: The Shields of Peace

Heraclitus, the grammarian or allegorist, to distinguish him from the other Heraclitus, the pre-Socratic philosopher, also known as the Obscure, wrote sometime between the first and second centuries AD the following about Homer in his *Homeric Problems*:

> I have come to feel amazed that the religious life, whose concern with the gods is stimulated by temples and precincts and annual festivals, should have embraced Homer's impiety so affectionately and learned to chant his abominable stories from memory. From the very first age of life, the foolishness of infants just beginning to learn is nurtured on the teaching given in his school. One might almost say that his poems are our baby clothes, and we nourish our mind by draughts of his milk. He stands at our side as we each grow up and

shares our youth as we gradually come to manhood; when we are mature, his presence within us is at its prime; and even in old age, we never weary of him. When we stop, we thirst to being him again. In a word, the only end of Homer for human beings is the end of life.[7]

This passage abounds in allegories, metaphors and metonyms, but there are two that I want to foreground as justifications for my own turning to Homer when wanting to make an argument about the poesis of peace. First, there is the allegory that Homer's poems are our own baby's clothes. Indeed, Homer's poems clothed our mind when it began to emerge from the fog of myth and superstition. Second, that his poems have been our teacher to guide us through our mental maturation into what Kant called 'sapere aude' (the injunction to dare to think on our own) but that we nevertheless never cease to draw from them nourishment. Heraclitus is right because Homer's poems capture two of the key metaphors, the most elemental metaphors that we have to make sense of life. These two metaphors exemplify what Hans Blumenberg called the irreducible metaphoricity of human existence.[8] One metaphor is that life is a relentless, chaotic and arbitrary 'struggle' in which we are at the mercy of blind fate. The other is that life is a blind, uncertain and circuitous 'journey'.[9] Here, however, I want to focus on the *Iliad*, and I want to contend that far from being a poem about life as an implacable struggle against a blind force that reduces humans into objects, mere relays of destructive force – as Simone Weil argued in her important essay *The Iliad or the Poem of Force* – the *Iliad* is a poem that shows how peace is to be created and attained. At the heart of the *Iliad* is an allegory of peace. Let me focus on four key scenes in order to make my case.[10]

Book 6 of the *Iliad* is titled in some translations as 'Hector and Andromache', as the pivot of the chapter is what we may call Hector's farewell to his wife and son.[11] The chapter, however, begin with the Argives or Greeks making advances against the Trojans. The chapter begins with a long list of individualized killings, led by Agamemnon, before it turns to the exploits of Diomedes, until Diomedes encounters Glaucus. As always in the *Iliad* both men taunt each other and celebrate their exploits and give us their lineage. If you are about to kill me, you need to know who it is that you are killing, and what lineage you are severing, Homer seems to be saying. This is one of the rare moments in the *Iliad* when two warriors give truce to each other, for in giving their respective genealogies, they recognized that their families have been guests of each other. At the core of Greek culture was the ethics of host-guest reciprocity, which established inviolable links of peace making but also reciprocity and mutual aid. As a sign of their truce and vow of peace, Glaucus and Diomedes exchange armours, sustaining and extending the rules of host-guest hospitality. Following M.I. Finley, we could offer a political-economic reading of this particular passage, and suggest that this is really an economic exchange. Armour was both a sign of economic prowess but also of social standing. The more elaborate, reliable, sturdy, and elegant, the wealthier and honourable its wearer was taken to be. Armour is a metonymy for both honour and wealth, which is why Patroclus will borrow Achilles' to lead the Greeks on a counter-offensive, and this is why when Hector kills Patroclus he must take Achilles' armour. I want to suggest, however, that the exchange of armour in the middle of a battlefield is like the handshake to us today: namely to reveal that we do not conceal a weapon, and that by reaching out to another, we are making ourselves vulnerable. What could be more of a gesture of peace than to partially make yourself naked – to expose your flesh to the possible deadly violence of swords and arrows?

In the midst of the agony of men dying on the battlefield, immortal horses crying for dying soldiers, rivers revolted against the carnage of war, in the din and cacophony of the clashing of weapons, there is still great tenderness, love, solicitude for the freedom and life of others. Nothing exemplifies this better than Hector's relationship to Andromache, his wife. She has suffered greatly at the hands of Achilles and the Greeks in general. She is an orphan of the wars of men. As she implores to Hector: '…you are my everything now: my father, my mother, my brother – and my beloved husband. Have pity on me. Stay with me here on the tower. Don't make your child an orphan, your wife a widow' (6.432–5). Andromache embodies the horrors of all wars and her supplication is that of every mother, wife, and sister. Hector tellingly replies, foreshadowing his demise and that of Troy. He knows deep in his heart that his beloved city will succumb and will be destroyed and that his Father, Priam, and brother will all also become victims of the war that is raging outside the walls of Troy. But, the one thing that distresses him more deeply than all of these losses is that Andromache will lose her freedom and that he sees her in his mind's eye: 'Then, all your life, in the Argives' land, you will work long days, bent over the loom of some stern mistress or carrying water up from her well – hating it but having no choice, for harsh fate will press down upon you' (6.453–6).

He is standing in his full armour, helmet in his head. As he reaches to hold his son from the nurse's arms, the child pulls back and cries. He is terrified by his father's appearance and does not recognize him. Both Hector and Andromache laugh. He takes his helmet and then holds his child and kisses him, as he commends and pleads to Zeus that his son may become 'outstanding among Trojans', and that he become a great warrior who will 'gladden his mother's heart' by bringing the 'gore-stained armor' of the enemy (6.476–81). This is a complex scene, if not self-contradictory. On the one hand, there is the tenderness of a husband for his wife. It is certainly unusual for those times that Hector would be so concerned about the freedom of his wife. He is not treating Andromache as either property or a servant. This is a relation of equals, or at least a relation in which there is solicitous concern for the one he loves. Hector loves Andromache in her freedom, for her freedom. When he is about to leave, he hands his son to Andromache, who smiles but is quietly crying. Hector is moved by her gentle and stoic sadness. Homer then sings: 'her husband was touched by pity, and he stroked her face, and he said, "My foolish darling, please do not take these things too greatly to heart…"' (6.484–6). This is a scene of incredible gentleness and intimacy that reveals their deep mutual love.

On the other hand, the child does not recognize his father in his armour. He is terrified. The theme of misrecognition and recognition run through Homer's *Iliad* and *Odyssey*. We only have to think of the ruses Odysseus plays on several on his antagonists. But in the *Iliad*, we have the key misrecognition of Patroclus by Hector that leads to the dénouement of the battle. Here Homer seems to suggest that war disfigures us as much as it makes us shine in our true character. If Achilles revels in war and drinks from the well of its passions, Hector is a reluctant warrior, who is a gentle father and a loving husband. For Hector, war is not an end itself, but a means to secure the freedom of others.

I turn now to the last book of the *Iliad*, which is about the encounter between Priam, Hector's father, and Achilles, the swift killer of men and women. Achilles has killed Hector and in his blind rage, has been desecrating his body by dragging it around Patroclus' funeral pyre. Priam has come to Achilles' hut, guided by Hermes, to implore for the return of Hector's body, so that he may receive a proper burial. Priam, the King and Patriarch of Troy, kneels before Achilles, grasps his knees, kisses his hands, and implores to him:

> 'Remember your father, Achilles. He is an old man like me, approaching the end of his life. Perhaps he too is being worn down by enemy troops, with no one there to protect him from chaos and ruin. Yet he at least, since he knows that you are alive, feels joy in his heart and, every day, can look forward to seeing his child, whom he loves so dearly, come home. *My* fate is less happy.... Have pity on me; remember your father. For I am more to be pitied than he is, since I have endured what no mortal ever endured: I have kissed the hands of the man who slaughtered all my children'.... Priam, crouched at Achilles' feet, sobbed for Hector; Achilles wept now for his father, now for Patroclus. And every room in the house rang with the sound of their mourning and lamentation. (24.476–83, 24.494–7, 24.501–4)

This is an extremely powerful and pivotal scene in the entire book. Coming at the end of a book about a terrible war, it tells us that war has costs that will weigh on survivors, victors and victims alike. There is always sorrow, mourning and lamentation, on both sides. War may have victors, but all sides have victims. On the other hand, this scene is a great moment of empathy. Even as enemies, there can be emotional reciprocity. Achilles, who is so often presented as irascible and full of fury, hate and rage, is brought out of his violent passion for killing and made to empathize. What keeps us humans, in the midst of carnage, is our ability to empathize across warring camps.[12] Achilles has not lost sight that Priam is still another human being, with passions, loves and cares like those of his father. Two enemies, together in their pathos and in their suffering together, reaffirm their humanity. Their humanity resides precisely in this ability to empathize. In fact, the majestic grace of this scene is what raises the book beyond tragedy. Against the violence of time and the violence of war, Homer gives us these moments that as it were raise these characters above time into the eternity of memory. As Stephen Mitchell put it in the introduction to his translation of the *Iliad*:

> At the end of the *Iliad* Homer gives Priam and Achilles a reprieve of infinite time. The final agony, the appalling misery that is fate to happen in the traditional account of the Trojan War, will never happen within the confines of the *Iliad*. The great city of Troy still stands, forever poised on the brink of disaster. Andromache will never become a slave, nor will her child be hurled of the wall of Troy. Hecuba will see Hector's body come home, as she desired. Priam will forever sit at the funeral feast, eating, drinking, and mourning over his fallen son to his heart's content. Achilles will sleep with his beloved Briseïs forever.[13]

It is our capacity to love, to empathize, to remember others and to yearn for their well being that generates another time than that of war, the time of our humanity, which is the reprieve of the infinite time of collective memory. For it is in collective memory, as the performance of a collective poesis, that we generate time by both memorializing and hoping. We remember to project a future. The future shines light on the past so that we can see it better, differently, more humanely. This time of collective memory is the infinite time of poesis. Here is where the imagination and the ethical converge to generate what we can call, following Jürgen Habermas and Hannah Arendt, the communicative power of collective poesis.

I now come to what I take to be the most visionary and utopian moment in the *Iliad*, the moment that in my view reveals this book to be about peace and not war. This moment also reveals Homer at the heights of his poetic and literary powers. The scene is in book 18, which in some translations is titled 'Achilles' Shield', or, 'The Shield of Achilles' (Rees and Fagles translations),[14] or the 'Immortal Shield' (Fitzgerald translation).[15] As was already indicated, when Hector killed Patroclus, thinking that he was Achilles, he had taken his armour as his badge of honour. Achilles wants to return to battle, but he cannot, as he no longer has his armour. His mother Thetis goes to Hephaestus, the great-maimed God, to implore that he smith a new armour for her son. He assents. Homer proceeds to describe how he makes Achilles' shield. Let me summarize this incredible description of what Hephaestus fashions. He first makes a shield that is five layers thick, with a triple layered rim. On the wide surface of the shield, he proceeds to forge and make some lovely scenes. Although none of the five translations I consulted make this clear or imply it, I will suggest that Hephaestus is constructing the front of the shield from the centre outward towards the rim, creating what seem to be six concentric circles. The innermost circle is where the God fashions the sky, with its sun, moon and constellations. In the next circle, he draws two lovely cities: the city of peace and the city of war. The city of peace is made up of two important scenes. On one side is depicted a marriage ceremony with all of its joy and festivities. On the other is of a court case in which two litigants stand before the judges, pleading their case. The city of war is also made up of two scenes. In one, a city is represented as being besieged by soldiers, while inside the walls of the city, solider are readying for an ambush, and the ambush is portrayed. The next circle represents farmers toiling the land. It is the scene of ploughing and the harvesting at the end of the season. The next circle portrays the festival of the harvest of the vineyard with young men and women are dancing, singing and playing the lyre. Around the vineyard Hephaestus also smiths cattle, which are moving from farmyard to pasture, guided by herdsmen and long green valleys with sheep and shepherds. The next and final circle depicts the powerful river Oceanus. The descriptions are dynamic, full of colour and gaiety. They have the power of animations. We can almost see the scenes dancing on the page.

My argument is that Achilles' shield is the synecdoche for the entire *Iliad*, for in the shield is represented the drama that the entire book tells. Achilles' shield is the visual representation of the story of the fall of Troy. But more than that, here we also find what I would call Homer's philosophy, using myth in order to go beyond myth. In fact, while the *Iliad* includes the story of the Gods meddling in the lives of humans, Achilles' shield is framed, or more accurately circled by a post-mythical worldview, what I would call a post-theistic and an *avant la lettre* secular view of human existence. The scenes are bookended by the sky and its constellations, in its eternal serenity, regularity and fixity, on one end, and the ceaseless motion and change of the river and seas, on the other end. In between, we have the rhythms of nature and humans. The shield thus portrays for us cosmic time, natural time and human time, or alternatively, Homer is portraying the rhythms of nature, the rhythms of sociality and the rhythms of history.

I want, however, to briefly focus on what is the core of the Shield, namely the representation of the two cities. The city of peace moves, literally, around two axes, each with its own telos. One axis is the pivot around which the wedding takes place, with its focus on individuals, who moved by love commit to procreation. This is the axis of the generation of generations. The other axis is the pivot around which the court takes place, where individuals come together as a collectivity, as a community that addresses itself through its laws. This is the axis of justice. The city of peace is precisely the synthesis of love and justice, or the generation of generations under the sun of the justice secured by law.

The city of war also moves, again literally, around two axes. One is the axis around which the amassed soldiers take place. Here are soldiers moved by courage, discipline, prowess, fearlessness and honour waiting to charge against a city. This is the axis of loyalty, which unites all the martial virtues. The other axis here is the one around which the ambush take place, with individuals using subterfuge, deception and dishonour. This is the axis of disloyalty and betrayal. Like the axes of the city of peace, with their own harmony and resonance, the axes of the city of war resonate but in a negative way. Homer seems to be insisting that the logic of war leads to the destruction of the very virtue that makes it possible. War becomes the very condition of its impossibility. I want to argue that Achilles' shield is the vision of a world passing away and one being born. In fact, *pace* Plato, Homer is closer to the world of Socrates, Plato and Aristotle, than to the world that the book itself portrays: the world of king-soldiers bound by loyalty and honour. In fact, the Shield is a utopian window into the world of peace, which here is portrayed as the world generated by the gift of love and the labour of justice.

The Legal Orthopedia of Peace

In order to articulate my second main theses in this chapter, I turn now turn to Ernst Bloch's *Natural Law and Human Dignity*, and his generative thesis that while social utopias are oriented towards *happiness*, natural law theories are oriented towards *dignity*. In what we should consider the key chapter in this magnificent, though neglected, book that is titled 'The Marxist Distance to Right', under a section titled 'Social Utopias and Natural Law', Bloch offers an analysis of what he takes to be their fundamental differences, which in fact allow them to complement each other in what he calls the project of the upright carriage of the human. He identifies three differences. The first difference is *temporal*. While natural law theories reached their apogee in the seventeenth and eighteenth centuries, social utopias reached their summit in the nineteenth century, that is, in the thick of the industrial revolution. The temporal difference here is a marker for two moments of the bourgeoisie. In the seventeenth and eighteenth centuries the bourgeoisie is still progressive, in fact, it is revolutionary. By the nineteenth century, with its triumph over the nobility and clergy and its opposition to the worker's movement, the bourgeoisie had already become conservative, reactionary and counter-revolutionary. The next fundamental difference is a *methodological one*. While social utopia operate in the medium of stories, pictures, representations, and images, natural law theories operate in the medium of logical deduction, 'with the zeal and rigor of a demonstrative science'.[16] The complement here is between the pedagogy of affect through the imagination and the mobilization of solidarity through rational persuasion. The third difference, and thus complementarity, between social utopias and natural law theories, is their *object*. As we noted before, social utopias aim at happiness, while natural law theories aim at dignity. Here, I must quote a beautiful passage that shows Bloch at the height of his philosophical poesis:

> Social utopias are primarily directed toward *Happiness*, at least towards the abolition of misery and the conditions that preserve and produce misery. Natural law theories, as is so readily apparent, are primarily oriented towards *dignity*, toward human rights, toward juridical guarantees of human security or freedom as categories of human pride. Accordingly, social utopias are oriented above all toward the abolition of human *suffering*; natural law is oriented above all toward the abolition of human *degration*. Social utopia want to clear away all that stands in the way of the *eudaemonia of everyone*; natural law wants to do away with all that stands in the way of *autonomy* and *eunomia*.[17]

There are two key ideas I want to highlight in this passage that will allow me to build my case for the legal *orthopedia* of peace. Natural law aims at dignity by way of law, and above all to law as it is embodied in human rights, which secures 'security' and 'freedom', always the two first and major casualties of war. Social utopias, in contrast but complementing natural law theories, aim at the abolition of suffering, not pain, but human inflicted suffering through exploitation. Exploitation is the cause of the suffering that brings humans to their knees, or strips them of their humanity. Both degradation and suffering bend the upright carriage of the human. The second idea has to do with the dynamic relationship between *eudaemonia* and *eunomia*, that is between the happy and flourishing life, and the good and proper law. There is no integral human flourishing without good and proper law, and the good law is legitimated by its securing human happiness. As Bloch puts it: '... there can be no human dignity without the end of misery and need, but also no human happiness without the end of old and new forms of servitude'.[18]

For Bloch, as for Habermas who recently has taken up his work, there is a dialectic between misery and degradation, on the one hand, and *eunomia*, the good law, the law that shines on Kallipolis. For both, misery and degradation must be able to speak, to be given voice and to be heard. This calls for the priority of the one who suffers both misery and degradation in their flesh in addressing the just or unjust law. As Bloch put it: 'Without the impulse of justice from below, no human rights would be installed',[19] but also and at the same time, 'An absolute, general injustice, as such, can be neither characterized nor measured nor repaired if no absolute, general justice, no legal utopia, is envisioned'.[20] Habermas agrees, when he writes: 'Our intuition tells us anyway that human rights have always been product of resistance to despotism, oppression, and humiliation.... The appeal to human rights feeds off the outrage of the humiliated at the violation of their human dignity',[21] or when he writes later on in the same article:

> The first human rights declaration set a standard that inspires refugees, people who have been thrust into misery, and those that have been ostracized and humiliated, a standard that can give them the assurance that their suffering is not a natural destiny. The translation of the first human right into a positive law gave rise to a *legal duty* to realize exacting moral requirements, and that has become engraved into the collective memory of humanity.[22]

For Habermas, as for Bloch, human rights are translated into positive law, then set a standard, a bar, and more importantly, a horizon of expectations that enable those who have become victims of degradation, humiliation, ostracism and violation to not only not be reconciled and endure their condition, but to actually seek to transform it, to make an appeal. But, at the same time, without the struggle from below, from those who are the victims of any given socio-economic-political order, the law cannot be transformed from moral outrage and moral solidarity into positive law. Law itself undergoes correction, a kind of rectifying. Law itself must be submitted to an orthopedia. I content that this orthopedia is performed through the poesis of collective memory, the communal act of remembering past suffering and hoping for future liberation and release from the degradation and misery that inflicted that suffering. At the heart of the communicative power of collective memory is the creation of an affective response to the suffering of others. The poesis of collective memory, as the mobilization of an affective response to the corporeal suffering of others, becomes the workshop for the orthopedia of law.

Law, on the other hand, aims at the utopia of perpetual peace, that is, the abolition of those conditions that bend the upright carriage of the human, to use Bloch's beautifully evocative expression. Law in the form of human rights, at the core of which is the spectre of 'crimes against humanity', is the first and most powerful means for the constraining and, hopefully, abolition of war. Human rights in fact should be seen as utopian projections that have efficacy in the real world. They are at least one of the very obvious cases where the utopian imagination is not mere wishful thinking or idle speculation. This has led Habermas to talk about human rights in an oxymoronic fashion as a 'realistic utopia'. Still, Habermas' coinage is entirely apt. Human rights set a 'standard', an ever receding, but always visible, line in the horizon of justice. Human rights are empty without the voice of moral outrage at the violation of human dignity, but human dignity is blind without the light shined on by positive law that turns moral intuitions into legal efficacy.

The dialectic between social utopia and natural law theories that Bloch sketched is also traced by Habermas in terms of the dialectic between dignity and human rights.[23] Ultimately, both are concerned with the mutual orthopedia of *eudaimonia* and *eunomia*, the mutual correcting between flourishing human excellence and justice. It is for this reason that I want to postulate that we speak of a legal orthopedia of peace. If peace is not simply the absence of war, but something positive that exceeds the negativity of war, it is because it is something that has to be attained, invented, fashioned and sustained. The poesis of peace presupposes then the education of our moral imaginary through a collective memory that is open to the suffering of others, as well as to the orthopedia of law that assures that we are entitled to live uprightly, with dignity. This is what natural law aimed at and now human rights seek to both entitle and enforce, namely '*uprightness as a right*, so that it be respected in *persons* and guaranteed in their *collective*'.[24]

Conclusion: Peace the Vernacular of the Humanum

In his 1517 text *Querela Pacis* [The Complaint of Peace], the great humanist Desiderius Erasmus personifies peace and makes her speak, in her own person. There Peace complains that she is perplexed by why she is insulted and maligned by humans, of all the animals on Earth best disposed to embrace her. As Fred Dallmayr notes in his book *Peace Talks*, peace speaks, but so few of us hear her.[25] As much as one should quote some extremely beautiful passages from this powerful text, we must refrain for the sake of space. Still, in a very interesting way Erasmus converges with a contemporary thinker, the maverick and heterodox cultural critic Ivan Illich.

In a speech he gave in 1980, titled 'The De-linking of Peace and Development', Illich makes the following perspicacious and provocative claims:

> You have invited me to speak on a subject which eludes the modern use of certain English terms. Violence now lurks in many key words of the English language. John F. Kennedy could wage *war* on poverty; pacifists now plan *strategies* (literally, war plans) for peace. In this language, currently shaped for aggression, I must talk to you about the recovery of a true sense of peace, while bearing in mind always that I know nothing about your vernacular tongue. Therefore, each word I speak today will remind me of the difficulty of putting peace into words. To me, it seems that each people's peace is as distinct as each people's poetry. Hence, the translation of peace is a task as arduous as the translation of poetry.... Peace is as vernacular as speech.[26]

This last formulation gets to the heart of the theme of this incredibly timely and important anthology: the poesis of peace. Illich also notes that while war homogenizes cultures, peace heterogenizes them. One could add that peace is to poesis as war is to techne, as plurality is to sameness. Peace is the condition of possibility for diversity, while war is the condition of its impossibility.[27] Peace that is the work of collective memory and yearning is for that very reason the work of different cultures, with their respective and unique life-worlds, and practices of memorializing. Peace is plural, precisely because humanity is plural. It is that plurality that is the ground for the poesis of peace. The plurality of humanity is not only an alpha, a point of departure, a reflection on the very condition of our humanity; it is also an omega, a goal, and a telos. Plurality is simultaneously humanity's *terminus a quo* and *terminus ad quem*. Peace, then, is the vernacular of plural humanity.

To close, I would like to return to Bloch's reflections on three differences between social utopia and natural law theories, namely the temporal, the methodological, and in so far as they aim at different objects. In light of Illich, and Dallmayr, we could add that there is a fourth complementary difference that unleashed another dialectic. This difference I would call the *terminus a quo* of collective memory as it is crystallized in social utopias, and the *terminus ad quem* of dignity as it enshrined in the protective sheltering of human rights. We begin from the ineradicable singularity of a people's collective memory to arrive at a construct, an invention, a fiction by means of which we force ourselves to treat each other, foreign and strange others, equally so that we can all dwell in dignity. The utopia of perpetual peace requires the plural vernaculars of humanity. The poesis of peace is the poesis of plural humanity in its remembering and hoping.

Notes

1 Sir Richard Howard, *The Invention of Peace: Reflections on War and International Order* (New Haven: Yale University Press, 2001), 5.

2 See Dave Grossman, *On Killing: The Psychological Costs of Learning to Kill in War and Society*, rev. ed. (New York: Back Bay Books/Little, Brown & Company, 2009) for a psychosocial study of how soldiers are educated to kill.

3 Susan Sontag, *At the Same Time: Essays and Speeches* (New York: Farrar, Straus, and Giroux, 2007), 155.
4 Theodor W. Adorno, *Negative Dialectics*, trans. E.B. Ashton (New York and London: Routledge, 2004 [1973]), 320.
5 Theodor W. Adorno, *Gesammelte Schriften*, vol. 6 (Frankfurt am Main: Suhrkamp Verlag, 1997), 314.
6 Ernst Bloch, *Natural Law and Human Dignity*, trans. Dennis J. Schmidt (Cambridge, MA: The MIT Press, 1986), xxix, 205.
7 Heraclitus, *Homeric Problems*, trans. Donald A. Russell and David Konstan (Atlanta: Society of Biblical Literature, 2005), 3.
8 See specifically Hans Blumenberg, *Paradigms for a Metaphorology*, trans. Robert L. Savage (Stanford: Stanford University Press, 2010).
9 See Alberto Manguel, *Homer's The Iliad and The Odyssey. A Biography* (New York: Grove Press, 2007).
10 See Simone Weil, *War and the Iliad*, trans. Mary McCarthy (New York: The New York Review of Books, 2005). This is an excellent edition that in addition contains an essay by Rachel Bespaloff and Hermann Broch.
11 Henceforth I will use the following translation: Homer, *The Illiad*, trans. Stephen Mitchell (New York: Free Press, 2011).
12 Spanish philologist Carlos García Gaul in fact has argued that Homer, in this key scene invents the 'victory of humanism over cruelty and destruction'. Gaul, in general, has written one of the most beautiful readings of this final meeting between Priam and Achiless, as well as between Hector and Andromache. See Carlos García Gaul, *Encuentros Heroicos: Seis escenas griegas* (Madrid: Fondo de Cultura Económica de España, 2009), 38.
13 Homer, *The Iliad*, trans. Stephen Mitchell (New York: Free Press, 2011), lii–liii.
14 Homer, *The Illiad*, trans. Ennis Rees (New York: Barnes & Noble Classics, 2005); Homer, *The Illiad*, trans. Robert Fagles, introduction and notes by Bernard Knox (New York: Penguin Books, 1998).
15 Homer, *The Illiad*, trans. Robert Fitzgerald (New York: Farrar, Straus and Giroux, 2004).
16 Ernst Bloch, *Natural Law and Human Dignity*, 205.
17 Ernst Bloch, *Natural Law and Human Dignity*, 205.
18 Ernst Bloch, *Natural Law and Human Dignity*, 208.
19 Ernst Bloch, *Natural Law and Human Dignity*, 202.
20 Ernst Bloch, *Natural Law and Human Dignity*, 208.
21 Jürgen Habermas, 'The Concept of Human Dignity and the Realistic Utopia of Human Rights', *Metaphilosophy* 41, no. 4 (July 2010), 466.
22 Habermas, 'The Concept of Human Dignity', 476.
23 I have developed in greater detail this argument in my essay 'The Legal Orthopedia of Human Dignity: Thinking with Axel Honneth', *Philosophy and Social Criticism* 40, no. 8 (Fall 2014): 799–815.
24 Bloch, *Natural Law and Human Dignity*, 208.
25 Fred Dallmayr, *Peace Talks: Who Will Listen?* (Notre Dame, IN: University of Notre Dame Press, 2004).
26 Ivan Illich, *In the Mirror of the Past: Lectures and Addresses 1978–1990* (New York and London: Marion Boyars, 1991), 15–6.
27 With more space we should develop this idea in dialogue with Emmanuel Levinas, especially what he has to say about peace as a form of *fraternal* proximity to alterity that is not a failure to coincide with the other, but is instead the *surplus* of sociality, a surplus that is love. See Emmanuel Levinas, 'Peace and Proximity', in *Basic Philosophical Writings*, ed. Adriaan T. Peperzak, Simon Critchley and Robert Bernasconi (Bloomington and Indianapolis: Indiana University Press, 1996): 161–9.

References

Adorno, Theodor W. *Gesammelte Schriften*. Vol. 6. Frankfurt am Main: Suhrkamp Verlag, 1997.

Adorno, Theodor W. *Negative Dialectics*. Translated by E.B. Ashton. New York and London: Routledge, 2004 [1973].

Bloch, Ernst. *Natural Law and Human Dignity*. Translated by Dennis J. Schmidt. Cambridge, MA: The MIT Press, 1986.

Blumenberg, Hans. *Paradigms for a Metaphorology*. Translated by Robert L. Savage. Stanford: Stanford University Press, 2010.

Dallmayr, Fred. *Peace Talks: Who Will Listen?* Notre Dame, IN: University of Notre Dame Press, 2004.

García Gaul, Carlos. *Encuentros Heroicos: Seis escenas griegas*. Madrid: Fondo de Cultura Económica de España, 2009.

Grossman, Dave. *On Killing: The Psychological Costs of Learning to Kill in War and Society*. Rev. ed. New York: Back Bay Books/Little, Brown & Company, 2009.

Habermas, Jürgen. 'The Concept of Human Dignity and the Realistic Utopia of Human Rights'. *Metaphilosophy* 41, no. 4 (July 2010): 464–80.

Heraclitus. *Homeric Problems*. Translated by Donald A. Russell and David Konstan. Atlanta: Society of Biblical Literature, 2005.

Homer. *The Illiad*. Translated by Ennis Rees. New York: Barnes & Noble Classics, 2005.

Homer. *The Illiad*. Translated by Robert Fagles, introduction and notes by Bernard Knox. New York: Penguin Books, 1998.

Homer. *The Illiad*. Translated by Robert Fitzgerald. New York: Farrar, Straus and Giroux, 2004.

Homer. *The Illiad*. Translated by Stephen Mitchell. New York: Free Press, 2011.

Howard, Richard. *The Invention of Peace: Reflections on War and International Order*. New Haven: Yale University Press, 2001.

Illich, Ivan. *In the Mirror of the Past: Lectures and Addresses 1978–1990*. New York and London: Marion Boyars, 1991.

Levinas, Emmanuel. 'Peace and Proximity'. In *Basic Philosophical Writings*, edited by Adriaan T. Peperzak, Simon Critchley and Robert Bernasconi, 161–9. Bloomington and Indianapolis: Indiana University Press, 1996.

Manguel, Alberto. *Homer's The Iliad and The Odyssey. A Biography*. New York: Grove Press, 2007.

Mendieta, Eduardo. 'The Legal Orthopedia of Human Dignity: Thinking with Axel Honneth'. *Philosophy and Social Criticism* 40, no. 8 (Fall 2014): 799–815.

Sontag, Susan. *At the Same Time: Essays & Speeches*. New York: Farrar Straus Giroux, 2007.

Weil, Simone. *War and the Iliad*. Translated by Mary McCarthy. New York: The New York Review of Books, 2005.

2 Peace, Vulnerability, and the Human Imagination

Clemens Sedmak

The main point of this chapter is the claim that genuine peace is realized within a culture of peacefulness. I define 'peacefulness' as a second-order resource to cope with human vulnerability in social situations and I define 'peace' as a social situation characterized by the stakeholders' readiness and capability to deal with questions of conflict and coordination in a way that preserves Co-Being. I will try to show that a culture of peacefulness can only be realized on the basis of the recognition of our human vulnerability.

I

Issa Grace lived from June 2013 until March 2014. She was the fourth child of her parents Sean and Felicia. The pregnancy was difficult and Issa was born with *Trisomy 18*; the doctors did not give the baby girl more than a few hours or a maximum of a few days to live. She beat the odds! Issa lived her life in the constant imminence of death to which more than once she came extremely close. Due to her condition she could not lie down and had to be held, 24 hours a day. More than 90 people supported Issa's family in a 'sleep relief fund' to hold the baby so that Sean and Felicia could get some sleep, while others cooked meals or took care of household chores. Issa's obituary verifies: 'Issa guided and taught her family all the way through her final breaths'.

We might now ask the question: What was this tiny baby able to convey as a guide and teacher? It was in February 2014 that I was privileged to have the experience of holding Issa. I was invited to her family's home and there she was, a tiny baby, breathing with difficulties. When I was holding Issa something happened to me: A feeling of peacefulness, a sense of protecting the vulnerable, also an understanding of the fragility of humanity and my own fragility. And in the usual mode of over-intellectualizing and having one thought too many I asked myself whether this experience could not be seen as a peace-making experience that would change the thinking of those who go to war. So here was Issa as a teacher and a guide.

Issa demonstrated, one could say, '*the pedagogy of the weak*' – she taught those around her important lessons about life in a way that only the most vulnerable, weak and fragile can do. We must not underestimate the role of the seemingly powerless in the context of peace building. Who does not, for instance, recall the 'sex strike' by Liberian women called on to intensify the 'powerful' men's peace talks?[1] There is the power of the seemingly powerless. This is the power Issa had so much to teach about. She inspired an attitude of peacefulness by being fragile and by bringing people together because of her fragility. Issa taught her elders a vital aspect in the lesson about love. In her blog about her daughter, Issa's mother wrote, 'One of the most challenging aspects of loving Issa is … trying to hold on and let go at the same time. We are learning that the experience of holding and letting go at the same time teaches us about the meaning of love' (28 July 2013). Issa was herself a lesson in the mystery of love – what does it mean to love a child as the greatest of gifts, and at the same time know that she will not live long? She proved how powerful the connecting force of love is: 'We are so thrilled to share Issa with the world and to expand her circle of love' (2 October 2013). Issa taught her family and friends about humility. 'It's humbling for me that I need so much help for our family to function' (19 January 2014). She taught her parents the humbling experience of understanding the reality and depth of dependency. This was a way of bringing people together, of showing solidarity, of reaching out and thereby a sense of 'being in there together' was strengthened. Issa made her family experience 'the opposite of loneliness'.[2]

Issa also taught important lessons about '*polyglotty*', about the many languages of love (and peacefulness); a polyglot person speaks many different languages. This may refer to English, French and German, but it can also refer to the languages of encounter. There are different 'styles' of being with a person, there are different ways of expressing closeness and distance, concern and commitment. In other words: Different people want to be loved and need to be loved in different ways. This was an experience of Sheila Barton, mother to a boy who was diagnosed on the autism spectrum. In her memoirs about what it meant to raise a special child like her son Jonathan, she talks about that she had to learn how to love her boy since autism means being in a different country, customs different, language strange. In situations where Jonathan was banging his head against the wall his mother was not supposed to hug him, speak to him or even to look at him, she had to learn to sing softly.[3] This is a lesson in a 'language of love'. There is a grammar to this language (the explicit or implicit rules) and a vocabulary (the ways of expression), as well as symbolic depth and a horizon of meanings. Human persons want to be loved in different ways – some people want to keep a certain distance, others prefer closeness, some like refined talk, others don't. It can be considered a sign of 'magnanimity' to effortlessly switch languages in interacting with people. British philosopher Iris Murdoch once observed that loving a person is like learning a foreign language which asks for accepting authority, attention, patience and what could be called self-forgetfulness:

> I am learning, for instance, Russian. I am confronted by an authoritative structure, which commands my respect. The task is difficult and the goal is distant and perhaps never entirely attainable. My work is a progressive revelation of

something which is independently of me. Attention is rewarded by knowledge of reality. Love of Russian leads me away from myself towards something alien to me, something that my consciousness cannot take over, swallow up, deny or make unreal.[4]

Sheila Barton had to learn a foreign language to be able to raise her son. Peace-building is an art of polyglotty in the sense that different people will have to be fully considered if peace is to become real. In post-Apartheid South Africa you will have to find different ways of addressing the different addressees of the peace process. Finding a unifying language requires polyglotty: There are lessons about this kind of polyglotty in Issa's life. People had to become polyglot in known and unknown languages of love; they had to learn new languages of love in taking care of Issa – she had to be loved in a special way which made some people very creative:

> On Friday, a bouquet of a dozen red roses arrived for Issa from our college friend, Deanna, with a message that took our breath away: 'Every girl should receive some roses at least once in her life. These are red for the love that you embody and the love that surrounds you. Issa Grace – stop and smell the roses, little one'. (11 August 2013)

Issa by her very being made people expand their language skills in speaking languages of love.

Issa's life also offered important insights into '*permeability*'– this is to say that the family system, the system of neighbourhoods, the system of official institutions and the health care system had to find and open up new ways of interacting with each other, had to be permeable to one another so that Issa could survive for almost nine months. Closed systems with a predominant spirit of independence would have threatened her life. This is another dimension of peace-building and peacekeeping: Different levels and different systems have to come together, have to be reconciled, the more personal with the more structural dimension. In the theological tradition the term 'structural sin' points to this dynamic of a permeability between the personal, the social and the structural.[5] Peace cannot be sustained without the proper environment with its political and social dimension, but also not without the proper personal involvement. A culture of peacefulness needs to permeate the private, the social, and the public.[6] Otherwise, peace is a fragile condition, vulnerable to structural weaknesses, social crises and also personal ill-will.

And, finally, Issa's life teaches us the meaning of '*polyphony*'; Dietrich Bonhoeffer used the term in the letters he wrote to describe the multifariousness of life, the colourfulness of human existence with its many dimensions even in a narrow prison cell.[7] Issa was a vulnerable baby in need of care, but she was so much more than that, she was a teacher and a guide, a mystery and a gift, a human being created in the image of God and a sign of God's presence. Her life was much more than a life of medically motivated attention – she was so much more than a 'medical case'. Here again, this is an important dimension for peace-building. Genuine peace is not a technical solution to a problem that can be fixed, but a change in attitude. There may be readings of peace that are more structural-technological and others that are more personalist; given the emphasis on interiority I put in this chapter I will opt for a personalist reading of peace where the structures are seen as attitude-enhancing environments rather than technical matters.[8] True peace respects the polyphony of life and cannot be one-dimensional. 'One-dimensonal peace', to borrow a term from Herbert Marcuse's analysis of the human person, is peace that responds to dimensions of life that can be changed in a predictable manner. This can be done with all those aspects that follow clear laws, but not with the fragility of human nature. We cannot predict how a person will act or react in a particular situation. One-dimensional peace can be predicted, but not as genuine 'peace'. Taking the polyphony of life seriously, makes peace, at the same time, easier and more difficult – more difficult because peace then seems to become this distant and not reachable goal, easier because polyphony of life with its sources for peace can be sustained even under adverse circumstances.

Issa's life, we can conclude, can teach us important points that are relevant for a discussion of peace: (i) the pedagogy of the weak who can contribute to peace-building in a unique way, (ii) the role of polyglotty in a social situation involving several stakeholders, (iii) the relevance of permeability for enduring peace, and (iv) the importance of considering the polyphony of life.

II

Issa's main lesson was a lesson in vulnerability. We talk about peace because we talk about human vulnerability; peace is a fragile good precisely because of human vulnerability. Peace is a good because the absence of peace is an evil. And the absence of peace is an evil because of human vulnerability. This may sound trivial, but seems to go to the heart of the matter. We need peace because we are fragile. If we were unwoundable we would not need peace; if we were unscathed we would not need peace. But since we are vulnerable, peace becomes precious. Similarly, because of our vulnerability peace is fragile.

Vulnerability is part of the human condition; and vulnerability also plays an important role in the reality of politics. Hannah Arendt describes the political as the art of holding conversations about differences. The ability to make promises and the ability to forgive are key capabilities for the possibility of public human interactions. In other words, the basis of citizenship is the recognition of dependence on other and vulnerability to other. Issa's story illustrates this point well – life is full of disruptions which are expressions of our vulnerability.

Vulnerability can be characterized as the condition 'to be susceptible to harm, injury, failure, or misuse'.[9] You can be damaged, even destroyed. Violence can be defined as use of force against persons or things intending to damage or destroy. Vulnerability in this sense is part of the human condition. It means that we cannot reduce the life risks to zero – risks, understood as potential impediments to reaching important life goals. And this means that we are not in full control over our lives. Or in Robert Goodin's words: 'Vulnerability amounts to one person being able to cause consequences that matter to the other'.[10] The fact that our actions have consequences for other people creates a sense of interconnectedness. It is against this background that Hannah Arendt suggested we see forgiving and promising as two fundamental acts of the person because of the fragility of our condition and its social nature.[11] Because of the boundlessness of the consequences of our actions, human agency falls in the category of the unpredictable. 'The reason why we are never able to foretell with certainty the outcome and end of any action is simply that action has no end'.[12] There is, we could say, a 'natality' to each action as well, a sense of 'new beginnings with uncertain outcomes'.

This also implies that a peaceful act can have harmful consequences, neither intended nor desired. And here again, we encounter the importance of attitudes – the acts of promising and forgiving are fruits of an inner attitude; promises are connected to the virtue of prudence with a clear sense of the 'now' and a clear enough sense of the 'then'. Acts of forgiveness express a certain 'inner structure', an inner situation with its emotions, beliefs, desires, and memories; this inner situation is structured in a way that people are open to forgiveness – this implies lack of inner bitterness or desires for revenge. William Blake wrote a famous poem, *A Poison Tree*, describing the dynamics of the inability to forgive as an act of planting a poisonous tree in the depth of your heart.[13] If one cannot forgive a person, this attitude is like a tree that grows and grows, but this tree is poisonous and spreads this poison, sowing embitterment and frustration that will affect the inner situation, the way people perceive, judge, desire, and remember. A poison tree, to use this image again, can infiltrate every memory, every thought, every emotion, every desire. 'As Blake says, it is concealed anger that plants the poison tree. ... It may exclude all other concerns from our attention so that we can't work or play or love as we would wish'.[14] That is why there are good reasons in the spiritual tradition to call for a cleansing of will and thought. 'Purity of heart' – mentioned by John Rawls at the very end of his *Theory of Justice*[15] – is the basis for 'justice beyond fairness', for a social situation that allows for breaking the cycle of action and reaction, for a situation that is open to forgiveness and the promise of peace. The experience of holding Issa was a peace-filling and, in a sense, purifying experience. Vulnerability (in that case, Issa's vulnerability) can be healing.

Vulnerability, however, can also be a source of social unrest. Peace, I have said, is fragile because of our vulnerability. The levels of vulnerability are unequally distributed: 'A person is vulnerable to the extent to which she is not in a position to prevent occurrences that would undermine what she takes to be important to her'.[16] People with more assets, people with more power, people with better health, people with more cultural resources, are less vulnerable. Jon Sobrino showed that an earthquake may be seen as a 'natural disaster', but is still affecting poor people to a much greater extent.[17] Catriona Mackenzie introduces the term 'pathogenic vulnerability' talking about social pathologies that create vulnerabilities.[18] Social pathologies undermine the conditions for an environment that is appropriate for a culture of peacefulness. Social pathologies are forms of social suffering and destructive forms of social development that inhibit human flourishing. One particular aspect of social pathologies is people's inability to make proper judgments. Social pathologies operate, according to Christoph Zurn's reconstruction of Honneth's approach, 'by means of second-order disorders, that is, by means of constitutive disconnects between first-order contents and second-order reflexive comprehension of those contents, where those disconnects are pervasive and socially caused'.[19] There is a gap between reflection and experience. This analysis views a social pathology in terms of 'ideology', i.e. as false beliefs on a first-order level connected with the social inability on a second-order level to identify (let alone satisfy) the need for reflexivity. A social pathology prevents a person from understanding the mechanisms that caused the condition. A person's vulnerability is increased but the person does not deconstruct this status as pathogenic. Many villagers in rural India would not question the status quo – they are caught in an inner prison, as Martin Kaempchen, a German theologian who has been living in an Indian village for more than four decades, once observed.[20] There may be an absence of political and social resistance, no obvious conflicts, but this is a matter of cheap peace, a peace bought with ignorance and epistemic neglect. So again, vulnerability is a double-edged sword with regard to peace: Peace is precious and fragile because of our vulnerability, but also empowered and made possible through vulnerability.

Vulnerability is part of the human condition and permeates all spheres of our existence – vulnerability, one could suggest, has four dimensions: (i) the capacity to be wounded, (ii) the contingency of the world, (iii) the fragility of our existence, and (iv) our human fallibility. There is the dimension of potential direct damage, there is the dimension of the unpredictability of the world which is characterized by a horizon of possibilities, there is the dimension of the unprotectedness of our finite existences, and there is the dimension of moral fragility in the sense that we make mistakes and become guilty. One could also say that there is a pragmatic, an ontological, an existential, and a moral dimension to vulnerability. It affects aspects of our lives, but also our life as a whole.

The recognition of vulnerability as part of the human condition is not just 'yet another thought about life'; it can be seen as an existential marker constituting impacts on an existential level. Let me illustrate: We are familiar with John Rawls' 'veil of ignorance' motif and scenario. It is a situation that is 'thin' and epistemically empty where those invited to judge can be substituted for each other. The key notion at stake is 'fairness'; but peace is not about fairness, this category does not seem appropriate when talking about human vulnerability. Issa's life can also not properly be described in terms of 'fairness'. Furthermore, looking at Rawls' approach, there is a sense, not only in this scenario, but throughout the theory that persons are, to borrow Michael Sandel's term, 'unencumbered selves'.[21] Let us change this scenario in the light of Issa's life. Let me call this scenario 'wound of knowledge'. Suppose Felicia, Issa's mother, had known from the very beginning of her life that she would give birth to Issa – how, then, would she have lived her life?[22] What does it mean to live life with a wound of knowledge that makes the experience of vulnerability tangible and thick and unavoidable? Or, suppose I know now that I will end my life suffering from Alzheimer's disease, in dependence and helplessness, suffering from experiences of loss and confusion – how would I live my life now? What does it mean to live life with a wound of knowledge? What does it mean to live with a thick account of vulnerability? What does it mean to live with a personal, non-substitutable sense of vulnerability?

I want to provide a personal answer: If I were to know now that I will end my life in a state of dementia, I would rethink key categories such as 'autonomy', 'life goals', 'structures of relevance' and 'compassion'. On the basis of this personal and thick understanding of vulnerability I would deal with my own vulnerability and with the vulnerability of others differently. If I were to recognize my vulnerability on a deep level, I would see myself as a person, not only wounded, but also one who has wounded others. And this can mean a fundamental change in self-perception.[23] Recognizing my own vulnerability changes my attitude vis-à-vis those who are especially vulnerable. Accepting my own vulnerability helps me to see myself more fully. It was Jean Vanier, founder of *l'Arche* communities, who reflected upon this point:

> If we deny our weakness and the reality of death, if we want to be powerful and strong always, we deny a part of who we are, this mixture of strength and weakness. To be human is to accept and love others just as they are, weaknesses and strengths, because we need each other. Weakness, recognized, accepted, and offered, is at the heart of belonging, so it is at the heart of communion with another.[24]

A wound of knowledge makes it easier for us to accept that 'behind our roles, and the masks we often wear, we are all vulnerable and struggling human beings whose hearts are more needy than we would dare to admit at times'.[25] So a first effect of recognizing vulnerability as part of the human condition is an understanding of 'relational autonomy', of dependence and connectedness or, of kinship.[26] Recognizing my vulnerability with its four dimensions will instil in me a sense of dependence, a sense of what it means to be a zoon politicón, a social and political being in need of community.

A second effect of the recognition of vulnerability could be the recognition of vulnerability of others and thus the cultivation of a 'caring attitude' or of moral demands. Facing the vulnerability of other puts us in a different place when embracing a second person perspective. This recognition would give rise to a protective attitude, an attitude even of tenderness. This was an experience people who encountered Issa were privileged to make. This encounter was, in many instances, transformative. Robert Jonas describes this effect from his experience with his daughter Rebecca, who lived for less than four hours. Eventually gratitude was the dominating attitude in Rebecca's father since his daughter had changed so many lives during and because of her life.[27] The encounter with a vulnerable person does something to the moral situation a person finds herself in: 'It is dependency and vulnerability rather than voluntary acts of will which give rise ... to our most fundamental moral duties'.[28] The vulnerability of others asks for a response that does justice to the protective and caring needs of the human person.

A third effect of the recognition of vulnerability is the recognition of depth and beauty in the world; there is not only a new self-understanding, a new way of embracing a second person perspective, but also a new way of being in the world, a new attitude towards the world as a whole. Just think of Issa: She was vulnerable, she made her family vulnerable, and at the same time there was the experience of depth and beauty, of deep beauty and beautiful depth. Simone Weil reflected upon the connection between vulnerability and beauty when she observed: 'The vulnerability of precious things is beautiful because vulnerability is a mark of existence'.[29] There is a depth that only fragility can give.

Now, of course, someone could say: But what about people who recognize the vulnerability of others and exploit that by displaying cruelty and violence? What about those who recognize their own vulnerability and become defensive about it? One possible answer to this rejoinder could be: Can we say that we have a 'deep understanding' of vulnerability if we are open to those kinds of reactions? Can we say that we have a 'substantial understanding' of vulnerability since vulnerability also implies fallibility, the fragility of our existence, and the capacity to be wounded? Can we say that we have really 'recognized' our vulnerability? If we recognize vulnerability with its four dimensions we will embrace a deeper understanding of relational autonomy, caring kinship, and a sense of depth and beauty of the world. And these are essential building blocks for a culture of peacefulness.

III

The peacefulness felt when holding Issa was more than just a mood, it was an attitude coming through; it was an attitude based on beliefs as well as emotions, an attitude that changed 'the inner situation'. The inner situation is painfully relevant in situations of war. Napoleon's war against Russia in 1812 was strategically unwise and politically unnecessary and was based on Napoleon's hubris.[30] World War I was orchestrated on the basis of an inner situation of cheerful recklessness and careless lack of judgment, as aptly described in Christopher Clark's well-received study *Sleepwalkers*.[31] Peace is based on and embedded in a culture of peacefulness. Peacefulness is part of the inner situation, it is a fundamental attitude that can be defined as 'a second-order resource to cope with human vulnerability in social situations'; this definition is built in conversation with Lennard Nordenfelt's definition of health as a second-order capability.[32] Hence, peacefulness is a resource that coordinates, connects, organizes and weights first-order resources such as memories, emotions, beliefs, actions and plans. It is an attitude that is relevant because of human vulnerability – if the human person were not vulnerable, we would not have to worry about matters of peace and war. The category of peacefulness makes a statement about the inner situation of a person.

How does one foster an inner situation of peacefulness? Let me briefly turn to early Christian sources for this question; they reflected on the sources of peacefulness against the background of a deep understanding of human interiority.[33] Furthermore, they were writing in a time characterized by conflicts on the microlevel (interpersonal conflicts) as well as on the macrolevel (wars, political instability). One could take 'anger' to be the absence of the attitude of peacefulness. Evagrius Ponticus in his *Texts on Discrimination in respect of Passion and Thoughts* mentions three main sources for anger, namely food, wealth and honour. He suggests that an important source for anger are memories which means that lack of social order (lack of food) or lack of inner order (greed) undermine peacefulness. John Cassian in his text *On the Eight Vices* sees anger as a dangerous situation that clouds our judgment, confuses justice, and obstructs decency – there is a need for community, hence a need for recognizing our connectedness in order to overcome peace. Anger can be seen as an 'inflation of spirit' that goes hand in hand with the despising of another person.[34] A culture of peacefulness will be challenged to overcome those kinds of dispositions leading to this kind of anger.

The aim of this attitude of peacefulness is peace which I suggest to define as 'a social situation characterized by the stakeholders' readiness and capability to deal with questions of conflict and coordination in a way that preserves Co-Being'. This is to say that peace is a social situation shaped by an inner situation; the inner situation is characterized by dispositions to preserve not only co-existence but also co-existence in the strong sense of recognizing vulnerability and mutual dependency ('Co-Being'). And this deep sense of oneself in the face of another is key to my reading of the concept of 'peace'.

A concept such as 'peace' has different properties such as its cultural anchoring (How is the concept rooted in a culture? Which cultural activities are possible owing to the concept?), its role in language games and its imaginative force. The latter is the capability of a concept to transform our imagination. 'Imagination' is the capability to conceive of alternatives to the status quo, of possible or impossible states and circumstances; this capability involves a sense of the real (as reference point for the construction of possible worlds) and a sense of possibilities. Immanuel Kant introduced 'imagination' as the bridging faculty between understanding and sense, and the faculty of representing an object even without its presence in intuition.[35] The senses lack intellectual content, understanding lacks sensual content – imagination connects the two. One could speculate that imagination could be 'cultivated' in that particular alternatives to the present are made the basis for ordering present experience; this could mean that a particular 'habit of imagination' (i.e. guided by 'obtained' or 'cultural' categories) helps to shape ways of perception and ordering the perceived. Deep encounters such as the one I described in the beginning shape the imagination, and may be starting points for new ways of perception, self-perception and imagination.

We might call the dynamics involved in the cultural refinement of imagination 'bounded imagination'. The Swiss philosopher, Peter Bieri, suggests in his book on human dignity that the concept of human dignity opens up the possibility for a new way of perceiving, a new form of life.[36] In other words, 'human dignity' implies ordering principles that 'bind' imagination in a particular way. A new kind of imagination, a refined 'sense of possibilities' (especially possibilities with a normative force insofar as they are acknowledged as points of orientation and direction) opens up a new way of 'being in the world'. A moving example of these dynamics is the story of Shin Dong-hyuk, who was born inside Camp 14, a huge political prison north of Pyongyang as a son of two prisoners. He was raised in the Camp but was never given a sense of 'context' or 'alternatives'; only with the arrival of another inmate, who told him about the outside world and the possibility of escape, was his imagination ('sense of possibilities') triggered for the first time and a whole new way of being in the world opened up before him.[37] His imagination was triggered by a deep understanding of the contingency of the world: Things could be different!

One of the dimensions of vulnerability, as suggested, is the contingency of the word. The recognition of vulnerability is a door that would allow the proper shaping of our imagination enabling peace. Or, in other words, peace is a concept that helps us to rethink vulnerability. The encounter with Issa was an experience that changed my inner situation; my understanding of vulnerability as well as my understanding of peacefulness were transformed. The inner situation is politically relevant, especially the sense of possibilities. There is a political relevance and depth to the imagination. Peter Brown talks about 'a revolution in the social imagination', which occurred after the fourth century, in dealing with famine and destitution from a Christian perspective.[38] Czech President Vaclav Havel, for example, in his *Summer Meditations*, imagined what a possible future of the Czech Republic could and should look like. He explored possible future developments for his country by applying bounded imagination,[39] that is imagination based on commitments (on values). Such exercises in 'bounded imagination' for political purposes have become rare in a climate of short-term oriented politics. 'Deep politics' is a kind of politics that respects the importance of the inner situation and asks tough questions of truth and meaning. A deep understanding of vulnerability will offer insights into our capacity to be wounded and thus into the importance of prudence, into the fragility of our existence and thus into the value of connectedness, into the contingence of the world and thus into the key challenge of a sense of possibilities, and into our fallibility and thus into the importance of promising and forgiving.

Building a culture of peacefulness as the experiential framework for peace will require a consideration of the lessons Issa taught us, including recognizing the pedagogy of the weak (the insight that there cannot be true peace without proper consideration of the victims as subjects is one of the key insights of the South African Peace Process lead by Desmond Tutu), polyglotty (offering communication in many forms, on different levels and with a clear perspective of honouring differences: the importance of language has been politically recognized in the linguistic debates around 'the politics of apologies', for instance), permeability as the connectedness of different systems and levels, and polyphony: having a sense of the nuances of life – peace is not only a contract that can be negotiated, but more of a covenant if the inner situation is part of the story, if the human imagination is informed by the concept of peace, and if the concept of peace is anchored in cultural practices of 'doing peace'. The latter, however, makes the challenges raised by Evagrius Ponticus and John Cassian relevant. Peace starts at home (and in a person's soul, if I may use this language). This is also the point where 'poetry' can be powerful; just think of Gerard Manley Hopkins' poem *Peace*[40] where we find the first lines tell us: 'When will you ever, Peace, wild wooddove, shy wings shut, Your round me roaming end, and under be my boughs? When, when, Peace, will you, Peace? I'll not play hypocrite to my own heart: I yield you do come sometimes; but that piecemeal peace is poor peace'.

Notes

1 Leymah Gbowee, *Might Be Our Powers: How Sisterhood, Prayer, and Sex Changed a Nation at War*, with Carol Mithers (New York: Beast Books, 2011).
2 See the first essay in Marina Keegan, *The Opposite of Loneliness* (New York: Scribner, 2014).
3 Sheila Barton, *Living with Jonathan: Lessons in Love, Life and Autism* (London: Watkins Publishing, 2011).
4 Iris Murdoch, *Metaphysics as a Guide to Morals* (London: Allen Lane/Penguin, 1997), 373.
5 Daniel J. Daly, 'Structures of Virtue and Vice', *New Blackfriars* 92 (2011): 341–57.
6 We owe this thought of placing the social as a third dimension between the private and the public to Hannah Arendt – Seyla Benhabib, 'Feminist Theory and Hannah Arendt's Concept of Public Space', *History of the Human Sciences* 6, no. 2 (1993): 108–11.
7 Dietrich Bonhoeffer, *Widerstand und Ergebung: Briefe und Aufzeichnungen aus der Haft; Vollständige Ausgabe, versehen mit Einleitung, Anmerkungen und Kommentaren*, ed. by Christian Gremmels, Eberhard Bethge and Renate Bethge in cooperation with Ise Tödt. Dietrich Bonhoeffer Werke, vol. 8 (n.p.: Gütersloher Verlaghaus, 2011), 444. English edition: life, even in prison, 'is kept multi-dimensional and polyphonous' (Dietrich Bonhoeffer, *Letters and Papers from Prison* [London: SCM, 1971], 3311).
8 There is a similar discussion, for instance, in the question of world hunger – is world hunger more a technological-scientific issue or more a moral-political one? I would clearly opt for the latter and not the former; similarly, in poverty studies, is poverty more a technological issue that can be fixed or rather a political challenge that finds its roots in the fragility of goodness? Here again, I opt for the latter. This is not to undermine the importance of structures – no sustainable peace without proper legal frameworks and economic conditions; but without a change in attitude, structures can only curb violence and minimize damage, they cannot 'create' peace.
9 Paul Formosa, 'The Role of Vulnerability in Kantian Ethics', in *Vulnerability: New Essays in Ethics and Feminist Philosophy*, ed. Catriona Mackenzie, Wendy Rogers and Susan Dodds (Oxford: Oxford University Press, 2014), 89.
10 Robert E. Goodin, *Protecting the Vulnerable* (Chicago: University of Chicago Press, 1985), 114.
11 Hannah Arendt, *The Human Condition* (Chicago: Chicago University Press, 1958), 237.
12 Arendt, *The Human Condition*, 233.
13 Cf. John Brenkman, 'The Concrete Utopia of Poetry: Blake's "A Poison Tree"', in *Lyric Poetry: Beyond Criticism*, ed. Chaviva Hošek and Patricia Parker (Ithaca, NY: Cornell University Press, 1985), 182–93.
14 L. William Countryman, *Forgiven and Forgiving* (Harrisburg, PA: Morehouse Publishing, 1998), 99.
15 'Purity of heart, if one could attain it, would be to see clearly and to act with grace and self-command' (John Rawls, *A Theory of Justice* [Cambridge, MA: Harvard University Press, 1971], 514). This is an inner situation clearly without a poison tree.

16 Joel Anderson, 'Autonomy and Vulnerability Intertwined', in *Vulnerability: New Essays in Ethics and Feminist Philosophy*, ed. Catriona Mackenzie, Wendy Rogers and Susan Dodds (Oxford: Oxford University Press, 2014), 135.

17 Jon Sobrino, *Terremoto, terrorismo, barbarie y utopia.* (El Salvador: UCA Editores, 2003), chap. 1.

18 Catriona Mackenzie, Wendy Rogers and Susan Dodds, introduction to *Vulnerability: New Essays in Ethics and Feminist Philosophy*, ed. Catriona Mackenzie, Wendy Rogers and Susan Dodds (Oxford: Oxford University Press, 2014), 7–9.

19 Christopher F. Zurn, 'Social Pathologies as Second-Order Disorders', in *Axel Honneth: Critical Essays*, ed. Danielle Petherbridge (Leiden: Brill, 2011), 345f. A. Honneth in his rejoinder in the same volume (417f) accepts this analysis as exceptionally fruitful. A more basic reconstruction of Honneth's concept of social pathologies is provided by Jean-Philippe Deranty, *Beyond Communication: A Critical Study of Axel Honneth's Social Philosophy* (Leiden: Brill, 2009), 319–24.

20 Martin Kaempchen, Leben ohne Armut. Wie Hilfe wirklich helfen kann – meine Erfahrungen in Indien (Freiburg/Br: Herder Publishers, 2011), 52, 63.

21 Michael J. Sandel, 'The Procedural Republic and the Unencumbered Self', *Political Theory* 12, no. 1 (1984): 81–96.

22 By way of a footnote: I do not think it would have made a difference in this case; it would have for the Putins and Maos and Napoleons of this world (maybe, hopefully).

23 A mythical illustration of this journey towards a deep sense of vulnerability can be found in the Jewish tradition in the biblical story of Jacob's wrestling with an angel (Genesis 32:23–32). Jacob is wounded, limps after that night-long encounter, but assumes a new identity, with a new name and a blessing. If I recognize my vulnerability on a deep level, I am also, in a sense, limping, but with a new name and identity.

24 Jean Vanier, *Drawn into the Mystery of Jesus through the Gospel of John* (Mahwah, NJ: Paulist Press, 2004), 191.

25 Tim Kearney, *A Prophetic Cry: Stories of Spirituality and Healing Inspired by L'Arche* (Dublin: Veritas, 2000), 76.

26 Gregory Boyle, *Tattoos on the Heart* (New York: Free Press, 2010), chap. 9.

27 Robert A. Jonas, *Rebecca: A Father's Journey from Grief to Gratitude* (New York: Crossroad, 1996).

28 Goodin, *Protecting the Vulnerable*, 34.

29 Simone Weil, *Gravity and Grace* (n.p.: University of Nebraska Press, 1997), 161.

30 Cf., Mark J. Kroll, Leslie A. Toombs and Peter Wright, 'Napoleon's Tragic March Home from Moscow: Lessons in Hubris', *Academy of Management Executive* 14, no. 1 (2000): 117–28.

31 Christopher Clark, *The Sleepwalkers: How Europe Went to War in 1914* (London: Allen Lane, 2012).

32 'A is completely helathy, if and only if A is in a bodily or mental state which is such that A has the second order ability to realize all his or her vital goals given standard or reasonable circumstances' (Lennart Nordenfelt, 'Standard Circumstances and Vital Goals', *Bioethics* 27, no. 5 (2013): 280–4).

33 It can be argued that one of the key contributions of Christian thinking to our understanding of 'Self' is the dimension of interiority – Charles Taylor, *Sources of the Self* (Cambridge, MA: Harvard University Press, 1989), chap. 2.

34 Cf. Thomas Aquinas, *Summa Theologica II-II*, 158, resp.

35 Immanuel Kant, *Critique of Pure Reason*, B 151.

36 Peter Bieri, *Eine Art zu leben: Über die Vielfalt menschlicher Würde* (Munich: Hanser, 2013).

37 Blaine Harden, *Escape from Camp 14* (London: Pan Books, 2013).

38 Peter Brown, *Poverty and Leadership in the Later Roman Era* (Hanover, NH: University Press of New England, 2002), 1.

39 Vaclav Havel, *Summer Meditations* (London: Vintage, 1993).

40 Gerard Manley Hopkins, *Poems* (London: Penguin, 1985), 42.

References

Anderson, Joel. 'Autonomy and Vulnerability Intertwined'. In *Vulnerability: New Essays in Ethics and Feminist Philosophy*, edited by Catriona Mackenzie, Wendy Rogers and Susan Dodds, 134–61. Oxford: Oxford University Press, 2014.

Aquinas, Thomas. *Summa Theologica.* New York: Benzinger, 1947–1948.

Arendt, Hannah. *The Human Condition.* Chicago: Chicago University Press, 1958.

Barton, Sheila. *Living with Jonathan: Lessons in Love, Life and Autism.* London: Watkins Publishing, 2011.

Benhabib, Seyla. 'Feminist Theory and Hannah Arendt's Concept of Public Space'. *History of the Human Sciences* 6, no. 2 (1993): 97–114.

Bieri, Peter. *Eine Art zu leben: Über die Vielfalt menschlicher Würde.* Munich: Hanser, 2013.

Bonhoeffer, Dietrich. *Widerstand und Ergebung: Briefe und Aufzeichnungen aus der Haft; Vollständige Ausgabe, versehen mit Einleitung, Anmerkungen und Kommentaren.* Edited by Christian Gremmels, Eberhard Bethge and Renate Bethge in cooperation with Ise Tödt. Dietrich Bonhoeffer Werke, vol. 8. N.p.: Gütersloher Verlaghaus, 2011. Translated as *Letters and Papers from Prison* (London: SCM, 1971).

Boyle, Gregory. *Tattoos on the Heart.* New York: Free Press, 2010.

Brenkman, John. 'The Concrete Utopia of Poetry: Blake's "A Poison Tree."' In *Lyric Poetry: Beyond New Criticism*, edited by Chaviva Hošek and Patricia Parker, 182–93. Ithaca, NY: Cornell University Press, 1985.

Brown, Peter. *Poverty and Leadership in the Later Roman Era.* Hanover, NH: University Press of New England, 2002.

Clark, Christopher. *The Sleepwalkers: How Europe Went to War in 1914.* London: Allen Lane, 2012.

Countryman, L. William. *Forgiven and Forgiving.* Harrisburg, PA: Morehouse Publishing, 1998.

Daly, Daniel J. 'Structures of Virtue and Vice'. *New Blackfriars* 92 (2011): 341–57.

Deranty, Jean-Philippe. *Beyond Communication: A Critical Study of Axel Honneth's Social Philosophy.* Leiden: Brill, 2009.

Formosa, Paul. 'The Role of Vulnerability in Kantian Ethics'. In *Vulnerability: New Essays in Ethics and Feminist Philosophy*, edited by Catriona Mackenzie, Wendy Rogers and Susan Dodds, 88–109. Oxford: Oxford University Press, 2014.

Gbowee, Leymah. *Might Be Our Powers: How Sisterhood, Prayer, and Sex Changed a Nation at War.* With Carol Mithers. New York: Beast Books, 2011.

Goodin, Robert E. *Protecting the Vulnerable.* Chicago: University of Chicago Press, 1985.

Harden, Blaine. *Escape from Camp 14.* London: Pan Books, 2013.

Havel, Vaclav. *Summer Meditations.* London: Vintage, 1993.

Hopkins, Gerard Manley. *Poems.* London: Penguin, 1985.

Jonas, Robert A. *Rebecca: A Father's Journey from Grief to Gratitude.* New York: Crossroad, 1996.

Kaempchen, Martin. *Leben ohne Armut: Wie Hilfe wirklich helfen kann – meine Erfahrungen in Indien.* Freiburg/Br: Herder Publishers, 2011.

Kant, Immanuel. *Critique of Pure Reason.* London: Macmillan, 1881.

Kearney, Tim. *A Prophetic Cry: Stories of Spirituality and Healing Inspired by L'Arche.* Dublin: Veritas, 2000.

Keegan, Marina. *The Opposite of Loneliness: Essays and Stories.* New York: Scribner, 2014.

Kroll, Mark J., Leslie A. Toombs and Peter Wright. 'Napoleon's Tragic March Home from Moscow: Lessons in Hubris'. *Academy of Management Executive* 14, no. 1 (2000): 117–28.

Mackenzie, Catriona, Wendy Rogers and Susan Dodds. Introduction to *Vulnerability: New Essays in Ethics and Feminist Philosophy*, edited by Catriona Mackenzie, Wendy Rogers and Susan Dodds, 1–32. Oxford: Oxford University Press, 2014.

Murdoch, Iris. *Metaphysics as a Guide to Morals.* London: Allen Lane/Penguin, 1997.

Nordenfelt, Lennart. 'Standard Circumstances and Vital Goals'. *Bioethics* 27, no. 5 (2013): 280–4.

Rawls, John. *A Theory of Justice*. Cambridge, MA: Harvard University Press, 1971.

Sandel, Michael J. 'The Procedural Republic and the Unencumbered Self'. *Political Theory* 12, no. 1 (1984): 81–96.

Sobrino, Jon. *Terremoto, terrorismo, barbarie y utopia*. El Salvador: UCA Editores, 2003. Translated by Margaret Wilde as *Where Is God? Earthquake, Terrorism, Barbarity, and Hope* (Maryknoll, NY: Orbis, 2004).

Taylor, Charles. *Sources of the Self*. Cambridge, MA: Harvard University Press, 1989.

Vanier, Jean. *Drawn into the Mystery of Jesus through the Gospel of John*. Mahwah, NJ: Paulist Press, 2004.

Weil, Simone. *Gravity and Grace*. N.p.: University of Nebraska Press, 1997.

Zurn, Christopher F. 'Social Pathologies as Second-Order Disorders'. In *Axel Honneth: Critical Essays*, edited by Danielle Petherbridge, 345–70. Leiden: Brill, 2011.

3   Aesthetic Imagination and Animate Peace

Pauline von Bonsdorff[1]

1. Introduction

It has been suggested that our civilisation is in a state of prolonged moral crisis in its relationship to nature, environment and non-human species. The crisis is not, then, just about material resources but about fundamental values that affect us as much as the natural environment. Philosophers and scholars have described the crisis in terms of a war between humankind and nature, or between humans and other species.[2] If there is a war it is fought in blindness: without an explicit will to harm nature yet with a profound negligence of how our lifestyles and societal structures – such as global trade, agriculture, foresting, urban land-use, mining for communication technology – affect local ecosystems and the earth as a whole, its ground, air and water systems. One might see the crisis as one of misplaced priorities where care and protection of non-human habitats is not seen as important enough as compared to economic growth or political power; or of an inability to grasp the big picture, or of not caring for our non-human companions. Other reasons could certainly be named as well.

Looking especially at the educated middle class in contemporary Western societies our nature relationship is indeed paradoxical. Many people 'love'[3] nature: some enjoy beautiful landscapes and travel far to see them, others seek adventure in nature, some grow gardens, and some breed and train animals in order to participate in competitions where aesthetic qualities such as skill, force, beauty and courage are at stake. Yet through our very lifestyle we consume natural habitats, as if our individual life and the broader environment were disconnected, as if what is not seen did not exist. There is however also a growing insight and an increasing sense of urgency to it, that humans can live only in interdependence with other species. In philosophy a turn towards interdependence is linked to criticisms of the dualistic traditions that separate mind and body, human and animal.[4] Writing on the animal 'that I am' and the absence of the animal as a philosophical theme in the West, Jacques Derrida shows how the idea that thinking alone constitutes the subject keeps the question of life, of living and breathing, of the animate and animals firmly outside 'the subject'. For Derrida, unlike Descartes, it is not thinking but animal that 'therefore I am'.[5]

In this chapter my aim is to contribute to the discussion about the nature crisis through looking at how we might work towards dynamic coexistence with non-human nature through communicating and bonding with domestic mammals, thereby anchoring ourselves in the world. Ultimately my contribution is about building peace with nature. I start, in Section 2, with a discussion of negative and positive peace between humans and non-human nature, and introduce 'animate peace' to suggest that peace is a dynamic, complex and challenging, in addition to rewarding, state of affairs. In Section 3 I turn to our interaction and communication with domestic animals. Using personal experience I show the multimodal, holistic character of such communication; how it is temporally layered and emerging in a relationship that transforms both parts; and how it marginalises verbal language as a means of communication. In Section 4 I argue that our communication with animals calls for aesthetic imagination: an imagination that is affected by and partly parallel with actual interactions, and operates with images more than concepts. Aesthetic imagination provides an alternative to the striving for control, with its implications of unilateral power and violence, and a poetic home for animal affections. I end, in Section 5, by addressing one possible limitation of the outlined approach, basically pointing out that self-education is an active process.

2. Animate Peace

In his book *Le contrat naturel*, written when worries about global warming and climate change had recently entered public consciousness, Michel Serres argues that we should realise that humans at present are at war with nature. Such an insight might make us more aware of nature and enable us to draw a peace treaty, e.g. a contract between humans and nature. Serres claims that our culture is fundamentally alienated from nature, which we do not know concretely.[6] In a sense then, Martin Heidegger's suggestion that humans are world-creating (*weltbildend*) while (other) animals are 'poor in world' (*weltarm*)[7] is turned upside down: it is not animals but contemporary humans whose world is impoverished and thin. The suggestion could be criticised for ignoring what Heidegger means by 'world'. Yet what I want to do is precisely to bypass the hegemony of a particular form of human culture and self-understanding in setting the limits for culturally significant communication between animate beings, including non-humans.

If humans at present are at war with nature, how can we work towards peace? We might start with the distinction between negative and positive peace. Johan Galtung describes negative peace as 'the absence of violence of all kinds', the cure of which is various means of violence reduction.[8] Focused as it is on the absence and reduction of its opposites, violence and war, negative peace leaves the substance of peace undefined. Furthermore, while negative peace implies the absence of violence of all kinds the boundary between negative peace, structural violence and explicit violence may in practice be rather open. Thus Hans Magnus Enzensberger describes violence and hatred in contemporary capitalist society as 'molecular civil war' and points to a cultural vacuum as its root cause.[9] A negative approach to peace, although necessary, is far from sufficient.

Fortunately Galtung gives directions for positive peace. It comprises qualities such as kindness and love to self and other, freedom, dialogue and solidarity. It is 'a cooperative system beyond "passive peaceful coexistence" ... that can bring forth positively synergistic fruits of the harmony'. Finally the means towards positive peace are in '*processes of life enhancement*'.[10] Several important points are involved here. I would however like to stress the dynamic aspects, including antagonisms and conflicting interests, even more than Galtung, who puts the 'bliss' of sexual union at the positive end of a continuum from total separation to total association (while observing that the latter may not be sustainable in the long run). Developing the concept animate peace I agree with Galtung about the need to think about what peace is rather than about what it is not, but I find it necessary to guard the heterogeneity and even messiness of life as *multum in parvo*.[11] This will lead, as I show later, to seeing peace as sustained through aesthetic imagination.

Where and how can we then preliminarily find processes of life enhancement – the building of positive peace – in our interaction with non-human mammals? First, the ideal of negative peace is, at least in practice, connected to control. Control is a constituent part of negative peace in and between societies as well, implemented through rules, borders, police and security forces, and so forth. With domestic animals this implies a demand of obedience, and communication defined unilaterally by humans. The problem is not that such methods of working with animals do not work: they can lead to calm, safe and predictable interactions. However, they are also rigid, and there is no real dialogue in such situations, no looking from the other side or imagining oneself in the other's place. Such methods often do not enhance the life and flourishing of the other. Second, positive peace is precisely about dialogue in dynamic relationships where the actors are allowed to change rather than stick to roles defined by rules and current opinion. Genuine dialogue is a way towards life enhancement and flourishing.[12] It demands a reflective relationship to oneself and the other: a willingness to change and adapt. Positive peace must be continuously sustained, performed and exercised: it is an individual and intersubjective practice, a personal task we do with others. In a fundamental sense, it is about culture, education and self-education.[13]

Positive peace, then, is not passive but involves dynamic acts of balancing, including risks and communicational failures. This is evident in 'animate peace', which is my take on the possibility of positive peace between humans and nature. I want to emphasise its lively and unpredictable character. Unlike when we think of peace as an end to war there are no treaties here; the game never stops. Animate peace has the potential of making us more aware of the conflicting interests that are part of life, where the challenge is not to eradicate them or make others give up what they want, but to find ways of living together in mutual enjoyment. With Donna Haraway, it is about 'how worldly actors might ... love each other less violently',[14] and it reminds us of what we share with non-human animate beings. Finally the idea is inspired by Luce Irigaray's call for a sexual culture:[15] a culture of dialogue instead of juxtaposition and stereotypes, a reflective culture with awareness of how language affects the relationship between the sexes, a cultivation of sexual relationships in the broadest sense. Animate peace, accordingly, is the cultivation of our philosophical, practical and poetical relationships with other species towards more insight, fairness and enjoyment.

Animate peace points us in a direction where communication broadens beyond words towards other forms of communication. Next I want to indicate how dialogues can arise by non-verbal means, where communication is more a making 'in common' rather than only 'making common' what one part desires.[16] Such exchanges demand that we recognise the embodied, multi-sensuous and often unintentional ways in which we share our state of being with other mammals that are more sensitive than we in many ways. We then have to become more worldly; more attached to the natural world through affectionate ties with fellow creatures and their ways of co-inhabiting our shared environment. Often this comes naturally, for despite difficulties and sometimes frustrations, grace, joy and playfulness are significant ingredients of animate peace, and mostly near at hand.[17]

3. Living with Animals

In reflecting on communication with animals more attention has been given to whether they understand what we want than on whether we understand what they want. Whether the animal responds to the human has been discussed in depth as compared to the virtually inexistent issue of whether the human responds to the animal.[18] Yet either way communication can be understood as information exchange or 'making common'. For understanding our life with animals, and for animate peace, the model of dialogue as making *in* common is more fruitful, and underexplored. Refreshingly, in her book on infants and intersubjectivity Vasudevi Reddy introduces the 'two-person model' of understanding other persons, where the starting point is that we are who we are in relation to others, and the presumed gap between self and other is a theoretical construction.[19] Recent multidisciplinary infant research shows that embodiment and intersubjectivity are fundamental conditions of what we are rather than add-ons; and early communication is rhythmic and aesthetic before it is verbal.[20] Language develops from vocal and multimodal gestures, and gestural, expressive elements remain part of verbal discourse.[21]

Relationality and the reciprocal creation of situations, including meaning, are key to our interaction with animals. As I argue below, we understand the other animal largely because we share contexts and in fact co-create them. This acting together can involve various aims, and is also a tuning of the intersubjective relationship. Personal, embodied communication is perhaps always to some extent the modulation of feelings shared in a situation, but together with animals this aspect is emphasised. Who we are is influenced by our relation to animals at least when we share our life with them.[22]

Another preliminary point is that the role of words is transformed when we speak to animals. They do react to names and other words, such as 'come', 'food' or 'wait', but what accompanies the word is as important as the word itself. I can say 'Mindi' in a factual tone: the cat half asleep on my desk shows no reaction. But when I repeat her name in the soft, melodious tone that is common between us her ear moves: she recognises that I address her. The linguistic system as such is not there for the animal, but emotional modulations and contextual meanings, and the style of a particular human person are recognised. Thus one answer to Serres' question on how to find a common language with nature[23] is to give up the primacy of the verbal. When Mindi rolls over I abandon the keyboard and caress her, entering her purring playful state. This takes place without any conscious decision: I just respond to her gestures as she invites me. In communicating with animals, movements, gestures and sounds are much more important than words. And vision, unquestionably central for us humans, is just one sense in a web of multimodal attention and response.[24]

I will reflect on my experience of interacting with domestic animals, mainly horses and cats, highlighting aspects of companionship, of sharing and influencing the other's life. The temporal and autobiographical dimension – the prolonged, dynamic conversation between individuals – is crucial. In this case my personal history with cats, cattle and horses provides familiarity with the character and body language of these creatures. The tacit knowledge that experience provides is the background from which I am frustrated, happy or puzzled with the animal companion or myself. Experience affects both the actual instances of communication and their interpretation. The narratives, on the other hand, also reveal some aspects of me as a person. Different styles of communication yield different outcomes that again influence who we are. The idea is to indicate aspects that are relevant for aesthetic imagination and animate peace. While I consider species and sex as existential conditions for the animal itself, and recognise that they influence our perceptions, my intention is not to generalise but to highlight interactions with individual animals.[25]

A feature that stands out in the human–equine relationship is the intimacy of human actions on the horse. Horses are groomed and ridden; when working they mostly wear iron shoes and iron bits in their sensitive mouths. There is much in riding and driving that relies on the threat of pain. At the same time, trust and reliability are necessary because the animal is big and strong, and potentially dangerous.

Today riders have more opportunities than ever to develop their skills in theory and practice through a wide variety of approaches. The biomechanical approach is especially useful because it looks at the dynamics of rider and horse through careful microanalyses of anatomy and movement.[26] The basic philosophy however varies from behaviourism to respect for the horse as an intelligent individual. Thus a dressage simulator – a life-size robot that reacts to the aids of the rider mechanically – can certainly help the rider to improve her actions on the horse, but it marginalises the individuality of horses and the temporally extended relationship between particular humans and particular horses. It leads to seeing the animal as the representative of a species, a token of a type.

The focus of riding instruction is often on control and obedience.[27] This obscures the personality of the animal, its initiatives, suggestions and emotions, and dialogue through a human response. A horse can suggest canter by taking a few strides when being asked for a trot: if she accepts trot the human can thank her by suggesting canter. This is however hindered by the rule that the human should always, with unfaltering consequence, stay with her own idea of what to do. Accordingly the horse's ideas must not be accepted and the relationship is competitive, even conflictual: one of at most negative peace between two separate parties.

Another rule, emphasised by virtually every instructor, is that the horse must not enter the space of the human unless invited. Yet if we accept exceptions in some situations another horse can appear. *One May afternoon I bring fresh willows to the two horses, and we spend time together. I talk to one at a time and stroke them. While I stand with Esteri, Suijari approaches. I surmise he is bossy and jealous and wave my arms to make him go away. Then I turn toward Esteri again. Surprised I then feel him scrubbing his head against my hip, without aggression. I look down and perceive the thick winter fell on his forehead. I scrub it and it comes off in balls. 'So this is what you meant' I say.* It should be added that Suijari has a reputation of not accepting to be touched on his head as he was probably beaten during his years as a trotter.

Sharing a space with horses requires willingness to see their side of the space as different from ours, and to accept their invitations. When dialogues take place the human and the equine are no longer separate entities, but more like fluids in a bucket, matters that mix.[28] Sharing can be, like with Suijari, tinged with a sense of vulnerability and affection, and gratefulness for being trusted as someone to turn to when there is an itch. On the other hand I doubt that we can ever not share space with domestic animals whenever they perceive us – and they almost always perceive us before we perceive them. When perceived we are present to them and in their space.

When humans train animals the emphasis is often on teaching the animal to react immediately to unambiguous signals. But while it is useful to become more aware of one's body, a side effect of focusing only on performance is neglect about the shared space. Yet the other mammal's perception of the human relies on cues beyond what we are aware of (for physiological or perspectival reasons) such as smells, patterns of movement, body language, tone of voice and gaze direction. Animals perceive us through multimodal, holistic attention to movements, sounds and smells where our feelings, such as kindness, fear or nervousness are immediately recognised. If Esteri lowers her head to smell my breath she probably trusts and maybe even enjoys me; and when I allow her to lick my hands (not recommended by horse professionals), to taste and feel me with her muzzle, I trust and enjoy her touch.[29] Human kisses are bleak, in a sensorial perspective, compared to the thorough appreciation of the other performed by most sniffing mammals. And inter-species interpretation is prone to mistakes because different species communicate differently.[30]

With companion animals there are however many situations where we spend time together without a particular goal, and where communication has a better chance of becoming more reciprocal. This is typical with cats since they co-operate only when they like to. Compared to most domestic animals the cat is a feral species.[31] More than serving humans it shares a symbiotic relationship with us: optimally peaceful co-existence with mutual enjoyment of material goods (like mice and rats: to eat or get rid of) and affection. Like the species once did, individual cats, if they can move freely, can choose their human host and move to a better home. In happy human–feline relationships there is a gift of friendship as the cat has no pressing psychological need of bonding with others. The cat's affection is far from given: the human therefore feels accepted, even chosen, and sustained. To train a cat is possible, yet cats challenge behaviourism by following their own judgement rather than human rules, especially when no one is around.

Perhaps it is no coincidence that the cat has been favoured by philosophers and poets.[32] Writing perspicuously on the naming and 'ad-dressing' of cats T.S. Eliot indicated their integrity and dignity.[33] Yet cats are not asocial. Like most other domestic animals they address us, sometimes in a simple greeting. But they also create a language intended for humans, typically with situated gestures and vocalisations to ask for specific things, and they train us to understand it. The communication they initiate has different functions and is taught through shared contexts in patient iteration. To Alice in Wonderland, who complained that 'whatever you say, they always purr'[34] we should point out that it is unrealistic to expect animals to communicate according to a code where meaning is preserved while the context changes. Inter-species communication especially is relational, contextual and situational. I shall shortly give an example of its difficulties. Let me first note however that a basic meaning of purring is emotional connection.[35] A feline mother purrs when she nurses, and kittens purr while pumping her tissues with their paws. This maternal eroticism is present when the cat purrs and pumps its human host, who might prefer to move the claws off her skin. Yet a purring cat on the lap is a basic figure of feline–human contentment.

Mindi, my present cat companion, is a small-sized black-and-white female, born in the countryside and trained in feline skills by her mother – to play, kill, and enjoy human company. She is confident with humans and able to stay in a flat during the week but likes to go hunting on weekends. She is soft and purring but also unpredictable and violent, or so it may seem. Her behaviour exemplifies much of the cultural mythology about cats.

Mindi comes towards me as I am sitting at the kitchen table. I take her up and stroke her, she purrs. But then I turn her on her back. Her pupils widen, her body stiffens; she still purrs but meows and gives my hand a bite. I scold her and put her on the floor. Now her movements become predator-like. Jumping sideways, she attacks my leg with front paws and teeth. It does not hurt much but I am offended and get up, talking angrily to her. She runs and hides in another room. I persecute her and throw an object along the floor. Almost immediately I am struck by shame, and call her name in a repentant tone. My mind is flooded with awareness of the innocence of the animals that we bring into our lives and expose to our practices, and the suffering of animals, and my own stupid behaviour. Five minutes later, she is at the other end of the hall. I squat and we look at each other, both hesitant but

*willing to approach. She allows me to come and stroke her on the back. She purrs
again, and her eyes are more normal, her body relaxed.*

In this example many things happen in a short time and the human is forced, if
she wants to continue a good relationship, to face her own actions from the point
of view of a much smaller animal. Cats are not just hunters, they are also prey,
and while Mindi can expose her belly when she stretches on a couch, to just turn
her over and touch her in this area is intrusive. Her feline dignity was offended
even if she, at some level, perhaps still trusted me (continued purring).[36] Shame,
a theme that Derrida approaches from the experience of being stared at, naked, by
his (female) cat,[37] is here a shame about what I did. While shame about nakedness
in front of the animal's gaze could be a projection of an interest that is not there
my shame hit me from the other side. With her bite Mindi disapproved, two times,
and I responded like a giant idiot.

The example casts a light of vulnerability on the 'ferocious' and 'unpredictable' character of cats, and exposes human–feline emotional interdependence in
a domestic relationship. Finally I would like to add some reflections on the asym-
metrical basis of all relationships to domestic animals, however close, as we are
the arbiters of their life and death. This is emphasised with production animals
that are put to death when they no longer earn their living, or earn their living
through death. My own experience of cattle goes back to working on a dairy farm
with roughly 100 animals. Responsibility, worries and mourning are an integral
part of caring for the cows, whose health and well-being are keys to productivity.
What attracts us to them, however, as with other mammals, is emotional, mutual
attachment, fascination and admiration. With cows the collective aspect of belonging, to some extent, to a herd, and the perception of how human and animal life
unfold in parallel, at best harmoniously and for mutual enhancement of daily life,
come to the fore. Attachment to the herd is, in addition, also attachment to a particular environment and to the cycles of nature which become significant in new
ways.[38] My body remembers walking with the herd, inhabiting the land with them,
sharing rhythms, at best in an atmosphere of peace and generosity, in symbiosis
and individual appreciation. Those moments are precious as life is finite. Despair,
sleeplessness, self-accusations, memories of pain and suffering are part of that
life as well.

4. Aesthetic Imagination

Perhaps we need not imagine in order to perceive mammals as individuals. Perhaps
we simply recognise the animal's agency, at least if we have freed ourselves from
cultural prejudice that suggests otherwise. While this may be true there is still
reason to describe many processes of understanding and interacting with mammals
in terms of aesthetic imagination, and reasons why such an approach is fruitful in
a process of self-education aiming at animate peace. In this section I first point to
aesthetic elements of human–animal interaction, and then suggest that we can fruit-
fully understand the thought processes that are involved as aesthetic imagination.

First, the communication between humans and animals is often disinterested in the sense of not being focused on particular practical or cognitive goals.[39] The human does not ask the animal to perform, nor does the animal ask for particular goods. Curiosity, sympathetic responses and playfulness are part of such communication, with reciprocity through improvisation and shared rhythms in a being-together that is also a transformation and modulation of feeling. Second, communication is multimodal, with looks, movements and vocalisations, not to forget touch and, probably, sniffing. Both the sensuous and the emotional are integral parts of an aesthetic mode of experience which is also thoroughly embodied and concretely worldly. We connect to the world through sharing sensuous practices and affirming sensuous and emotional – rather than narrowly rational, let alone verbal – forms of agency with animals.

Third, aesthetic admiration and value are central ingredients of the love of animals. Animals indeed do more than suffer: they show grace, joy and dignity, and many more ways of being. They are admired for strength and beauty; in all mammals shiny furs and lively eyes are appreciated. While domestic animals are evaluated in competitions and for breeding purposes on the basis of how they look, the look is never separated from performance. The kind of beauty varies with species and kinds but performance and personal character are, as a rule, evaluated together with apparition. An inclusively aesthetic take on life and the living is thus already in place – in practice – as an alternative to the philosophical perspective on the subject which, as Derrida argues, has missed life, the animate and the animal by focusing on thinking only.[40] Animate beauty is primarily a beauty of actions and processes, not objects; and it needs to be analysed from that point of view.[41] This beauty is also expressive of feelings – like joy, intense concentration, curiosity, relaxation – and helps us realise what they are, and what is involved in a flourishing life. Animals bring values and awareness of values into the world.

Fourth, reflectivity[42] is part of the appreciation and interaction with animals in at least three ways, all of which can be memorable. The first is admiration: we are struck by the animal's expressive beauty and pause, even briefly, to appreciate it. This kind of appreciation takes a distance, if not physical, then at least mental, to its object. Second, reflectivity is involved when humans and animals address and respond to each other – whenever there is response rather than just mechanical reaction. Co-creating situations we recognise the other's initiatives and responses; we touch and are touched. This can take place in a situation without major challenges, as in riding on a forest path in mutual modulation of care and courage, informed by rhythms of stepping, breathing and singing. Here I am with the animal, and the constant reciprocity as such makes me aware of my position. Third, we become reflective when animals surprise, frustrate or challenge us: when things do not run smoothly. This is where interpretation and self-scrutiny step in, and such situations can haunt us for weeks, months, or a lifetime. Remembering and recalling, we return to the situation and try to capture what happened and what we might have done differently. The potential for doing differently provides space for imaginative self-formation.

While the aesthetic element of admiration is hopefully evident, the necessity of conceiving the two other kinds of reflectivity as aesthetic may be less so. I shall however argue that we draw upon aesthetic imagination in order to reconnect and find ways of living with the other animal. Already questions of how they are like us or different demand imaginative acting. Our understanding is informed by biology; yet scientific explanations, especially if simplified, can hamper our understanding of particular animals. For example, all animals perceive the world according to sensorial styles affected by the placement, sharpness and functions of sense organs, which condition how the world appears. But each domestic animal's style of being is also contextually shaped in relation to humans, and for some humans the reverse is true as well. Memories, narratives, images need to be engaged in addition to facts.

Many theories of imagination emphasise its cognitive value for the exploration and study of phenomena, and the creation of novel questions and solutions.[43] Imagination is then typically described as intentional: the subject relates actively to objects of thought. It is also independent from reality. Imagination is a mental activity, unaffected by actual contexts, where sensuous and emotional aspects are part of the content rather than providing its very structure and space. With animals we need another emphasis, since we typically imagine in the situation, whether present or past, and future-oriented imaginings are also affected by real contexts of experience. Imagination is informed by feelings and by the sensuous feedback of our own and other's bodies; it is both active and passive. It is about actual experience as well as novel interpretations and possibilities of acting differently. Not knowing the other animal – i.e. the difficulty of rationalising, explaining or predicting behaviour – invites imaginative and intuitive thought with practical rather than theoretical hypotheses. Therefore aesthetic imagination with the animate other is an embodied practice while also a mental activity. It is a practice often driven by love; or at least by the desire to become more skilful and have more enjoyable interactions with animals, and fused with actual interactions with the other. In addition it is a practising of imagination as such.

We need then to understand imagination as more open, dialogical and rooted in the world than cognitively biased theories suggest. Gaston Bachelard's work offers some resources for this. Following Bachelard, imagination is a process of activity and passivity where thoughts are interdependent with and affected by previous experiences, cultural ideas and our existential situation as singular, embodied creatures. His discussion of 'material imagination' is particularly fruitful in its emphasis on how 'images of matter' affect us, put our thoughts into motion, and are dreamt 'substantially, intimately'.[44] Bachelard's conceptualisation of imagination as reverie emphasises children and childhood, and suggests that imagination is more fundamental than language.[45] On these lines and with Derrida we may venture to think (or imagine) that precisely the imaginative mode of thought might be shared among verbal and non-verbal mammals.[46] Yet whether we accept this or not, looking at imagination's material and sensuous dimension helps us see how it places us in the world, with other animals, and confirms our existence as situated, topological subjects.

Bachelard also indicates the close connection between imagination and poetry. The arts of language in particular shape our ideas because language serves many functions, including philosophical and political. As Irigaray argues, words shape our imaginings and values. Thus 'bovine' is commonly used as a derogatory term, and 'cattle' suggests lump-like matter rather than living individuals.[47] In the connotations voices that do not know, like or care for the family of cows overpower the voices of those who admire and respect them. This comes in the way of building peace *with* nature. But poetry also gives room for animals, articulates and invites naming and addressing, and helps us imagine the animal that addresses us. I call my horse friends the guinea pig and the hamster, and the nicknames cast light on their fears and vulnerability in the face of imagined predators and real human violence. Imagined mammalian overlaps play with what we take to be real, and transform it.

According to Bachelard, the imagination of childhood is an exploration of the world that finds values.[48] If imagination is material, felt and sensed, then it is not axiologically neutral. Aesthetic qualities invite us to imagine. Lars Spuybroek argues that beauty creates 'spheres of action and cycles of exchange':[49] it is a gift economy of giving and receiving, and it invites us to participate. In interactions with companion mammals this applies to situations where the clarity of the animal's gestures creates in us feelings of joy, surprise, admiration and curiosity.[50] We react positively, not so much in affirmation as in making ourselves available. Beauty is then animate and animating, and animals invite us into their world, which is parallel to ours although often not perceived by us.

5. Conclusions: Imagining Conviviality

I have argued that engagement with domestic animals provides opportunities for reciprocal interactions that call for imagination; and that this imagination is aesthetic in being informed by the expressive behaviour of animals that address and touch us physically, mentally and existentially. This gives insights that can sustain life enhancement and animate peace in our personal world. But does this affect the war between humankind and non-human nature on the species level, or does the war continue while some of us enjoy the company of inter-species families? I can think of three ways to respond to this worry.

First, while the path towards animate peace that I have indicated may not be sufficient, it, or some equivalent, might be necessary for change towards it. If the present crisis has a fundamental moral dimension we need change on that level. Remember now that while animals attract us through grace and joy the relationship has darker sides as well. Our failures and shortcomings become precisely 'images of matter' that, with Bachelard, 'have a weight [and] are a heart'.[51] We may find here a key to moral motivation if we accept the call to extend our life and responsibilities towards the nature that we are and the natural world we inhabit. The second point is precisely that while our relationship to animals can sustain us in self-education towards animate peace, this process needs active work from our side. Education is never mechanical; peace does not just happen. Something similar is true of imagination. If we want animate peace we need to practice imagination towards flexibility and situational wisdom, relying on intuitions and experiences of trust and non-violence.[52] Practising imagination is thinking and dreaming, acting and experimenting, perceiving and reflecting in alterations of 'doing and undergoing'.[53] The third and final point is that benevolent imagination, its intuitions and insights, needs to be communicated more widely, for only if the imagination of people who know and like animals is made common and culturally legitimate can it influence the societal and global balance between human and non-human nature.

Notes

1 I thank participants in the *Poesis of Peace* conference for valuable comments and suggestions, especially Tomaž Grušovnik, who challenged me on the need to introduce imagination in order to see animals as agents. More personally, this piece is dedicated to my cousin Gunilla Donner, with whom I have shared animal friendships and narratives from childhood on. Significantly, she was given her nickname Dure by an older brother who saw his baby sister as an 'animal' (*djur*). I should also thank the late cows at Ahdenkallio who made me realise the similarities between bovine and human herds, not to forget my present inter-species community.

2 See Michel Serres, *Le contrat naturel* (Paris: Flammarion, 1990); and Jacques Derrida, *L'animal que donc je suis* (Paris: Galilée, 2006), 46, 140. I use 'nature' to refer to both the environment, organic and inorganic, and to nature as part of our own physiology. Agreeing with Donna Haraway in *The Companion Species Manifesto: Dogs, People, and Significant Otherness* (Chicago: Prickly Paradigm Press, 2003) that nature and human culture are intertwined, I find the conceptual distinction useful.

3 For a critical discussion of the 'love' of pet animals see Haraway, *Companion Species Manifesto*, 33–40.

4 For an in-depth discussion of animals' role in Western philosophy, see Kelly Oliver, *Animal Lessons: How They Teach Us to Be Human* (New York: Columbia University Press, 2009).

5 Derrida, *L'animal*. This work importantly opens the philosophical significance of animals. Yet the emphasis is more on philosophy than on animals.

6 Serres, *Le contrat*, e.g. 16. For similar views, see David Abram, *The Spell of the Sensuous: Perception and Language in a More-Than-Human World* (New York: Vintage Books, 1996); Gernot Böhme, *Die Natur vor uns: Naturphilosophie in pragmatischer Hinsicht* (Zug: Die Graue Edition, 2002); and Wolfgang Welsch, *Mensch und Welt: Eine evolutionäre Perspektiv der Philosophie* (München: C.H. Beck, 2012).

7 Heidegger's view is discussed critically by Derrida, *L'animal*, 193–219, and refuted by Stephen David Ross, "Living with the animals ... In the fullness of our nonidentities ...', *Poligrafi* 17, no. 65–6 (2012): 217.

8 Johan Galtung, *Peace by Peaceful Means: Peace and Conflict, Development and Civilization* (London: Sage, 1996), 31, 30.

9 Hans Magnus Enzensberger, *Civil War*, trans. Piers Spence and Martin Chalmers (London: Granta Books 1994), 19–31.

10 Galtung, *Peace by Peaceful Means*, 32, 61, 30. Italics mine.

11 Oliver is critical of the animal rights discourse because it is 'oppositional and exclusionary' as compared to an emphasis on relationships and responsivity. Quoting Derrida she later indicates that difference does not imply opposition; *Animal Lessons*, 29, 25–48, 137.

12 David Bohm, *On Dialogue*, ed. Lee Nichol (London and New York: Routledge, 1996).

13 Cf. Galtung, *Peace by Peaceful Means*, 196–210.

14 Haraway, *Companion Species Manifesto*, 7. She also points out that the human–animal relationship is far from easy, e.g. 12.
15 E.g. Luce Irigaray, *J'aime à toi. Esquisse d'une félicité dans l'histoire* (Paris: Grasset, 1992).
16 Bohm, *On Dialogue*, 2.
17 Haraway, in *The Companion Species Manifesto*, argues that precisely play, actual enjoyment and affection between humans and dogs contribute to making us more worldly. I follow her, with other animal companions.
18 Derrida, *L'animal*, 24ff. Oliver, in *Animal Lessons*, 77, reverses the question that preoccupies Derrida by asking 'What if the human responded?'
19 Vasudevi Reddy, *How Infants Know Minds* (Cambridge and London: Harvard University Press, 2008); See also Maurice Merleau-Ponty, *Phénoménologie de la perception* (Paris: Gallimard, 1992), 398–419.
20 Stephen Malloch and Colwyn Trevarthen, eds., *Communicative Musicality: Exploring the Basis of Human Companionship* (Oxford: Oxford University Press, 2009); Daniel N. Stern, *Forms of Vitality: Exploring Dynamic Experience in Psychology, the Arts, Psychotherapy, and Development* (Oxford: Oxford University Press, 2010).
21 See also Abram, *Spell of the Sensuous*; and Pauline von Bonsdorff, 'Language and emotion in Merleau-Ponty', in *Emotion and Language: Theory, Research, Application*, ed. Ulrike Lüdtke (Amsterdam: John Benjamins, 2015).
22 This also applies among animals. Reddy describes how the sheep Isis started to behave like a dog after losing her sheep companion but returned to being sheep-like when there was a new sheep, *How Infants Know Minds*, 31.
23 Serres, *Le contrat*, 22–3.
24 While Derrida recognises that non-human animals may use other senses than humans in their social relationships, his reflections might on the whole be too preoccupied with vision to do justice to an interspecies perspective.
25 Derrida observes that for philosophers animals have no sex; *L'animal*, 59. But for people who have or work with animals they are mostly strongly sexed, sometimes to the point where human gender stereotypes are projected on them.
26 Centered riding is classical in this field but by no means the only one. See, e.g. Sally Swift, *Centered Riding 2: Further Exploration* (North Pomfret: Trafalgar Square Publishing, 2002); Mary Wanless, *Ride with Your Mind Clinic: Rider Biomechanics – Basics to Brilliance* (Wykey: Kenilworth Press, 2008); Jean-Luc Cornille, *Science of Motion*, accessed 27 September 2015, www.scienceofmotion.com/index.html.
27 For discourses that respect the horse's intelligence, see Cornille, *Science of Motion*; also Perry Wood, *Real Riding: How to Ride in Harmony with Horses* (Addington: Kenilworth Press, 2002); and Mark Rashid, *Horses Never Lie: The Heart of Passive Leadership* (Cincinnati: David & Charles, 2007). A more daring narrative is Anna Clemence Mews and Julie Dicker, *What Horses Say: How to Hear, Help and Heal Them* (Addington: Kenilworth Press, 2005). While Cornille relies on imagination and narrative to give a horse's point of view that differs from popular theories, Mews and Dicker address the imagination at least of a sympathetic if also sceptical reader. These authors break cultural and quasi-scientific assumptions about what horses are capable of thinking and feeling.
28 Cf. Ross, 'Living with the animals', 217: 'Bodies are proximate, relational, embedded, and entangled'.
29 The horse's muzzle is in some respects comparable to human hands. Horses use it to investigate, including manipulating things. Suijari has opened more than one 'horse-safe' door.
30 Wagging the tail is a well-known example: for the dog it is a friendly greeting whereas the cat's tail moves from side to side in tension just before attack; see, e.g., Desmond Morris, *Catwatching* (New York: Three Rivers Press, 1986).

31 Derrida points out that a cat cannot be owned, and while a domestic species, it is not domesticated; *L'animal*, 23, 214.

32 In addition to Derrida, one could mention Oliver's *Animal Lessons*, dedicated to a cat and with cats as chapter vignettes.

33 T.S. Eliot, *The Illustrated Old Possum: Old Possum's Book of Practical Cats* (London and Boston: Faber and Faber, 1981), 9–10, 61–3. 'What would it mean if we granted dignity to all things?' asks Ross, 'Living with the animals', 220.

34 Quoted in Derrida. *L'animal*, 25.

35 Another instance of intimacy is when the cat rubs her cheeks against a human leg, marking it with her smell. The cat probably does not realise how relatively poor our olfactory organs are.

36 The functions of purring are certainly manifold and not enough known.

37 Derrida, *L'animal*, 18–21.

38 Pauline von Bonsdorff, 'Agriculture, aesthetic appreciation and the worlds of nature', *Contemporary Aesthetics* 3 (2005), accessed 15 September 2015, www.contempaesthetics.org/newvolume/pages/article.php?articleID=325.

39 Disinterestedness has been a hallmark, although disputed, in modern aesthetics since its inception; Immanuel Kant, *Kritik der Urteilskraft* (Hamburg: Felix Meiner Verlag, 1990), 39–48. Against Kant I understand aesthetic experience as embodied, even material; and giving rise to a pleasure that can be informed, even fused with affective or other interests while not being driven by instrumentality. See von Bonsdorff, 'Agriculture'.

40 Derrida, *L'animal*, 104, 173.

41 For accounts of beauty that emphasise movement and life, see Friedrich von Schiller, 'Über Anmut und Würde', in *Über das Schöne und die Kunst. Schriften zur Ästhetik* (München: Deutscher Taschenbuch Verlag, 1984), 44–93; Guy Sircello, *Love and Beauty* (Princeton: Princeton University Press, 1989); or Lars Spuybroek, 'Charis and Radiance: The ontological dimensions of beauty', in *Giving and Taking: Antidotes to a Culture of Greed*, ed. Sjoerd van Tuinen and Joke Brouwer (Rotterdam: V2 / NAi Publishers, 2014), 119–49.

42 For Kant aesthetic judgement is fundamentally a form of reflective judgement; *Kritik der Urteilskraft*.

43 E.g. 'propositional imagination' in Shaun Nichols, ed., *The Architecture of the Imagination: New Essays on Pretence, Possibility, and Fiction* (Oxford: Clarendon Press, 2006). Paul Crowther is closer to my approach, yet limited for the purpose of this chapter, 'Imagination, language, and the perceptual world: a post-analytic phenomenology', *Continental Philosophy Review* 46 (2013): 37–56.

44 Gaston Bachelard, *L'eau et les rêves. Essai sur l'imagination de la matière* (Paris: Librairie José Corti, 2003), 8.

45 Gaston Bachelard, *La poétique de la reverie* (Paris: Presses Universitaires de France, 1999). That imagination precedes language is confirmed by infant research, see Malloch and Trevarthen, *Communicative Musicality*; also Crowther, 'Imagination, language', 4n7.

46 Derrida, *L'animal*, 23, 90–100; se also Oliver on Merleau-Ponty, *Animal Lessons*, 212–3. Space does not allow me to go deeper into animals' imagination here.

47 In addition, to call someone a 'cow' sadly reveals misogyny, and is also an offence towards the animal. As Oliver writes: 'As it has been used in patriarchal literature, the term *female* is an insult to women and female animals alike'. *Animal Lessons*, 155.

48 Bachelard, *La poétique*, 84–123.

49 Spuybroek, 'Charis and Radiance', 132.

50 As Haraway puts it, 'we might hope for the creative grace of play', *Companion Species Manifesto*, 98.

51 Bachelard, *L'eau et les rêves*, 8. Enzensberger suggests that narratives might be the way for steering culture away from violence; *Civil War*, 70–1, 87, 115.

52 Violent imagination construes the other as an adversary. A juxtaposition of imagination as either violent or non-violent however runs the risk of simplification. Imaginative processes often include conflictual elements.
53 The expression is from John Dewey, *Art as Experience* (New York: Perigree, 1980), 50ff.

References

Abram, David. *The Spell of the Sensuous: Perception and Language in a More-Than-Human World*. New York: Vintage Books, 1996.

Bachelard, Gaston. *La poétique de la rêverie*. Paris: Presses Universitaires de France, 1999. First published 1960.

Bachelard, Gaston. *L'eau et les rêves: Essai sur l'imagination de la matière*. Paris: Librairie José Corti, 2003. First published 1942.

Bohm, David. *On Dialogue*. Edited by Lee Nichol. London and New York: Routledge, 1996.

Böhme, Gernot. *Die Natur vor uns: Naturphilosophie in pragmatischer Hinsicht*. Zug: Die Graue Edition, 2002.

von Bonsdorff, Pauline. 'Agriculture, aesthetic appreciation and the worlds of nature'. *Contemporary Aesthetics* 3 (2005). Accessed 15 September 2015. www.contempaesthetics.org/newvolume/pages/article.php?articleID=325.

von Bonsdorff, Pauline. 'Language and emotion in Merleau-Ponty'. In *Emotion and Language: Theory, Research, Application*, edited by Ulrike Lüdtke. Amsterdam: John Benjamins, 2015.

Cornille, Jean-Luc. *Science of Motion*. Accessed 27 September 2015. www.scienceofmotion.com/index.html.

Crowther, Paul. 'Imagination, language, and the perceptual world: a post-analytic phenomenology'. *Continental Philosophy Review* 46 (2013): 37–56.

Derrida, Jacques. *L'animal que donc je suis*. Paris: Galilée, 2006.

Dewey, John. *Art as Experience*. New York: Perigree, 1980. First published 1934.

Eliot, T.S. *The Illustrated Old Possum: Old Possum's Book of Practical Cats*. Illustrations by Nicolas Bentley. London and Boston: Faber and Faber, 1981.

Enzensberger, Hans Magnus. *Civil War*. Translated by Piers Spence and Martin Chalmers. London: Granta Books, 1994.

Galtung, Johan. *Peace by Peaceful Means: Peace and Conflict, Development and Civilization*. London: Sage, 1996.

Haraway, Donna. *The Companion Species Manifesto: Dogs, People, and Significant Otherness*. Chicago: Prickly Paradigm Press, 2003.

Irigaray, Luce. *J'aime à toi: Esquisse d'une félicité dans l'histoire*. Paris: Grasset, 1992.

Kant, Immanuel. *Kritik der Urteilskraft*. Hamburg: Felix Meiner Verlag, 1990. First published 1790.

Malloch, Stephen and Colwyn Trevarthen, eds. *Communicative Musicality: Exploring the Basis of Human Companionship*. Oxford: Oxford University Press, 2009.

Merleau-Ponty, Maurice. *Phénoménologie de la perception*. Paris: Gallimard, 1992. First published 1945.

Mews, Anna Clemence and Julie Dicker. *What Horses Say: How to Hear, Help and Heal Them*. Addington: Kenilworth Press, 2005.

Morris, Desmond. *Catwatching*. New York: Three Rivers Press, 1986.

Nichols, Shaun, ed. *The Architecture of the Imagination: New Essays on Pretence, Possibility, and Fiction*. Oxford: Clarendon Press, 2006.

Oliver, Kelly. *Animal Lessons: How They Teach Us to Be Human*. New York: Columbia University Press, 2009.

Rashid, Mark. *Horses Never Lie: The Heart of Passive Leadership*. Cincinnati: David & Charles, 2007.

Reddy, Vasudevi. *How Infants Know Minds*. Cambridge and London: Harvard University Press, 2008.

Ross, Stephen David. 'Living with the animals … In the fullness of our nonidentities …'. *Poligrafi* 17, no. 65–6 (2012): 211–26.

von Schiller, Friedrich. 'Über Anmut und Würde'. In *Über das Schöne und die Kunst: Schriften zur Ästhetik*, 44–93. München: Deutscher Taschenbuch Verlag, 1984.

Serres, Michel. *Le contrat naturel*. Paris: Flammarion, 1990.

Sircello, Guy. *Love and Beauty*. Princeton: Princeton University Press, 1989.

Spuybroek, Lars. 'Charis and Radiance: the ontological dimensions of beauty'. In *Giving and Taking: Antidotes to a Culture of Greed*, edited by Sjoerd van Tuinen and Joke Brouwer, 119–49. Rotterdam: V2 / NAi Publishers, 2014.

Stern, Daniel N. *Forms of Vitality: Exploring Dynamic Experience in Psychology, the Arts, Psychotherapy, and Development*. Oxford: Oxford University Press, 2010.

Swift, Sally. *Centered Riding 2: Further Exploration*. North Pomfret: Trafalgar Square Publishing, 2002.

Wanless, Mary. *Ride With Your Mind Clinic: Rider Biomechanics – Basics to Brilliance*. Wykey: Kenilworth Press, 2008.

Welsch, Wolfgang. *Mensch und Welt: Eine evolutionäre Perspektiv der Philosophie*. München: C.H. Beck, 2012.

Wood, Perry. *Real Riding: How to Ride in Harmony with Horses*. Addington: Kenilworth Press, 2002.

4 The Primordial Respiratory Peace and the Possibility of Cultivation of Breathing as a Method of Peacemaking

Petri Berndtson

In this chapter I will concentrate my efforts to inspire the beginning of a conversation concerning the possibility of peaceful coexistence from the perspective of breathing. Here we will interrogate the phenomenon of *primordial respiratory peace*, an idea that is based upon a new way of thinking that I call the *philosophical task of respiratory thinking*. This way of thinking always thinks all phenomena of being-in-the-world with and within the respiratory atmosphere of *We Breathe Air*. As such this respiratory thinking is a form of 'cultivation of breathing'.[1] The initial inspiration for this idea of primordial respiratory peace comes from two quotations from Maurice Merleau-Ponty's book *Phenomenology of Perception*. In the first of these two citations Merleau-Ponty does not use explicitly the notion of 'peaceful coexistence', but instead speaks of an 'ancient pact established between X and the world in general'. The explicit usage of the wording 'peaceful coexistence' will only occur in the second one of these citations. Let us air the first one of these quotations:

> [M]y first perception and my first hold on the world must appear to me as the execution of a more ancient pact established between X and the world in general; my history must be the sequel to a pre-history whose acquired results it uses; my personal existence must be the taking up of a pre-personal tradition. There is, then, another subject beneath me, for whom a world exists before I am there, and who marks out my place in that world. This captive or natural spirit is my body.[2]

Here Merleau-Ponty argues that there is something more primordial than 'my first perception and my first hold on the world' as these fundamental relations with the world become possible only as an execution, that is, as a result, or a performance, of 'a more ancient pact established between X and the world in general'.[3] What, or who, is this mysterious 'X', this something unknown, this unknown person? This 'X' refers to 'another subject beneath me' whom Merleau-Ponty names as 'my body'. The ordinary interpretation in the Merleau-Pontian context would be that this body as a body-subject is, in the first place, 'the subject of perception'.[4] I would suggest that we dig deeper than this and take seriously

Merleau-Ponty's words from his text 'The Child's Relations with Others' in which he says that 'at the beginning of the child's life ... the body is already a respiratory body. Not only the mouth but the whole respiratory apparatus gives the child a kind of experience of space. After that, other regions of the body intervene and come into prominence'.[5] So according to Merleau-Ponty it is a 'respiratory body' which is there always 'already' before and beneath everything else in our bodily existence and all the 'other regions of the body' 'come into prominence' afterwards, for example, seeing, hearing, grasping, crawling, and speaking. As the body is always already a respiratory body I would suggest that we would interpret Merleau-Ponty's 'X' as a respiratory body which would mean that then this 'ancient pact established between X and the world in general' would actually speak of an ancient pact established between the respiratory body and the world in general. This would also mean that the rest of this quotation would now receive a respiratory meaning and as such would now state in a reformulated manner the following: my history must be the sequel to a respiratory pre-history whose acquired results it uses; my personal existence must be the taking up of a pre-personal respiratory tradition. There is, then, a respiratory body as another subject beneath me, for whom a world exists before I am there, and who marks out my place in that world.[6]

What does all of this have to do with peace, or peaceful coexistence, as a primordial respiratory peace? This 'ancient pact between X and the world in general' is, according to Merleau-Ponty, a 'primordial level'[7] which founds all the other levels of our being-in-the-world. This means that it is, in the words of *Phenomenology of Perception*, 'the origin of everything'[8] and as such we could call this pact also the primordial, or original, pact between X and the world in general. A pact is a covenant, or agreement, between two or more parties. Etymologically the word 'pact' is in a deep manner connected with 'peace' as the words like 'pacific' and 'pacifist' show. If we follow the etymological path we can say that the word 'pact' comes from the Latin *pactum* which means 'pact', 'agreement', 'contract' or 'covenant'. This word *pactum* is connected to the word *pacem* which means 'compact', 'agreement', 'treaty of peace', 'tranquillity' or 'absence of war'. Its nominative form is *pax* meaning 'peace', 'silence', 'harmony' and 'agreement'. The English word 'peace' comes from it via the old French word *pais* meaning 'peace', 'reconciliation' and 'silence'. Ultimately all of these words grow out of their Proto Indo-European root *pag-* 'to fix', 'join together', 'unite' and 'make firm' of which the Latin *pangere* is one example meaning 'to fix' and 'to fasten'. From all of this we can say, if we take these etymological considerations seriously, that Merleau-Ponty's 'ancient, or primordial, pact established between X and the world in general' is covenant, agreement, treaty of peace, peaceful joining together, harmony and fastening between the body and the world in general. To this originating conciliatory event we have given a respiratory meaning as a covenant or peaceful bringing together of the respiratory body and the world in general as the primordial level before and beneath all the other forms of being-in-the-world.

Let us then come to read the second quotation from *Phenomenology of Perception* which speaks explicitly of 'peaceful coexistence'. In it Merleau-Ponty writes:

> With the *cogito* begins the struggle between consciousnesses in which, as Hegel says, each one seeks the death of the other. So that this battle may begin, so that each consciousness may suspect the strange and external presences that it negates, they must have a common ground and they must remember their peaceful coexistence in the world of childhood.[9]

If we read these words within the respiratory atmosphere, which we have just opened, the 'common ground' of each rational subjectivity as a private, separate and opposing consciousness is in its most primordial level the ancient respiratory pact between the respiratory body and the world in general formed at the beginning of each child's life and the 'peaceful coexistence[10] in the world of childhood' that these consciousnesses must remember is the coexistence between them as respiratory body-subjects who each and everyone participate in harmonious agreement with the world in general. This remembrance that Merleau-Ponty is referring to is not any act of consciousness, but bodily memory which takes place beneath all the acts of consciousness and which makes all active remembering possible. This 'body memory' is, according to Edward S. Casey, 'memory that is intrinsic to the body, to its own ways of remembering: how we remember in and by and through the body'.[11] In the primordial level of our being-in-the-world this body memory is respiratory body's memory to which we already referred to previously when we stated following Merleau-Ponty that 'my history must be the sequel to a respiratory pre-history whose acquired results it uses; my personal existence must be the taking up of a pre-personal respiratory tradition. There is, then, a respiratory body-subject beneath me, from whom a world exists before I am there, and who marks out my place in that world'. This means that each and every historical and personal consciousness as rational subjectivity with its continuous struggles with other consciousnesses uses at each and every moment the acquired results of the respiratory pre-history starting from the formation of the primordial respiratory pact. So the execution of this pact established between the respiratory body-subject and the world in general and the life of peaceful respiratory coexistence between these respiratory body-subjects 'does not merely occur at the beginning of my life', but 'it is recommenced at each moment' giving 'every subsequent perception [and act of consciousness] its sense',[12] meaning and direction. This means that the primordial respiratory peace as agreement, harmony and peaceful covenant in the name of bringing together takes place always already before and beneath any possibility of disagreement, disharmony, conflict and war. There is no possibility of battle or disagreement between conscious subjectivities, or struggles and wars between nations, ideologies, religions, classes and races, in which they suspect each other and try to negate each other without them all first perpetually breathing together, that is, conspiring with each other and the world in general.

By conspiring I mean the etymological sense of the word which means 'breathing together' and in this sense our primordial respiratory peaceful coexistence with each other is a conspiracy, that is, *conspiration*[13] of our life, of our being-in-the-world in the true sense of the word. Respiration is always *conspiration* as breathing is never anybody's private, or separate, matter, but an event in which each and every respiratory body opens itself continuously in the process of inspiration and expiration to the atmosphere of air as our intersubjective world. The meaning of respiration as conspiracy is that we breathe together (*conspire*) with the shared and common atmosphere of air as with each cycle of inspiration and expiration the direction of the breath reverses from We Breathe Air to Air Breathes Us and back again from Air Breathes Us to We Breathe Air. This could perhaps be the true meaning of *re-spiration* as 'breathing again' and again and continuously again. This conspiracy as peaceful respiratory coexistence can be thought of as a respiratory Community of breathing body-subjects. The Community of conspirators is the most universal community, or communion, and in this sense it differs from our normal communities and fellowships, for example, national, cultural, political and religious groups, which are built on a principle of inclusion-exclusion, or of insiders-outsiders, as they include and exclude human beings through the criteria of race, nationality, language, social class, values, education and religion. This true conspiracy of peaceful coexistence as the Community of breathers differs radically from these normal communities as it does not exclude anybody based on their inheritance, values, beliefs or skills, but includes everybody who is a breathing being without any choice on the part of the breather himself or herself. One can choose not to be participant, not to be included into this respiratory communal covenant after one has already been initiated to it by holding one's breath as an act of negation of this primordial respiratory pact, but this act of disagreement leads one very fast into a deep state of anxiety, unrest and disharmony which makes all our human enterprises from the poetic creation to 'the most cruel forms of sadism',[14] from the lovemaking and peacemaking to the war making,[15] impossible.

This means that even violence and war between human beings are possible only within the primordial respiratory community of peaceful coexistence. It is impossible to try to win, suspect, negate or kill the other if I am not in the first place conspiring with this other that I wish to negate, win or kill. This means that it is actually this primordial respiratory peace which lets, or allows, us to negate others, that is, gives us freedom to nihilate them, from their membership to this conspiratory Community by killing them, which is the only way except the natural death to lose one's access to it as it is universally all-inclusive alliance of peace and freedom.

We have now here with the inspirational help of Merleau-Ponty stated that the ancient pact between the respiratory body and the world in general is the primordial level of our being-in-the-world, that is, the origin of our existence from which all the other forms of relating with the world become possible, such as speaking, moving, seeing, hearing and thinking. Within these perceptual, linguistic, motor, and intellectual horizons our human enterprises of ordinary and extraordinary patterns of life, work, love, war, science, art, commerce and religion take place. All of these personal, social, practical and theoretical dimensions of our being-in-the-world focus their attention to the things and objects in the world. What is essential to all of these human activities is that they all take place within the world of awakeness. The phenomenologist Erwin Strauss writes about this world of awakeness as follows: 'Awakeness is a primitive fact. It is the foundation upon which is erected the human world, in the praxis of life as in theoretical insight, in its interhuman intercourse as in its individual and common history'.[16] Let us take as an example of this world of awakeness a four-day academic conference on peace. Such a conference can take place only as an awakened project in which the speakers as well as the members of the audience as 'waking subjects' share together this common world of awakeness which, as Drew Leder points out, is 'the precondition for outer-directed perception, motility, and social engagement'.[17] Without these faculties of human embodiment being awake academic communication, or any other form of communicative activity, would be impossible. As this hypothetical academic conference of ours is concerned with the phenomenon of peace it means that our awakened faculties of embodiment are directed toward a shared goal, which is the question of peacemaking and matters related to it. But it is not only this *particular* question of peace that is particularized for us as also the manner of *how* we are directed towards this *particular phenomenon is particularized* to the sphere of academic discourse. This means that if somebody would start to give a speech about the art of cooking lasagna without any connection to the question of peace, or would perform his or her presentation suddenly naked, which would be opposed to all normal behavioral standards of academic morality, or would perhaps even just start to speak about peace in a way which has no relation to the standards of academic discourse, the conference participants as 'waking subjects' would become surprised and perplexed about what in the world is going on and how they should react to this strange situation. All of this means that any academic conference as an awakened project, like all our various awakened human enterprises, is very strictly narrowed into 'this or that world',[18] into 'a *particular* world, a *particular* spectacle',[19] to borrow Merleau-Ponty's notions, with its own particular standards, values and goals. Most of our awakened human experience is particularized in this manner to various cultural, scientific, religious, artistic, everyday and working worlds with their own particular objects of attention.

But this awakened experience is not the whole of our human existence. We are also beings who sleep. This means, in the case of our hypothetical academic conference that it does not continue perpetually as a particularized awaken spectacle of thinking of peace even if it would be the most exciting event in our lifetime. All the conference participants, or at least most of them, will during those four days withdraw from this awakened state into the mysterious world of sleep. And then the question is what happens when one tries to fall asleep? How does one enter from the world of awakeness to the dormant world? Let us once again ponder the words of Merleau-Ponty's *Phenomenology of Perception* concerning the event of falling asleep which according to this book is a respiratory journey:

I lie down in my bed, on my left side, with my knees drawn up; I close my eyes, *breathe slowly*, and distance myself from my projects. But this is where the power of my will or consciousness ends. Just as the faithful in Dionysian mysteries invoke the god by imitating the scenes of his life, *I too call forth the visitation of sleep by imitating the breathing and posture of the sleeper.*[20]

Later in this same book Merleau-Ponty continues his description as follows:

[S]leep arrives when a certain voluntary attitude suddenly receives from the outside the very confirmation that it was expecting. *I breathe slowly and deeply to call forth sleep, and suddenly, one might say, my mouth communicates with some immense external lung that calls my breath forth and forces it back.* A certain respiratory rhythm, desired by me just a moment ago, becomes my very being, and sleep, intended until then as a signification, turns itself into a situation.[21]

These two citations are extremely powerful with their potential meaning in our journey to understand the primordial respiratory pact between the respiratory body and the world in general. How should we, then, understand these two dense pieces of text? In order to do so, let us see how Merleau-Ponty understands the phenomenon of sleep which in both of these quotations is called forth by slow and deep breathing and which in the second one of these pieces of texts is understood as a certain kind of respiratory event. In one place of *Phenomenology of Perception* the phenomenon of sleep is described as follows: 'During sleep ... I only keep the world present in order to hold it at a distance, I turn myself back toward the subjective sources of my existence'.[22] So during sleep the world is present to us, but it is at a distance. If the world is kept at the distance, does this mean that this turning back as a return 'toward the subjective sources of my existence' is a return toward a source, or origin, which is subjectivity outside of the world, or some kind of Augustinian, Cartesian, or Husserlian 'inner man'? The answer to this question is definitely: 'No!' as, according to Merleau-Ponty, 'there is no "inner man", [and as] man is in and toward the world, and it is in the world that he knows himself'.[23] Elsewhere in *Phenomenology of Perception* it is said that 'the sleeper is never completely enclosed within himself' and 'never absolutely cut off from the ... world'.[24] If this is the case, then this return 'toward the subjective sources of my existence' must still be a certain kind of relationship with the world and within the world. It is actually quite simple to understand what Merleau-Ponty means by 'the subjective sources of my existence' as in the depth dimension subjectivity, or the subject, refers to our body, that is, to the body-subject which is this 'another subject beneath me' to which we referred already earlier in this chapter. On the other hand, existence, for Merleau-Ponty, is synonymous with being-in-the-world. When one understands these key notions of *Phenomenology of Perception* it is fairly easy to say that 'during sleep I [actually] turn myself back toward the bodily sources of my being-in-the-world'. Would this mean then that in order to be able to turn back toward these sources of being-in-the-world one has to distance oneself from other dimensions of the world? This is exactly what takes place in the first quotation concerning the process of falling asleep which stated that 'I lie down in my bed, on my left side, with my knees drawn up; I close my eyes, breathe slowly, and distance myself from my projects'. In order to fall asleep one has to withdraw oneself as thoroughly as possible from all particularized projects of the world of awakeness which are based, as Leder pointed out, on 'outer-directed perception, motility, and social engagement'. If we do not withdraw from these dimensions of our being-in-the-world falling asleep becomes almost impossible. As one imitates the being of the sleeper one withdraws oneself from all the dimensions of the world of awakeness, from every 'particular world, particular spectacle' as thoroughly as it is possible in our human capabilities. One closes one's eyes as one withdraws from the world of 'outer-directed perception', that is, from the world of things and objects. One lies down in bed in stillness in order to withdraw from the world of 'motility'. One distances oneself from one's projects to withdraw oneself from the world of 'social engagement' and human enterprises.

After this distancing of the world comes the crucial point of the process of falling asleep. As one withdraws from everything in order to make oneself as still, calm and peaceful as possible, that is, as dead as possible to the awakened world of active life in order to fall asleep, the only relationship with the world that stays present as one cannot withdraw, or distance, oneself from it without causing oneself anxiety and unrest is breathing. To cause oneself unrest when one is trying to *rest in peace* makes the whole process of falling asleep, of course, completely impossible. And for this reason one calls forth sleep by breathing in a slow and deep rhythm. If one would breathe in a rapid and shallow manner this kind of breathing would not give us *rest in peace* as it would activate our relation with the world and would not allow us to return to the bodily sources, or roots, of our being-in-the-world. What are these sources? They are our respiratory origins of which Merleau-Ponty wrote: 'I breathe slowly and deeply to call forth sleep, and suddenly, one might say, my mouth communicates with some immense external lung that calls my breath forth and forces it back. A certain respiratory rhythm, desired by me just a moment ago, becomes my very being'. When sleep comes one returns to the primordial level of our being-in-the-world that we named in the beginning of this chapter the ancient pact, or agreement, between the respiratory body and the world in general in which all respiratory body-subjects conspire as a form of primordial peaceful coexistence establishing a universal dormant Community of the 'Primordial Breath',[25] or should we say, a *Communion of the Immense Lung*[26] with which every sleeping subject communicates continuously. This primordial respiratory coexistence is peaceful coexistence as in deep sleep it becomes almost impossible to continue the struggles and battles between conscious subjectivities except in some very rare cases of sleepwalking and sleep-talking. As the source, origin and lifeline of all particular worlds is 'the world in general', that is, the world of this primordial respiratory pact, I would suggest that we could also call this primordial world following Merleau-Ponty with the notion of 'some immense external lung'. This would mean that the primordial respiratory peace is the ancient, or original, pact between the respiratory body-subject and the world in general as some immense external lung. During sleep this primordial respiratory peace covenant 'becomes my very being'. Does this mean that the conspiring community of the sleeping subjects is the truest incarnation of the world peace today in our world?

This question challenges us to raise another question which I suggest should be one of the fundamental questions of human interest: would it be possible that during our awakened being-in-the-world this primordial respiratory pact could also 'become our very being' and if this could be possible what would it mean to our human existence and coexistence? To ponder this in a brief manner, I would say, it would mean, first of all, that in order to even think this possibility we need to reorient ourselves as waking subjects from our normal attitude of 'forgetting of breathing'[27] to the transformative attitude of 'cultivation of breathing'[28] to use the notions of Luce Irigaray. This would mean that in our awakened particular worlds we would always try to keep ourselves mindful that all our human enterprises are each and every moment founded upon the agreement between our respiratory body-subjects and the world in general as the immense lung. It would also mean that this awakened project of cultivation of breathing would understand itself always in a deep manner as cultivation of the primordial respiratory peace and as such its every act of thought, speech and gesture should promote realization of this respiratory peace in all dimensions of human existence. If we would take these basic respiratory principles as our guidelines for the future perhaps we could have hope as waking subjects to join our alter egos of the dormant world in celebration of *the Conspiracy of the World Peace*.

Notes

1 Luce Irigaray, *Between East and West: From Singularity to Community*, trans. Stephen Pluhácek (New York: Columbia University Press, 2002), 7.

2 Maurice Merleau-Ponty, *Phenomenology of Perception*, trans. Donald A. Landes (London: Routledge, 2012), 265. The translation has been slightly altered.

3 For Merleau-Ponty's usage of the notion of 'pact' see Merleau-Ponty, *Phenomenology of Perception*, 168, 261 and 373; Maurice Merleau-Ponty, *The Visible and the Invisible*, ed. Claude Lefort, trans. Alphonso Lingis (Evanston, IL: Northwestern University Press, 1968), 146; Maurice Merleau-Ponty, *The Primacy of Perception: And Other Essays on Phenomenological Psychology, the Philosophy of Art, History and Politics*, ed. James M. Eddie, trans. Arleen B. Dallery et al. (Evanston, IL: Northwestern University Press, 1964), 6 and 176; Maurice Merleau-Ponty, *Signs*, trans. Richard C. McCleary (Evanston, IL: Northwestern University Press, 1964), 31, 269, 272 and 293; Maurice Merleau-Ponty, *Humanism and Terror: An Essay on the Communist Problem*, trans. John O'Neill (Boston: Beacon Press, 1969) 35–7, 54, 60 and 66; Maurice Merleau-Ponty, *Adventures of the Dialectic*, trans. Joseph Bien (Evanston, IL: Northwestern University Press, 1973), 61, 159, 195 and 230.

4 Merleau-Ponty, *Phenomenology of Perception*, 213.

5 Merleau-Ponty, *The Primacy of Perception*, 122.

6 What about the pre-history before the birth, one could ask? Would that also be respiratory in its nature, that is, the pre-history before baby's first breath? Thanks to Pauline von Bonsdorff for raising these questions at *The Poesis of Peace Conference* in Gozd Martuljek, Slovenia in May of 2014. To these questions one could briefly note that from the very beginning of a foetus' existence the mother is breathing for the foetus as it 'receive[s] oxygen through the mother's blood' (Irigaray, *Between East and West*, 73)

and thus the foetus exists throughout the mother's pregnancy within the vital atmosphere of breathing even if it does not breathe itself. In addition to this the mother's breath creates a certain kind of perpetual respiratory rhythm throughout the foetus' life in the womb, as with every breath the mother takes her body expands and contracts. Thus the spatiality and temporality of the womb as the foetus 'home' has essential respiratory dimensions.

7 Merleau-Ponty, *Phenomenology of Perception*, 264.
8 Merleau-Ponty, *Phenomenology of Perception*, 264.
9 Merleau-Ponty, *Phenomenology of Perception*, 371–2. The translation has been altered.
10 Merleau-Ponty uses the expression of 'peaceful coexistence' also in *Adventures of the Dialectic*, 100; and *Signs*, 49.
11 Edward S. Casey, *Remembering: A Phenomenological Study*, 2nd ed. (Bloomington and Indianapolis: Indiana University Press, 2000), 147.
12 Merleau-Ponty, *Phenomenology of Perception*, 265. The translation has been altered. Here I give to these words of Merleau-Ponty a respiratory context.
13 Jason M. Wirth writes as follows of Schelling's use of the word *Konspiration*: 'In the 1809 *Freedom* essay, perhaps Schelling's most daring work and one of the treasures of the nineteenth-century German philosophical tradition, he spoke of a "unity and conspiracy", a *Konspiration* (I/7, 391). When something or someone falls out of the conspiracy, they become inflamed with sickness and fever, as "inflamed by an inner heat". Schelling used the Latinate-German *Konspiration*, which stems from *conspiro*, to breath or blow together. *Spiro*, to breathe, is related to *spiritus* (the German *Geist*), meaning spirit, but also breath. *Geist* is the progression of difference, the A, the breathing out of the dark abyss of nature into form and the simultaneous inhaling of this ground, the retraction of things away from themselves. The conspiracy is a simultaneous expiration and inspiration, and each thing of nature is both inspired yet expiring. This is what I call the conspiracy of life, that is, the life beyond and within life and death'. Jason M. Wirth, *The Conspiracy of Life: Meditations on Schelling and His Time* (Albany, NY: State University of New York Press, 2003), 2. My thanks to Lenart Škof for reminding me of this passage concerning the idea of conspiracy. In relation to this see also Lenart Škof, *Breath of Proximity: Intersubjectivity, Ethics and Peace* (Dordrecht: Springer, 2015), 42–3. In addition to these references to the theme of *conspiracy* Jean-Louis Chrétien writes in a theological context as follows: '[While] describing prayer as being at one and the same time a gift and a task (*Gabe, Aufgabe*), [Franz von Baader] compares it to the movement of the breath; we receive it from God, we "inspire" it from him, in order to give it back to him, to "expire" it into him. This circulation of the breath taken and given, received and returned, this "conspiration" of the human and the divine is of such a kind, for Baader, that prayer appears to him as a function that is no less vital for the spirit than is breathing for the life of the body'. Jean-Louis Chrétien, *The Ark of Speech*, trans. Andrew Brown (London: Routledge, 2003), 30. See also my own article on this theme of conspiracy, Petri Berndtson, 'The Temple of the Holy Breath as the Place of Conspiracy Between the Respiratory Body and the Space of Open Air', in *Art and Common Space*, ed. Anne-Karin Furunes, Simon Harvey and Maaretta Jaukkuri (Trondheim, NO: NTNU, 2013), 39–47.
14 Merleau-Ponty, *Signs*, 240.
15 Merleau-Ponty on the dialectic between war and peace see, for example, *Signs*, 31–2, 236–7 and *Adventures of the Dialectic*, 185–6.
16 Erwin Strauss quoted by Drew Leder, *The Absent Body* (Chicago: The University of Chicago Press, 1990), 57.
17 Leder, *Absent Body*, 57.
18 Maurice Merleau-Ponty, *Phenomenology of Perception*, trans. Colin Smith (London: Routledge, 1992), 160. Other quotations from Merleau-Ponty's book are taken from Landes' translation. See Landes' translation of these words, 162.

19 Merleau-Ponty, *Phenomenology of Perception*, 264.
20 Merleau-Ponty, *Phenomenology of Perception*, 166. My emphasis.
21 Merleau-Ponty, *Phenomenology of Perception*, 219. My emphasis.
22 Merleau-Ponty, *Phenomenology of Perception*, 297. The translation has been altered.
23 Merleau-Ponty, *Phenomenology of Perception*, lxxiv. See also lxxiii and 493n21. In addition to this see Edmund Husserl, *Cartesian Meditations: An Introduction to Phenomenology*, trans. Dorian Cairns (The Hague: Martinus Nijhoff Publishers, 1960), 157.
24 Merleau-Ponty, *Phenomenology of Perception*, 167.
25 Paul Klee quoted by Maurice Merleau-Ponty, *Notes des cours au Collège de France 1958–1959 et 1960–1961* (Paris: Éditions Gallimard, 1996), 56n4. See also William S. Hamrick and Jan Van der Veken, *Nature and Logos: A Whiteheadian Key to Merleau-Ponty's Fundamental Thought* (Albany, NY: State University of New York Press, 2011), 81n13.
26 I have elsewhere interrogated spatial and poetic dimensions of Merleau-Ponty's notion of 'some external immense lung'. See Petri Berndtson, 'The Respiratory Constitution of Space and Its Connection to the Origin of Space', *Philosophy: Consciousness and Thing, Scientific Papers University of Latvia* 765 (2011): 80–6; and Petri Berndtson, 'The Inspiration and the Expiration of Being: The Immense Lung and the Cosmic Breathing as the Sources of Dreams, Poetry and Philosophy', in *Thinking in Dialogue with Humanities: Paths into the Phenomenology of Merleau-Ponty*, ed. Karel Novotný et al. (Bucharest, RO: Zeta Books, 2010), 281–93.
27 Irigaray, *Between East and West*, 77.
28 Irigaray writes, for example, that in this transformative process of 'cultivation of breathing' 'our elemental vital breath [is transformed] little by little into a more subtle breath in the service of the heart, of thought, of speech and not only in the service of physiological survival'. Irigaray, *Between East and West*, 76. See also Emily A. Holmes and Lenart Škof, eds., *Breathing with Luce Irigaray* (London: Bloomsbury, 2013), which is a unique collection of articles interrogating the dimensionalities and possibilities of Irigaray's idea of 'cultivation of breathing'.

References

Berndtson, Petri. 'The Inspiration and the Expiration of Being: The Immense Lung and the Cosmic Breathing as the Sources of Dreams, Poetry and Philosophy'. In *Thinking in Dialogue with Humanities: Paths into the Phenomenology of Merleau-Ponty*, edited by Karel Novotný, Taylor S. Hammer, Anne Gléonec and Petr Specián, 281–93. Bucharest, RO: Zeta Books, 2010.

Berndtson, Petri. 'The Respiratory Constitution of Space and Its Connection to the Origin of Space'. *Philosophy: Consciousness and Thing. Scientific Papers University of Latvia* 765 (2011): 80–6.

Berndtson, Petri. 'The Temple of the Holy Breath as the Place of Conspiracy between the Respiratory Body and the Space of Open Air'. In *Art and Common Space*, edited by Anne-Karin Furunes, Simon Harvey and Maaretta Jaukkari, 39–47. Trondheim, NO: NTNU, 2013.

Casey, Edward S. *Remembering: A Phenomenological Study*. 2nd ed. Bloomington and Indianapolis: Indiana University Press, 2000.

Chrétien, Jean-Louis. *The Ark of Speech*. Translated by Andrew Brown. London: Routledge, 2003.

Hamrick, William S. and Jan Van der Veken. *Nature and Logos: A Whiteheadian Key to Merleau-Ponty's Fundamental Thought*. Albany, NY: State University of New York Press, 2011.

Holmes, Emily A. and Lenart Škof, eds. *Breathing with Luce Irigaray*. London: Bloomsbury, 2013.

Husserl, Edmund. *Cartesian Meditations: An Introduction to Phenomenology*. Translated by Dorian Cairns. The Hague: Martinus Nijhoff Publishers, 1960.

Irigaray, Luce. *Between East and West: From Singularity to Community*. Translated by Stephen Pluhácek. New York: Columbia University Press, 2002.

Leder, Drew. *The Absent Body*. Chicago, IL: The University of Chicago Press, 1990.

Merleau-Ponty, Maurice. *Adventures of the Dialectic*. Translated by Joseph Bien. Evanston, IL: Northwestern University Press, 1973.

Merleau-Ponty, Maurice. *Humanism and Terror: An Essay on the Communist Problem*. Translated by John O'Neill. Boston: Beacon Press, 1969.

Merleau-Ponty, Maurice. *Notes des cours au Collège de France 1958–1959 et 1960–1961*. Paris: Éditions Gallimard, 1996.

Merleau-Ponty, Maurice. *Phenomenology of Perception*. Translated by Colin Smith. London: Routledge, 1992.

Merleau-Ponty, Maurice. *Phenomenology of Perception*. Translated by Donald A. Landes. London: Routledge, 2012.

Merleau-Ponty, Maurice. *The Primacy of Perception: And Other Essays on Phenomenological Psychology, the Philosophy of Art, History and Politics*. Edited by James M. Eddie, translated by Arleen B. Dallery, James M. Edie, John Wild, William Cobb, Carleton Dallery, Nancy Metzel and John Flodstrom. Evanston, IL: Northwestern University Press, 1964.

Merleau-Ponty, Maurice. *Signs*. Translated by Richard C. McCleary. Evanston, IL: Northwestern University Press, 1964.

Merleau-Ponty, Maurice. *The Visible and the Invisible*. Edited by Claude Lefort, translated by Alphonso Lingis. Evanston, IL: Northwestern University Press, 1968.

Škof, Lenart. *Breath of Proximity: Intersubjectivity, Ethics and Peace*. Dordrecht: Springer, 2015.

Wirth, Jason M. *The Conspiracy of Life: Meditations of Schelling and His Time*. Albany, NY: State University of New York Press, 2003.

5   On Sacred Genealogies in Antigone and Sāvitrī

Lenart Škof

I

In this chapter I wish to delineate new ethical spaces, by following the deeds of two heroic women from the literary and religious tradition – namely Sophocles' Antigone and Sāvitrī from the *Māhabhārata*. What they have in common is that in their lives and/or deaths, and in their heroic deeds, they were in a close relationship to the deceased and to death. But also to life. In this, they were guardians of cosmic laws, with their sacred sexual and generational genealogies. Despite sometimes their tragic fate, they were and remained sacred guardians of basic cosmic laws, related to the living and deceased, heaven, earth and the underworld. In a Heideggerian language, they were, as it were, in a close vicinity of the elements of ancient cosmic order and cosmic laws; in their deeds they acted and spoke from out of a belonging to Being (*to deinon*).

Today, it seems that we have lost our relation to the cosmos and its ethical order. We live in a civilization offering us a plenitude of earthly goods, including various ethical and political laws, and justice in one of its forms. In this fabricated world we (who are *we*?[1]) (un)willingly tolerate evil and violence in one of its varied forms and are thus not able to posit an *unconditional* ethical demand against them. Being subjected to different forms of power, we cannot find a peaceful repose, a place to host (*hospitality*) and protect peace for the concrete living others. This chapter wishes to place Sophocles' *Antigone* into a new ethical framework and point towards some elements for a possible new cosmico-feminist interpretation of justice. It will elaborate on the logic of *agrapta nomima* (unwritten/divine laws) and the logic of ethical gestures towards mortals (both deceased persons and living beings). It will show how Antigone's sacred duty was to preserve the equilibrium of the cosmic order (with its sexual and generational genealogies), and how this equilibrium has been lost in our times, in fact, how it has been subjugated to various forms of power since Creon's political act. According to Luce Irigaray[2] – whose teachings have been my inspiration for years – this was possible only with the Greek substitution of ancient law and cosmic justice with an inauguration of new political laws, as defended by Creon, who finds ancient unwritten laws as obsolete. We know that even Hegel – by fully acknowledging this shift and by highly praising Antigone for her acts – was still not willing to support Antigone's adherence to those ancient laws, representing a sacred order of femininity. New ethical gestures, and a new view of justice are thus needed in our times, gestures which are more closely related to the human body, deceased (as in Polyneices), but also gestures *for* the living corpse (Agamben), any child, or a (wo)man on the very edge between life and death, or any other living body in pain. Universally then, no duty and no justice can be more important than our adherence to the deepest cosmico-ethical layers of both our faith and knowledge, an awareness, rooted in our bodily sensibilities and interiority.

II

From Hegel to Irigaray, Sophocles' Antigone has provoked major thinkers and raised key ethical questions: from divine law to the human law, from ethics to morality, from cosmic awareness to the modern political life; in all those contexts, interpreters such as Hegel, Lacan, Butler, Irigaray and Žižek have searched for the proper *measure*, delineating the most sensitive space of all – the space of proximity between the sexuate subjects, between kin members (even hinting at incestuous relationships between them), or, as in more politically invested readings – among the members of a political community. The languages of psychoanalysis, ethics, theology and law were used and merged in the many and varied reading of this ancient drama. But originally, *Antigone* is a tragedy about cosmic laws and hospitality towards others – members of a kin, but also others as strangers.

According to Irigaray, unveiling the meaning of Antigone is not an easy task in our culture.[3] It is a task requiring from us a descent into entirely different modes of our intersubjective thinking as we inhabited from our predecessors. Clearly, this also is an intercultural task for us Westerners: for example, Irigaray's awakening through Yoga and her dialogue with an ancient Indian culture of breath testify for this. Irigaray's awakening through yoga testifies for this. And there are only a few contemporary philosophers that are sensitive to this task in its entirety. I would dare and in this sense only add Jean-Luc Nancy (perhaps Agamben) to Irigaray. Now, at the very beginning of his *Being Singular Plural* Nancy cites Nietzsche from *Thus Spoke Zarathustra*:

> Like me, guide the virtue that has flown away back to the earth – yes, back to the body and life: so that it may give the earth its meaning, a human meaning! ... Let your spirit and your virtue serve the meaning of the earth ... Human being and human earth are still unexhausted and undiscovered.[4]

Nancy is right in his diagnosis: this earth – now at this moment – 'is anything but sharing community of humanity'.[5] There is no compassion on this earth, no sense of an *être-a-plusieurs*, as he states. Moreover, in his *Corpus*, first by enumerating the atrocities committed in the last century against humanity, Nancy – by reflecting the jurisdiction of bodies – rightly observes that we'd need a *corpus*, namely 'the areality of corpses: of bodies indeed, including the dead body'.[6] What Nancy is aiming at is to delineate spaces, places, topics, perhaps new grounds for bodies, being able to go beyond mere 'dialectical respiration from the "same" to the "other"'.[7] Here we can already sense another *justice*, coming from this sense (or sensitivity) for the bodies and their places. But we will stop here and return to *Antigone*.

What kind of love and justice is then revealed to us in this play of Sophocles? Authors of an excellent study on *Antigone* – namely Max Statkievicz and Valerie Reed – state, that Antigone is 'the turning point in the ethical thinking of our time' and 'an embodiment of the ethical value of the community',[8] in a sense of Agamben's *coming community* (*communità che viene*). Is it not that out from the Hegelian claim on the collision between two equally valid claims (Creon vs. Antigone) there comes our uncertainty regarding justice: '… familial love, the holy, the inward, intimate feelings – hence known also as the law of the nether gods – collides with the right of the state'.[9]

To be able then to view justice not as one-sided, but as an integral ethical law, we have to admit the inner logic of this collision. *But this is impossible.* Antigone's faith and her radical ethical care for the other, the brother-as-corpse, is deeper than any one-sided view, as proposed by Hegel, Lacan, Butler, Žižek, or many others. Antigone's ethics is best understood when confronted with Heidegger's and Irigaray's ontologies on one, and Levinas' and Derrida's views of justice on the other side. These are all thinkers, being in the close vicinity of an ancient Greek and Indian (Presocratic: as Heidegger and Irigaray with her relation to pre-Vedic cults and sources and Yoga) or divine (as in Levinas and Derrida) justice: this is the realm of divine law and *agrapta nomima*.[10]

According to Rémi Brague, we can understand the divinity of Greek law only beginning with Sophocles. For Brague, these divine laws (and accompanying justice, of course), are so old that 'they really did not appear, since they are so obvious, that there is no beginning in them'[11] (*qu'elles n'ont pas de point d'émergence*). For the double setting of an *ethical archeology* and *ethical anatomy*[12] – or relation between morality (with justice) and ethical gestures towards the other *in* her body, the other in pain, and equally the deceased and dead bodies – this simple but pregnant observation of Brague indeed is of a key importance. *Agrapta nomima* can only be inscribed in our hearts and our bodies. We all are the inheritors of this sacred message, being inaugurated by Antigone's act and – as we shall see later – having also important intercultural consequences. Divine laws and our bodies as sacred stelas, furthermore, the logic of a sacrificial body, the body as a tabernacle (M. Douglas):[13] this also is an inauguration of a plane where Derrida and Levinas meet with their interventions into the very logic of justice. In this tradition (Ancient Near East and Old Testament), washing the body – a living body – is 'an enactment that replicates atonement for restoring the sanctity of the tabernacle'.[14] The same holds for Antigone's – now ancient Greek – ancestral care for Polyneices' corpse: it is an act, needed in order to regain the lost cosmic order, to remove, or to wash out the impurity, brought into this world by Creon's political act. This is why there is no antagonism between two different ethical worlds (according to Hegel and his followers, *eine sittliche Macht gegen die andere*) in Antigone: her act rests in divine law and divine justice: it is an act, inscribed in the feminine body and as such it is *an-archic*. In the body as a microcosm a 'shared background knowledge'[15] is stored. According to Levinas, these ancient rights of the other person, and their justice, are *a priori*: they have an *ineluctable authority* and demand from us an *inexhaustible responsibility*, one compared to Antigone's claim.[16] Phenomenologically, they lead us towards radical proximity in intersubjectivity, towards the event of meeting, goodness, and peace.

In the pre-Homeric Greek world, the guardians of these ancient cosmic laws were Erinyes (and along them Gaia, Hades, Persephone/Demeter, Kore etc.). In the pre-Vedic, and later in the Vedic world, this place has been secured by deities from the Proto-Śakta-Tantric cults on one, and later from the Ādityas – Varuṇa, Mitra and Aryaman – on the other side. But let us wait for a moment with the intercultural aspects and firstly reflect upon the world of pre-Homeric deities and Irigaray's interpretation of the tragedy. According to Walter F. Otto,[17] pre-Homeric and pre-Olympic deities of the ancient chthonic religion testify for the close proximity of the Greek (wo)man to the elements of the nature. I wrote about the elements – i.e. air/breath/ether, water, earth, fire (and food, in India) – and the cosmico-ethical constellation arising from them in my last book.[18] These elements appear philosophically in the world of both pre-Socratic and Upanishadic philosophers, but later they reappear only in Schelling, Feuerbach, Heidegger (via Hölderlin), Irigaray and Caputo. Caputo, for example, pleads for greater respect for intuitions, based on the ancient mythic elements, forgotten all the way in our philosophies and theologies, and our view of justice – human and divine: invoking Irigaray, Caputo mentions 'sun and eye, air and breath, wind and spirit, sea and life, rock and god'; we may add, for the sake of our reading of Antigone, earth and the netherworld.[19] Now, to return to the Greek world: it seems that Antigone is a guardian of this sacred cosmic order, as represented within this elemental world. Otto mentions in this sense ancient laws, or, better, ancient justice, as an interruption into this world. The gods which belong to the Earth, argues Otto, all belong to the principles of femininity (perhaps matriarchy)[20] and stand against the later masculine orders of the Olympic gods. This ancient earthly order is a place where Antigone's act is also rooted. This is a magical world: with the corpse of Polyneices, lying there on the earth, unburied as a pray for the dogs, and any corpse or living dead (Agamben) in *our* world not being cared for, od being *deserted, betrayed, forgotten* … the sacred equilibrium of the cosmic order is broken. This intrusion of an injustice into the cosmic order means that sexual and generational orders, and of course also natural orders of fertility (food, grain), are unsettled and broken. The basic principles of *a life* are endangered, including death as its part. Twins (as Indian Yama and Yami), brothers and sisters, sharing the same womb, as in the case of Antigone and Polyneices; mother and a child … this now is not yet a world of morality (or, not any more), nor any form of 'justice': we may add that it is this cosmic order what is the meaning of *a priori* in the above-mentioned Levinasian sense, including the phenomenological consequences.

For Irigaray, Antigone represents the key point in the history of the mankind: as a woman and as a sister, she incorporates in herself three orders: of life and cosmic order, order of generations, and order of sexuate differentiation. This is how Irigaray summarizes this task:

> The law or the duty Antigone defends at the risk of her life includes three aspects that are linked together: respect for the order of the living universe and living beings, respect for the order of generation and not only genealogy, and respect for the order of sexuate difference. It is important to stress the word 'sexuate', and not 'sexual', because the duty of Antigone does not concern sexuality as such, nor even its restraint as Hegel thought. If this was the case, she ought to have privileged her fiancé Haimon and not the brother. Antigone undertakes the burial of her brother because he represents a singular concrete sexuate identity that must be respected as such: 'as the son of her mother'. For Antigone, human identity has not yet become one, neuter, universal as Creon's order will render it. Humanity is still two: man and woman, and this duality, already existent in the natural order, must be respected, as a sort of frame, before the fulfilment of sexual attraction or desire.[21]

Antigone's decision (famously, she gives precedence to brother over the potential child or husband) shows her cosmico-ethical intuition: she cannot substitute a potential other to the concrete living other, or, even more radically, his corpse. She must also secure an identity for herself, for her self-affection. But she must protect her dead brother, not only from the decay, but principally from his wandering as a ghost, being deprived of a memory, his past, and, paradoxically, his future. For Irigaray, brother and sister represent two horizontal identities: 'She must secure for her brother the memory of a valid sexuate identity, and not just of an anonymous and neutralized bodily matter'.[22] Again, she thus wants to preserve life and cosmic order.

Antigone's famous words 'My nature is to join in love, not hate'[23] represent the peak of the tragedy. Not only Hegel, but also Irigaray thinks that her mission might even be higher than that of Christ. Again, Antigone's problem stays at 'the turning point in the ethical thinking of our time'[24] being in the closest vicinity of the place of *hospitality*, perhaps the central topic of all today's ethics. *Hospitality, clearly, is justice.* Hospitality is closely related to the problem of Antigone: within ancient Greek, ancient Near Eastern, Vedic etc. contexts, hospitality clearly played a prominent role. Philosophically, hospitality first means that we are willing to acknowledge the other in his or her autonomy, without appropriating his or her subjectivity to our place, our interiority: this is what Derrida understood by unconditional hospitality. We also know that already for Levinas, the very essence of language *was* hospitality, but Irigaray, being heavily influenced by the teachings of Buddha and Yoga, will say that this place can only be secured from the *silence*.[25] Now, for Derrida, Antigone clearly had to transgress written laws 'in order to offer her brothers the hospitality of the land and of burial'.[26] This offering of an ultimate hospitality is furthermore accompanied with the possibility of its radicalization through what Anne Dufourmantelle has called in her commentary to Derrida's text *hospitality toward death*, which means, a hospitality offered to the dead one (as a burial), an act which of course can never be reciprocated. This act – hospitality toward death – testifies how closely tied Antigone was with the gods of the netherworld. This is also the essence of Patočka's reading of Antigone.[27] But it is not the night and death, which is feared by Creon; it is principally Antigone's mode of silence, her language and her values that he cannot understand or, ultimately, bear.

III

Now I intend to point to some interesting intercultural possibilities, as represented in the legend of Sāvitrī from the *Mahabhārata*. The Sāvitrī legend of course is itself a topic which deserves more space and more time and attention.[28] What is important to notice, firstly, is that what Irigaray denotes by sexual difference and (divine) couples is already represented within Indian religiosity in divine couples such as Brāhma and Sāvitrī, among many others (also Yama and Yami are closely related to what was in the forefront of my analyses of *Antigone*). It seems that Indian religiosity from the most ancient times (i.e. including pre-Vedic cults and traditions) is closely related to the task of gaining a sexuate identity through religion and is thus in the closest proximity to the ideal of justice I wish to propose. Secondly, upon King Aśvapati's wishing of the child and worshiping the goddess Sāvitrī with the Sāvitrī verse – *a daughter* has been born. For Irigaray, again, daughters play a special role within cosmic and generational orders: they are women, born of the women, and thus bearers of a different sexual genealogy as compared to men; it is a genealogy which is not accessible to men.[29] Princess Sāvitrī represents this genealogical element. Then there are other genealogies, such as represented in the rules of kinship, to whose Sāvitrī was subjugated (some of them have worked analogously to Antigone and have been stamped with the mark of an incestuous relationship),[30] but still, the autonomy of her acts relates her to the argumentative autonomy (according to A. Sen)[31] of key Upanishadic women such as Gārgī Vācaknavī from the Upanishadic brahmodyas. Last but not least, and this will be my point of departure here, Sāvitrī legend is marked by similar cosmic relations or cosmic markers as compared to the religious background of Antigone.

According to Parpola, as a Goddess and the daughter of the sun, Sāvitrī is connected 'with the first light of the day'. She is called *prasavitrī* (from *pra-savā*) referring to her roles as being the 'procreatrix, mother, bestowing progeny'.[32] In this, she inhabits the very threshold between the night and day, between *not-yet-life* and *life*, dying and creating/resurrecting, with femininity and masculinity represented in their different roles. In her role Sāvitrī as a person will also be comparable to what Irigaray prophetizes for the future task of philosophy – not as represented by the works of male philosophers (Irigaray mentions Sartre, Merleau-Ponty and Levinas), where woman is reduced to a certain mode of passivity and man (the philosopher, at least) to activity.

Now, in her role as bestowing progeny, Sāvitrī represents ancient cosmic generational and sexual orders, similar to those propounded by Irigaray in her reading of *Antigone*. Justice can only appear if there is care and compassion in the world, which comes both from the masculine as well as from the feminine, in woman, daughter, or wife. This latter element has nothing to do with the ritual of *satī* or heroic death as understood through this act. In this ritual, ancient cosmic respect for sexual difference has already been lost. Deshpande articulates the message of the legend in the sense of an incarnation of the goddess Sāvitrī, being in the world for the purpose of rescuing the *dharma*. For him, Sāvitrī is a symbol of Nature (*prakṛtī*), which is to be understood not in some philosophical explanation (such as Sāṃkhya-Yoga) but rather in a more primeval cosmico-ethical way: as a care for life, care for various generational orders, for progenity and growth.

We are inhabitants of a world in which suffering, death and evil form an equal part. Our task as humans, in our masculine and feminine identities, is to secure in our interiorities (through ethical gestures such as caress and compassion) and in our intersubjective relations the hospitable place for the others/guests/enemies, including animal others in this world. Only in this care does cosmic justice have the possibility to emerge in spaces between us – and enliven and ethically trespass the sacred threshold between Gods and mortals, nature/earth/nether/world and heavens.[33]

Let me wind up this essay with a beautiful passage of Irigaray, closely related to what I mentioned in the context of a justice for mothers and children, little brothers and sisters of this world, a view of justice most obviously missing or obscured in today's world:

> It suffices to listen to unwritten laws inscribed in nature itself: the respect for life, for its generation, growth and blossoming and the respect for a sexuate transcendence between us – first of all between children of the same mother, but more generally between all the children of our human species, of our mother nature, whose we are children on the side of or beyond all the more or less sacrificial sociological constructions that divide us.[34]

There is only one transcendence then: the transcendence of a cosmic order, securing to all cultures and all persons their identity, their unique, respected and hospitable place within cosmos, and one *justice*.

Notes

1 Upon referring to the 'we', it would be necessary to address what Jean-Luc Nancy refers to in his *Being Singular Plural* (Stanford, CA: Stanford University Press, 2000, 5ff), thinking of a coexistence, communication as a very essence of Being, which, for Nancy, ultimately is material – i.e. as an ontology of bodies, filling the empty space in ethics between the areas of Heidegger's/Irigaray's on one, and Levinas' thought on the other side. Let me add, that close to this constellation is the position of American pragmatism's processual and communicative ethics (Mead and Dewey).

2 Luce Irigaray, *Una nuova cultura dell'energia: Al di là di Oriente e Occidente* (Torino: Bollati Boringheri, 2013).

3 Luce Irigaray, *In the Beginning, She Was* (London: Bloomsbury, 2013), chap. 5, 'Between Myth and History'.

4 Friedrich Nietzsche, *Thus Spoke Zarathustra: A Book for All and None*, ed. Arian del Caro and Robert B. Pippin, trans. Adrian del Caro (Cambridge: Cambridge University Press, 2006), 57–8.

5 Nancy, *Being Singular Plural*, xiii.

6 Jean-Luc Nancy, *Corpus*, trans. Richard A. Rand (New York: Fordham University Press, 2008), 53.

7 Nancy, *Corpus*, 103. See also: 'Since the *First World War* (in other words, the simultaneous invention of a new juridical space for an international political economy, *and* a new combat-space for a whole new number of victims) these bodies, crowded wherever they go, are bodies primarily sacrificed'. Nancy, *Corpus*, 79.

8 Max Statkiewicz and Valerie Reed, 'Antigone's (Re)Turn: The Ēthos of the Coming Community', *Analecta Husserliana* LXXXV (2005), 788.

9 Georg Wilhelm Friedrich Hegel, *Lectures on the Philosophy of Religion*, part 2, ed. Peter C. Hodgson, trans. R.F. Brown, P.C. Hodgson and J.M. Stewart (Berkeley: University of California Press, 1984), 1087.

10 On the history of *agrapta nomima* see Rosalind Thomas, 'Writing, Law, and Written Law', in *The Cambridge Companion to Ancient Greek Law*, ed. Michael Gagarin and David Cohen (Cambridge: Cambridge University Press, 2005), 41–60.

11 Rémi Brague, *La loi de Dieu – Histoire philosophique d'une alliance* (Paris: Editions Gallimard, 2005), 43. Original passage: 'Mais c'est seulement Sophocle qui permet de comprendre ce que signifie le caractère divin d'une loi. Dans le célèbre passage de l'*Antigone*, l'héroïne dit des lois dont elle se réclame contre le décret de Créon que "personne ne sait d'où elles sont apparues". C'est qu'elles ne sont en fait jamais apparues du tout, elles sont si manifestes qu'elles n'ont pas de point d'émergence'.

12 On the very concept of *ethical anatomy* (with its elements: eye, heart, lungs, stomach, skin …), see my book *Breath of Proximity: Intersubjectivity, Ethics and Peace* (Dordrecht: Springer, 2015).

13 Mary Douglas, *Leviticus as Literature* (Oxford and New York: Oxford University Press, 2000), 67ff. It is an important observation of Douglas for our purpose, namely, that 'Leviticus focuses its metaphysical resources on that very point between life and death' and also 'that there has always been in the Jewish culture a strong association between body and tabernacle in respect of fertility'. Douglas, *Leviticus as Literature*, 67, 80.

14 Douglas, *Leviticus as Literature*, 188.

15 Douglas, *Leviticus as Literature*, 190.

16 Emmanuel Levinas, *Outside the Subject* (London: Continuum, 1993), 91, 98.

17 Walter F. Otto, *Die Götter Griechenlands: Das Bild des Göttlichen im Spiegel des griechischen Geistes* (Frankfurt/M: Klostermann, 1987). See Chapter 2 on the ancient religion ad myth.

18 Škof, *Breath of Proximity*.

19 John D. Caputo, *The Insistence of God: A Theology of Perhaps* (Bloomington and Indianapolis: Indiana University Press, 2013), 251. In this sense, Caputo's cosmic Jesus 'is a man of flesh and blood, with animal companions and with animal needs … a Judeo-pagan prophet and healer, in tune with the animals and the elements, in whose body the elements dance their cosmic dance, supplying as it does a conduit through which the elements flow, and I treat the elements as a cosmic grace which is channelled by the body of Jesus'. Caputo, *The Insistence of God*, 251–2.

20 W. Burkert seems to be more critical or at least reserved of this view in his *Griechische Religion der archaischen und klassischen Epoche* (Stuttgart: Kohlhammer, 2011). Burkert here contrasts chthonic religion with 'die Epiphanie der Gottheit von oben her im Tanz' which, for him, testifies for a different religious principle (70). Yet, he admits the importance of chthonic order in particular as related to the nutrition and life

circle (306). From Burkert one still gets the general impression that he was not willing to grant any greater importance to the deities of chthonic origin.

21 Irigaray, *In the Beginning, She Was*, 118–9.
22 Irigaray, *In the Beginning, She Was*, 119.
23 Sophocles, *Antigone*, ed. M. Griffith (Cambridge: Cambridge University Press, 1999), line 523. For the translation, see *Greek Tragedies*, vol. 1, ed. David Greene and Richmond Lattimore (Chicago: University of Chicago Press, 1991), 201.
24 Statkiewicz and Reed, 'Antigone's (Re)Turn', 788.
25 For Irigaray, silence is the speaking of the threshold. Already for Heidegger, the meaning of the threshold lies in difference. Difference between two subjectivities and other differences, which all, for Irigaray, have been inaugurated in the most basic of all differences, sexual difference. Upon her/him coming to my world, at the very threshold, silence is what must be 'preserved before meeting the other'; it is also 'openness that nothing occupies or preoccupies – no language, no values, no pre-established truth'. Luce Irigaray, 'Ethical Gestures toward the Other', *Poligrafi* 15, no. 57 (2008): 10. This securing of the place for silence in ourselves and in spaces of *between-us* presupposes that we remain two and demands from us a new kind of *self-affection* – one respectful to my self, for the difference and being attentive towards the needs of others.
26 Jacques Derrida, *Of Hospitality* (Stanford: Stanford University Press, 2000), 85. On law and justice see also Jacques Derrida, *Acts of Religion*, ed. Gil Anidjar (New York and London: Routledge, 2002), in particular the chapters 'Force of Law: The "Mystical Foundation of Authority"' and 'Hostipitality'.
27 See the A. Dufourmantelle invocation of Jan Patočka and his thought in *Of Hospitality*: 'She is one of those who love, not one of those who hate', wrote Patočka, but this love is not Christlike. It signifies 'love as foreign to the human condition, deriving from the portion of night which is the portion of the gods'. Derrida, *Of Hospitality*, 42. It seems that the difference between Antigone and Christ lies in their relation to the ancient religion. While Christ (as a man) revolutionized the ancient Judaic religion, it was Antigone's sacred duty that first came out from her sexual identity as a key cosmico-ethical impetus and was thus also closely related to the cosmic interiority of the divine law.
28 I rely on Asko Parpola, 'The Religious Background of the Sāvitrī Legend', in *Harānandalaharī – Volume in Honour of Professor Minoru Hara on his Seventieth Birthday*, ed. R. Tsuchida and A. Weber (Reinbeck: Dr. Inge Wezler Verlag für orientalische Fachpublikationen, 2000); see also the extended version of the essay: 'Sāvitrī and Ressurection', in *Changing Patterns of Family and Kinship in South Asia* (Studia Orientalia, vol. 84), ed. Asko Parpola and Sirka Tenhunen, Studia Orientalia 84 (Helsinki: Finnish Oriental Society, 1998). See also R.Y. Deshpande, *The Ancient Tale of Sāvitrī* (Sri Aurobindo International Centre of Education, Pondicherry, 1995).
29 See Luce Irigaray, *To Be Two* (New York: Routledge, 2001), 34: 'a woman gives birth to a woman'.
30 See Parpola, 'The Religious Background of the Sāvitrī Legend', 200.
31 Cf. Amartya Sen, *The Argumentative Indian: Writings on Indian History, Culture and Identity* (New York: Farrar, Straus and Giroux, 2005), 7–9.
32 Parpola, 'The Religious Background of the Sāvitrī Legend', 197.
33 Deshpande, *The Ancient Tale of Sāvitrī*.
34 Irigaray, *In the Beginning, She Was*, 137.

References

Brague, Rémi. *La loi de Dieu – Histoire philosophique d'une alliance*. Paris: Editions Gallimard, 2005.
Burkert, Walter. *Grieechische Religion der archaischen und klassischen Epoche*. Stuttgart: Kohlhammer, 2011.

Caputo, John D. *The Insistence of God: A Theology of Perhaps*. Bloomington and Indianapolis: Indiana University Press, 2013.

Derrida, Jacques. *Acts of Religion*. Edited by Gil Anidjar. New York and London: Routledge, 2002. See esp. chaps. 'Force of Law: The "Mystical Foundation of Authority"' and 'Hostipitality'.

Derrida, Jacques. *Of Hospitality*. Stanford: Stanford University Press, 2000.

Deshpande, Renukadas Yeshwantrao. *The Ancient Tale of Sāvitrī*. Sri Aurobindo International Centre of Education, Pondicherry, 1995.

Douglas, Mary. *Leviticus as Literature*. Oxford and New York: Oxford University Press, 2000.

Greene, David and Richmond Lattimore, eds. *Greek Tragedies*. Vol. 1. Chicago: University of Chicago Press, 1991.

Hegel, Georg Wilhelm Friedrich. *Lectures on the Philosophy of Religion*. Part 2. Edited by Peter C. Hodgson, translated by R.F. Brown, P.C. Hodgson and J.M. Stewart. Berkeley: University of California Press, 1984.

Irigaray, Luce. 'Ethical Gestures toward the Other'. *Poligrafi* 15, no. 57 (2008): 3–23.

Irigaray, Luce. *In the Beginning, She Was*. London: Bloomsbury, 2013. See esp. chap. 5, 'Between Myth and History'.

Irigaray, Luce. *To Be Two*. New York: Routledge, 2001. See esp. chap. 3, 'Daughter and Woman'.

Irigaray, Luce. *Una nuova cultura dell'energia: Al di là di Oriente e Occidente*. Torino: Bollati Boringheri, 2013.

Levinas, Emmanuel. *Outside the Subject*. London: Continuum, 1993. See esp. chap. 10, 'The Rights of Man and the Rights of the Other'.

Nancy, Jean-Luc. *Being Singular Plural*. Translated by Robert D. Richardson. Stanford, CA: Stanford University Press, 2000.

Nancy, Jean-Luc. *Corpus*. Translated by Richard A. Rand. New York: Fordham University Press, 2008.

Nietzsche, Friedrich. *Thus Spoke Zarathustra: A Book for All and None*. Edited by Arian del Caro and Robert B. Pippin, translated by Adrian del Caro. Cambridge: Cambridge University Press, 2006.

Otto, Walter F. *Die Götter Griechenlands: Das Bild des Göttlichen im Spiegel des griechischen Geistes*. Frankfurt: Klostermann, 1987.

Parpola, Asko. 'The Religious Background of the Sāvitrī Legend'. In *Harānandalaharī – Volume in Honour of Professor Minoru Hara on his Seventieth Birthday*, edited by R. Tsuchida and A. Weber, 193–216. Reinbeck: Dr. Inge Wezler Verlag für orientalische Fachpublikationen, 2000.

Parpola, Asko. 'Sāvitrī and Ressurection'. In *Changing Patterns of Family and Kinship in South Asia*, edited by Asko Parpola and Sirka Tenhunen, 167–312. Studia Orientalia 84. Helsinki: Finnish Oriental Society, 1998.

Škof, Lenart. *Breath of Proximity: Intersubjectivity, Ethics and Peace*. Dordrecht: Springer, 2015.

Sen, Amartya. *The Argumentative Indian: Writings on Indian History, Culture and Identity*. New York: Farrar, Straus and Giroux, 2005.

Sophocles. *Antigone*. Edited by Mark Griffith. Cambridge: Cambridge University Press, 1999.

Statkiewicz, Max and Valerie Reed. 'Antigone's (Re)Turn: The Ēthos of the Coming Community'. *Analecta Husserliana* LXXXV (2005): 787–811.

Thomas, Rosalind. 'Writing, Law, and Written Law'. In *The Cambridge Companion to Ancient Greek Law*, edited by Michael Gagarin and David Cohen, 41–60. Cambridge: Cambridge University Press, 2005.

Part II

Intercultural Approaches to Peace and Non-Violence

6   Islam Versus the West?

Muslim Challenges of a False Binary

Carool Kersten

As part of their efforts to find ways of overcoming – or perhaps more accurately subverting – the Islam–West dichotomy that dominates the post–Cold War world-views projected by advocates of an allegedly inescapable clash of civilizations, certain intellectuals from the Muslim world are engaging with the work of Western philosophers such as Dewey and Heidegger, Arendt and Gadamer, Agamben and Vattimo. The purpose of the resulting critiques is to develop alternative ways of looking at the role of religion – in this instance, Islam – in what is at one and the same time a de-centred, but also an increasingly interconnected world. These approaches stand in contrast to binary opposition of Islam versus the West that is not only feeding international discord, but also fuelling Islamophobia and sectarianism in domestic settings.

As examples I have chosen two Iranian-born intellectuals Hamid Dabashi and Ali Mirsepassi. Trained as sociologists of knowledge, their work on intellectual history is very much concerned with regimes of knowledge, that is, the relationship between knowledge and power. Ironically, both work in the metropole of Neoliberal Capitalism: New York, standing as a defiant symbol of global financial prowess and functioning as a lightning rod for the interlocutors on opposite sides of this Islam versus the West paradigm. While Mirsepassi draws on American pragmatists, Dabashi engages European poststructuralist thought and post-colonial theories from the Global South.[1] Whereas the heuristic apparatuses may differ in terms of Dabashi and Mirsepassi's respective *diagnostics*, their *diagnoses* point up certain commonalities, unified by their criticism of particular regimes of knowledge that underlie what both of them regard as an outdated, obsolete and unhelpful dichotomy. Focussing on intellectual conversations that have helped shape the oeuvres of Dabashi and Mirsepassi, the present chapter offers an exercise in intertextuality and epistemological genealogy.

In the case of Dabashi, this means tracing the development of an ideology of resistance defying the new globalized world order and challenging the projections of an allegedly inevitable Clash of Civilizations Thesis that is supposed to have replaced the Cold War East–West binary with a dichotomy between Islam and the West. Rejecting the totalizing aspirations of both Enlightenment modernity and parallel tendencies found in Islamist ideologies, Dabashi has developed a counternarrative that is in conversation with certain poststructuralist thinkers and critical theorists. Mirsepassi, in turn, refracts the intellectual virtues of the classical Enlightenment, the cultural truth claim of counter-Enlightenment thinking and parallel Islamic discourses through the lens of the inclusivist moral virtue found in John Dewey's conceptual pragmatism that was spawned by a more radical strand of Enlightenment thinking.

Despite epistemological differences and diverging ideological orientations, Dabashi and Mirsepassi's thinking about knowledge and power converge in their concerns with freedom, democracy and civil rights. For Mirsepassi these values are safeguarded by privileging a sociological and pragmatic anti-foundationalist interest in the experience of everyday life over a philosophical preoccupation with overarching epistemologies and ontologies. According to Dabashi, emancipation arises from a disposition of worldly cosmopolitanism which is found in the cultural traditions of Muslim literary humanism – or what is called *adab* in Arabic.[2] This shared orientation of Dabashi and Mirsepassi's work is also reflected in the similarity between the titles and concerns of their latest publications: *Being a Muslim in the World* and *Islam, Democracy and Cosmopolitanism: At Home and in the World*.

Transforming Islamic Liberation Theology into a Liberation Theodicy for a Decentred World

The increasingly prolific writings of Hamid Dabashi during the past decade all feed into a project he has been working on for many more years.[3] With his *Islamic Liberation Theology* of 2008 holding centre stage, the books published between 2006 and 2013 offer a contrarian – and often counterintuitive – account, sketching the emergence of a world order that is no longer just postcolonial and postmodern, but also post-Western and post-Islamist. Dabashi's interpretation not only declares the metaphysics of identity underlying the binary of Islam versus the West outdated; it also renders obsolete the totalizing tendencies of all regimes of knowledge that have so far shaped the understanding of historical events, such as the French Revolution, and that inform ideologies and trends like Bolshevism, as well as two hundred years of Islamic responses to colonization and subjugation in the name of Enlightenment modernity.[4]

By way of alternative, Dabashi formulates an oppositional discourse imaginatively attuned to the new geography of what has become in effect a decentred world, but which is now facing a truly global form of 'Empire' without any identifiable epicentre or gravitational point. Although he adopted Negri and Hardt's term, Dabashi criticizes their exposition as 'pathologically Eurocentric'.[5] Similar objections colour his account of what he calls 'the phenomenon code-named globalization', for which he has primarily drawn on select women authors.[6] Dismissing Julia Kristeva and Susan Sontag as European provincials, for the dismantling of what he calls an 'outdated geography of domination', Dabashi sides with Arundhati Roy, Judith Butler, and especially Zillah Eisenstein and Amy Kaplan's return to the writings of African-American intellectual W.E.B. Du Bois (1868–1963).[7] Their writings open up the prospect of an 'emancipatory remapping' in which the binaries of centre-periphery and colonizer–colonized collapse along with the 'meta-narratives of [...] Islamism, nationalism, [and] liberalism'.[8] Noting repeatedly that the colonial is now as much in the metropolis as the metropolis in the colonial, Dabashi announces a new solidarity that launches forward from early discourses of emancipation. These include Islamic ideologies (with central importance accorded to Malcolm X), Gustavo Guttierez's Catholic Liberation Theology, and Frantz Fanon's *Tiers-Mondisme*. In contrast to the kind of new transnational politics envisaged by Saskia Sassen, Dabashi foresees more localized instances of 'insurrectionary resistance'.[9] Dabashi's presentation of this new global confrontation echoes with the Marxist undertones of such poststructuralists as Louis Althusser and Michel Pêcheux, as he pitches the disenfranchised masses in both the global south and the former metropolises against predatory capitalism that is benefiting a select aggregate of interests represented by corporate multinationals and their political allies in the US, Europe and select regimes in Asia, Africa and Latin America.

Dabashi is very critical of what he refers to as the 'autonormativity' of Western thinking, which is the result of its self-proclamation as the benchmark for all critical thinking and intellectual rigour.[10] But at the same time he mines that legacy for the intellectual deposits needed to forge this counter discourse. Dabashi's new agenda is also very much the outcome of introspection and self-reflection. Based on critical examinations of the Iranian revolution and its religious underpinnings in historical Shi'a Islam, Dabashi's analysis concludes that the success of the Iranian revolution also heralds the failure of political Islam. This is the tragic consequence of what he calls the paradox of Shi'ism as a 'Religion of Protest': morally strong when politically weak, and the other way around. During two centuries of resisting European colonisation and the concomitant spread of Enlightenment modernity, the mutation of Islam into a counter ideology made sense, only to collapse under its own success after the Iranian revolution. Just as he continues to engage with European thinkers, Dabashi also does not disavow Islam. On the contrary, even; it is time to reconstitute the worldly cosmopolitanism of the various Muslim cultures and turn it into the underpinning of a new revolutionary ideology.

The acute necessity of this transformation is imposed by escalating levels of violence that have accompanied the emergence of Empire and the concomitant extremism of al-Qaeda. Both 9/11 and Donald Rumsfeld's subsequent campaign of 'shock and awe' in Iraq stand as the twin markers of the replacement of the kind of legitimate violence theorized by George Sorel, Karl Marx, Max Weber and Franz Fanon, as well as the idea of eternal enmity celebrated in the work of Carl Schmitt and Ernst Jünger.[11] To offset Schmitt's appropriation and misinterpretation of Walter Benjamin's notion of 'pure violence', Dabashi turns to Giorgio Agamben's rereading of the essay '*Kritik der Gewalt*'. His interpretation cautions against giving the oft-cited 'state of exception' a status of normalcy, because this results in a reduction of human life to the level of *zoë* – the bare life of *homo sacer*, elaborated in Agamben's life-long philosophical project of the same name.[12] Dabashi also notes with approval Agamben's dismay with the breakdown of communications between Foucault's *biopolitics*, the holocaust, and Hannah Arendt's *Human Condition*, as well as the latter's failure to see the relation between what Dabashi calls her own version of biopolitics and her writings on totalitarianism and revolution.[13] Dabashi advocates the opposition of these pathological mutations of violence with a new consciousness growing out of a parallel transformation of the liberation theologies from the colonial and postcolonial age into what he calls a liberation theodicy.[14] In parallel with the diametrically opposed ways in which Walter Benjamin and Carl Schmitt understood the notion of 'pure violence', Dabashi's interpretation of the theodicy does not account for evil in the world, but for diversity and alterity.[15] It is conceived as an 'other-based, not self-based' hermeneutics that goes back to Levinas rather than Heidegger or Husserl.[16]

In order to oppose both the metanarratives of Enlightenment modernity and Islamism, 'Muslims will have to learn the logic of their own inauthenticity, syncretism, pluralisms and alterities'.[17] Here Dabashi's thinking connects with Gianni Vattimo's celebration of difference and advocacy of embracing what he calls *pensiero debole* – 'weak thought'.[18] This notion can be traced back to the hermeneutics developed by Hans-Georg Gadamer in *Truth and Method*.[19] Vattimo adopted it as a – to his mind – better alternative to Deconstruction, because that strand of French poststructuralism still harbours 'too much nostalgia for metaphysics'.[20] Dabashi's use of Vattimo's 'weak thought' is not just to introduce yet another fanciful term into his writings. As I have demonstrated elsewhere, it pays to trace the genealogy of such seemingly arcane terminology to the wider oeuvre of the writer in question.[21]

In the present instance, reading Vattimo's other writings also offer an entry point for a critical interrogation of what Dabashi means by worldly cosmopolitanism. For example, in *The Transparent Society*, Vattimo's discussion of the transformation of the modern idea of linear-progressive 'utopia' into postmodern 'heterotopia' contains a cautionary note that is not only applicable to the Islamists' return to *al-salaf al-salih* or 'pious ancestors', but also to Dabashi's advocacy of a return to literary humanism, namely the danger that this will only lead to a celebration of literalist religious revivalism or literary nostalgia.[22] Another challenge posed by the use of Vattimo lies in the close connection of 'weak thought' with the nexus established in Vattimo's writings on religion between, on the one hand, the announcement of the 'Death of God' in Nietzsche's nihilism and Heidegger's end of metaphysics, and, on the other hand, the incarnation of Christ as the ultimate exponent of that event for Western culture, and the subsequent establishment of secularization as being inextricably tied up with the teachings of Jesus.[23] Invoking statements such as Benedetto Croce's 'we cannot not call ourselves Christians', Vattimo argues that the ultimate consequence of interpretation as the maximum possible degree of certainty we can achieve due to our condition as historicized beings offers him the opportunity to accept his Catholic faith and leaves Europeans no other option than to identify their culture as Christian.[24]

However, Vattimo also makes a few other points that offer a way out of this problematic – at least from the perspective of a Muslim thinker – preoccupation with Christianity. Vattimo has expanded the Pauline notion of *kenosis* – the 'emptying out' of the Transcendent into the world – from the incarnation in Christ to the revelation of scriptures. For Vattimo, the latter have not ended, because Vattimo says that 'revelation continues [...] by way of an increasingly "truer" interpretation of Scripture'.[25] This opens a window of opportunity for Muslims to join this conversation as well, since Muhammad's mission can be regarded as a continuation of the Judeo-Christian narrative for a new audience. Moreover, according to Vattimo, one of the effects of Nietzschean nihilism and the Heideggerian end of metaphysics is 'the end of Eurocentrism' and the 'pluralization of the agencies of information'.[26] This re-orientation fits with Dabashi's insistence that we live in a world that is at one and the same time postcolonial and post-Oriental, as well as post-Western and post-Islamist.

At this point it is also instructive to consider Gianni Vattimo's conversations and debates with John Caputo. There are strong resonances between Hamid Dabashi's subversion of the Islam versus West binary, where he posits the need for a restoration of Islam's worldly cosmopolitanism, and John Caputo's agreement with 'Vattimo's aim of disarming the metaphysics of apocalypticism, the dualism of two worlds, one immanent, lost, and secular, the other in-breaking, salvific, holy, and wholly other'.[27] At the same time, given the mocking tone in which he discusses the writings of Caputo, I detect on the part of Hamid Dabashi a clear preference for the thinking of Vattimo.[28] However, if one sets aside Caputo's occasional mystical rhetoric and sermon-like digressions, a closer inspection of his criticisms of Vattimo, in texts such as 'Spectral Hermeneutics', points up some problems with Vattimo's elaboration of 'weak thought', which Dabashi apparently chooses to ignore. In view of his criticism of Habermas's privileging of Western Enlightenment thinking, it is all the more remarkable that Dabashi has nothing to say about Vattimo's Christianity-centred elaboration or what Caputo calls a 'two-pronged process of weakening'.[29]

By way of prelude to his challenge of Gianni Vattimo's collaborative project on religion with Richard Rorty in *The Future of Religion*, Caputo highlights how the interpretation of Pauline *kenosis* and Nietzsche's nihilism as the constituent elements of a secularization theorem put Vattimo squarely in the camp of 'Death of God' theologians, who remain beholden to a grand narrative emerging from the Christian West that, since Joachim of Fiora, has been referred to as the doctrine of the theology of the 'Three Ages': the religion of the Father (Judaism), the Son (Christianity), and of the Spirit, which theologians T.J.J. Altizer and Mark Taylor associate with modernity and postmodernity.[30]

The consequences of this disposition are further unpacked in Caputo's dissection of Vattimo's slogan 'The West or Christianity' and a critical reading of Richard Rorty's *Achieving Our Country*.[31] Whereas Caputo is appreciative of the inclusivist rather than exclusivist disjunction intended by Vattimo's provocation and also of his and Rorty's ambition to achieve the universal ideals that are emblematized by the country and religion in question, he nevertheless maintains that within this framework, the transformation of Christianity from a ecclesiastic doctrine into a discourse of love, hospitality and pluralism remains an 'in-house debate', with no guarantee that it can be expanded onto a global scale.[32]

This Christian pedigree of the 'Death of God' theology and the fact that the plotted transitions from transcendence to immanence, from Fiora to Feuerbach, are beholden to Paul and Hegel, turn it not only into a '*grand récit* all of its own', but also exclude Jews and Muslims from this conversation.[33] Because of its spatiotemporal and linguistic particularities, there is an inherent violence to the 'Death of God' theology. This brings Caputo to the conclusion that 'when weak thinking works itself into its own story', it actually becomes 'too strong'.[34] For a way out of this conundrum, Caputo turns to French deconstructionist philosophers, noting – with an evident nod to Derrida – that: 'Deconstruction is something more of a Jewish science, that is, a deconstruction of idols that, while affirming flesh and the body – the Jewish Scriptures are all about land and children – is constantly worried about divine incarnations, because incarnations are always *local* occurrences'.[35]

Caputo's weakening of metaphysics into what he calls the 'ethicoreligious sense' of a theology of the event (the local occurrence) draws therefore much more on the thinking of Levinas and Derrida than Vattimo's 'lightening of the dogmatic burden' of the church.[36] Caputo observes that in Vattimo's work one looks in vain for 'what Derrida calls *khora*'. Aside from featuring in Plato's *Timaeus*, Derrida associates it also with the desert as the emblem of space into which human language and history are inscribed. Instead of the historicity of a periodization of a theology of the Three Ages, the interest of event theology in *kenosis* is 'not to distinguish two worlds but two different logics' – that is to say a 'structural analysis of the distinction between the name and the event'.[37] This makes it more into a epistemological question than a matter of ontology, which should resonate positively with Hamid Dabashi's anti-foundationalist reservations against the metaphysics of identity that shape the dichotomous view of the relationship between the West and the Muslim World. In Caputo's case this leads to a rhetorical question: 'Is not a radically weak theology a theology of desert?'[38] Rather than the 'robust and holy spirit', allegedly found in Gadamer and Vattimo, Caputo focuses on 'events inscribed in the weaker, more ghostly play of *différance*'.[39] This interest in event as not so much 'what happens as what is going on in what happens', extends to Caputo's interest in Gilles Deleuze and in particular his work, *The Logic of Sense*.[40]

While mentioning him only sporadically, Gilles Deleuze also looms large over Hamid Dabashi's writings, although – with a nod to his notion of the *rhizome* – when it comes to Deleuze, perhaps it is more appropriate to say that his ideas on difference burrow underneath. Rather than Caputo's reliance on *The Logic of Sense*, parallels between Deleuze and Dabashi's thinking are pointed up by the affinities between the latter's hermeneutics of alterity and Deleuze's opus magnus, *Difference and Repetition*. Where Gilles Deleuze's philosophy of difference reflect a 'desire to remain within the plane of immanence and refusal of any move to a transcendental or theological plane', Hamid Dabashi's hermeneutics of alterity is motivated by a similar desire to offset the metaphysics of identity that underlies the dominant dichotomy between Islam and the West, as manifested in the competition between the 'dogged dogmatism of nomocentric juridicalism' of Islamist ideology and the pretentious autonormativity of Enlightenment modernity.[41] This hermeneutics of alterity finds its most articulate expression in Muslim literary traditions, which are suffused with what Dabashi alternately refers to as 'worldly cosmopolitanism' or 'cosmopolitan worldliness'. Further echoes of such parallels are evinced by Dabashi's characterization of Iran's student protests of 1999 as a 'material, anti-oedipal, revolt' presaging later outbursts in the form of the 2009 Green Movement and the 2011 Arab uprisings.[42]

The sources then for an Islamic liberation theology that can be transformed into a theodicy are found in the logocentric and homocentric aspects of the Muslim world's philosophical and mystical traditions, thus turning Dabashi's hermeneutics of alterity into a new lightweight cross-cultural and non-essentialist 'guerrilla' ideology opposed to the homocentric orientation of Islamism. The cosmopolitanism of this new decentred world needs both a new geography of liberation and a new language. In his latest books *The World of Persian Literary Humanism* and *Being a Muslim in the World*, Dabashi suggests that the panacea of worldly cosmopolitanism finds its most celebratory manifestation in the vernacular literatures of the Muslim world. Here Dabashi's thinking enters more explicitly into a conversation with Hans-Georg Gadamer, because the hermeneutics of aesthetics explored in *Wahrheit und Methode* argues that our very being inhabits language ('the being that can be understood is language [...] who has language has the world').[43] At the risk of being accused of romanticizing what has become known as the Arab Spring of 2011, Dabashi also looks at these uprisings through a literary lens, suggesting reading these events as novels rather than epics, to the degree that – instead of taking them as monologues – they are understood as open-ended and dialogical in Bakhtin's sense. Dabashi sees the recent revolutions as heralds of an undetermined postcolonial and post-Western world, which parallel the novel in its 'textual facilities of heteroglossia' rather than an epic's 'teleological crescendo'.[44]

Taken together, Hamid Dabashi's oeuvre provides an interlocking – and therefore sometimes also repetitive and here and there even superfluous – narrative, driven by the deconstruction – or denarration, as he calls it – of both Islamist ideology and Enlightenment modernity. As a constructive contribution to formulating an alternative, Dabashi proposes the reconstitution of a cosmopolitan worldliness. His deliberate use of the term 'worldly' – as opposed to the Latin-based 'secular' – is integral to his rejection of European parochialism and his mission to dismantle binaries, like secular-religious or profane-sacred, which replicate the obsolete Islam versus the West ontology. It resonates with 'the affirmative spirit' underlying Gilles Deleuze's advancement of the cause of immanence, which in turn is informed by a Nietzsche-inspired subversion of transcendental values related to morality, conceiving of ethics as a set of rules for a 'way of existing'.[45] It also echoes Vattimo's 'ontology of decline' where ethics is put in 'the centre of the epistemological hierarchy' and in which 'final authority is attributed to *beings*' rather than 'metaphysical Being'.[46]

Against Dualism: From Philosophies of Despair to a Philosophy of Hope

Ali Mirsepassi's work is also geared towards a similar anti-teleological and open-ended human future. However, where Dabashi's hermeneutics of alterity as the counterpoint to the metaphysics of identity echoes a poststructuralist preoccupation with difference, Mirsepassi's anti-foundationalism remains attached to a certain type of Enlightenment thinking.

From the publication of *Intellectual Discourse and the Politics of Modernization* in 2000 onwards, Mirsepassi has challenged the hegemonic claims of both classical Enlightenment and the dubious influences of early twentieth-century anti-Enlightenment thinkers on the formation of Islamic ideologies.[47] He sees their shared totalizing and misconceived pretentions as parts of the same root cause of the West versus 'the Rest' binary.

Mirsepassi traces this dichotomous worldview to Montesquieu's *Persian Letters*, but singles out Hegel as the main culprit for the persistent misconception of the place of Western Enlightenment thinking in the totality of human intellectual history. He holds him responsible for the epistemic system known as Orientalism and for its political counterpart: imperialism – a way of thinking that continues to exercise influence through figures such as Bernard Lewis and Samuel Huntington.[48]

Unlike French Poststructuralists such as Gilles Deleuze, Mirsepassi does not play Nietzsche against Hegel, but posits his thinking – and Heidegger's too – not as a solution, but part of the problem.[49] Germany's counter-Enlightenment thinkers writing under the influence of Nietzsche, such as Martin Heidegger and Ernst Jünger, represent what Jeffrey Herf calls a 'reactionary modernism', thus demonstrating that – notwithstanding its claims to the contrary – the search for authenticity arises from within modernity itself.[50] The importance of the search for authenticity pursued in this strand of counter-Enlightenment thinking for the formation of contemporary Islamic ideologies has been generally overlooked.[51] Mirsepassi's study of these influences on Iran's religious intellectuals offers a corrective of the mistake made by many analysts of political Islam: that Islamism is anti-modern, an error that is also repeatedly pointed out by Hamid Dabashi.[52] Mirsepassi's invocation of what Martin Luther King called 'a world of geographical togetherness' underscores the formative importance of such a circulation of ideas for an accurate appreciation of the world we live in.[53] It also echoes Dabashi's call for a new 'liberation geography', which reflects that the West and Islam are not bounded geographical entities in a world that is not just postcolonial and postmodern, but also post-Western and post-Islamist.[54]

Mirsepassi continues this line of inquiry in *Political Islam, Iran and the Enlightenment* with the examination of the 'non-Islamic' elements in what he calls the 'politics of despair' manifested in Persian nativism and Islamism. In this later book, he traces these elements to the totalitarianism and inherent violence of both the Jacobin Enlightenment and the search of anti-Enlightenment thinkers, such as Jünger and Heidegger, for authenticity or cultural and religious truth.[55] For Mirsepassi, these findings affirm the conclusion that for classical Enlightenment thinkers and their adversaries alike:

> Everything fits in advance to a preconceived model, and in this unconscious imposition there is a blindness to specificity, detail, ultimately to actuality, and hence the possibility of dialogue and understanding is foreclosed. But these precepts do not arise from the breath of spirit; they are contained in a discourse and form an ingrained intellectual habit. As such, upon being identified, they can and should be transcended in favour of a more open and less totalizing horizon.[56]

For his alternative, presented under the header 'narrative of hope', Mirsepassi turns to the American pragmatist tradition – a third, relatively unexplored and underestimated strand within the Enlightenment heritage.[57] Here he finds a suitable substitute to the French Revolution paradigm from which grew the totalizing teleology of Jacobin Enlightenment against which Hannah Arendt had warned.[58]

Mirsepassi takes the 'Conceptual Pluralism' of John Dewey as his point of departure, because it offers not only a counterpoint to the metaphysical suppositions underpinning the erroneous idea of a single road to democratic modernity. With its anti-foundationalist appreciation of everyday life experience, Dewey's 'Conceptual Pluralism' also provides an antidote to the totalizing tendencies of anti-Enlightenment thinking that has infected Persian nativism and Islamism.[59] Dewey's philosophy presents an alternative that has also been practically adopted in social movements in India and the US itself under the direction of independence fighters and postcolonial politicians such as Nehru, emancipators like Ambedkar and civil rights activists like Martin Luther King. This alternative is based on the argument that: 'Secularism – as merely a formal and legal system – cannot by itself maintain democratic and egalitarian principles in a society, and some additional "common" or unifying ideals and moral traditions are required to help develop our communities toward the realization of freedom'.[60]

When elaborating Dewey's critique of the received paradigm of modernity and its dualist view of democracy and religion, Mirsepassi calls him a philosopher of openness and immanence with a certain affinity to certain poststructuralists who share some of Heidegger's preoccupations.[61] Although he leaves this unspecified, to my mind it suggests references to Italian poststructuralists schooled by Gadamer rather than their French counterparts. Ironically, with Mirsepassi's turn to Dewey, two aspects of Heidegger's thinking resurface, namely, the centrality of the experience of everyday life and the importance of this 'organic grasp' for 'what we call "home"'.[62] This brings to mind Richard Rorty's observation that continental philosophers such as Heidegger, Derrida and Foucault walked a different path to the same place already 'occupied by Dewey and pragmatism'.[63]

Dewey's conceptual pluralism also appears not that dissimilar from Nietzsche's *Genealogy of Morality* in the way it hinges on a complex understanding of a morality that is devoid of any of the 'grand plans' imposed from above by totalizing modern ideologies. Instead it builds a unity of ends and means from 'unfinished lived experience' or what Hilary Putnam called 'an ethics without ontology'.[64] It denounces 'dogmatic generalization', but retains a 'universalizing-critical function'.[65] Offering the prospect of emancipation from metaphysics because it opposes a conception of truth as a 'fixed object of knowledge', Dewey's conceptual pluralism seems not far removed from the antifoundationalism that also characterises Vattimo's 'weak thought'.[66] Finally, the centrality of imagination and its 'practical relation to our inherited traditional past' point up a disposition held in common with Hamid Dabashi's literary humanism.[67]

The epistemic modesty of Dewey's anthropocentrism, without a metaphysical ontology, but with an appreciation for the reflexivity and aesthetics of practical knowledge, as well as for everyday language and life, together with its focus on the richness of moral and poetic meaning rather than absolute truth claims, offers a coping mechanism for dealing with the uncertainty of human knowledge. This makes any single grand conception of modernity untenable. Modernity is composed of multiple singularities in which tradition is not a static stage of a past historical development, but a dynamic dimension of existing social life. This conceptual pragmatism presents an alternative to the 'dominant tradition of liberal Enlightenment as well as any radical "anti-Enlightenment" politics of being', regardless of whether it takes European antiquity, Persian nativism or Islam as its point of reference.[68]

Conclusion

In summary then, influenced by poststructuralist strands of thought emphasizing immanence and difference, Dabashi proposes a hermeneutics of alterity grounded in cosmopolitan worldliness as an alternative to the metaphysics of identity which informs this misconstrued opposition between the West and the Muslim world. To offset the totalizing effects of liberalism and Marxism as well as the philosophies of despair manifested in both European counter-Enlightenment thinking and Islamism, and avoid the pitfalls of the search for authenticity, Mirsepassi presents a Philosophy of Hope informed by John Dewey's conceptual pluralism which is hermeneutical in its recognition of difference as the starting point for a non-teleological dialectic.[69] In both cases the objective is to avoid the inherently violent tendencies of Enlightenment modernity, as well as supposedly primordial anti-Enlightenment thinking and Islamism which are actually equally modern ideologies of resistance.[70] Despite epistemological differences and diverging ideological orientations, Dabashi and Mirsepassi's thinking about knowledge and power converge in their concerns with freedom, democracy and civil rights.

As an intellectual historian I am more concerned with analysing the ways in which scholars and other intellectuals develop their ideas than judging their philosophical validity and persuasiveness per sé. In this instance, this leads me only to a tentative conclusion, as well as two questions that need further consideration. Critiques grounded in the sociology of knowledge, which are attentive to concrete lived experiences rather than abstractions, are certainly useful for challenging existing binaries and totalizing world views. But is privileging philosophies of hope or a hermeneutics of alterity over philosophies of despair or metaphysics of identity not also a totalizing worldview? And, does it not create another binary, because the only way we can think is in contrasts – opposing what a thing is with what it is not?

Notes

1 A distinction is made between hyphenated 'post-structuralism' and unhyphenated 'poststructuralism': the former refers to thinking that follows on from the structuralism developed in linguistics (Saussure) and anthropology (Lévi-Strauss), while the latter term refers to a distinct body of philosophical and theoretical work sharing certain premises, hypotheses, arguments, procedures and even writing styles.

2 Cf. F. Gabrieli, 'Adab', in *Encyclopaedia of Islam*, ed. P. Bearman et al. (Leiden: Brill, 1960–2007), Brill Online, 2015, accessed 7 September 2015, http://referenceworks. brillonline.com/entries/encyclopaedia-of-islam-2/adab-SIM_0293. For an interesting case study by a contemporary intellectual and scholar, cf. Mohammed Arkoun, *L'Humanisme Arabe au IVe/Xe Siécle: Miskaway, Philosophe et Historien* (Paris: Librarie Philosophique J. Vrin, 1982).

3 The texts in which this project is condensated include Dabashi's monographs, *Iran: A People Interrupted* (London and New York: The New Press, 2007); *Shi'ism: A Religion of Protest* (Cambridge, MA and London: Belknap, 2011); *Theology of Discontent: The Ideological Foundation of the Islamic Revolution in Iran* (New Brunswick, N: Transaction Publishers, 2006); *Islamic Liberation Theology: Resisting the Empire* (London and New York: Routledge, 2008); *Post-Orientalism: Knowledge and Power in a Time of Terror* (New Brunswick, N: Transaction Publishers, 2009); *Brown Skin, White Masks (The Islamic Mediterranean)* (London: Pluto Press, 2011); *The World of Persian Literary Humanism* (Cambridge, MA: Harvard University Press, 2012); *Being a Muslim in the World: Rethinking Islam for a Post-Western History* (London: Palgrave Macmillan, 2013); and, lastly, *Persophilia: Persian Culture on the Global Scene* (Cambridge, MA: Harvard University Press, 2015).

4 Mohammed Bamyeh's analysis of the Arab Uprisings also underscores the political *and* epistemic dimensions of these political revolts, cf. Mohammed Bamyeh, 'Anarchist Method, Liberal Intention, Authoritarian Lesson: The Arab Spring between Three Enlightenments', *Constellations* 20, no. 2 (2013): 188–202.

5 Hamid Dabashi, *Islamic Liberation Theology: Resisting the Empire*, 153. Gianni Vattimo echoes similar reservations against the work of Negri and Hardt: he rejects their self-proclaimed spokesmanship for the people without voice. With Noam Chomsky, he even adds the stronger charge that they do not wish to be understood by these very people: if Negri and Hardt want the so-called 'multitude' also to experience the increased mobility, indeterminacy and hybridity that characterizes the global spread of postmodern condition as a liberation rather than a suffering, 'Why did they need to say in a

complicated way what you can say in an easier way?' Cf. Gianni Vattimo, 'A Prayer for Silence', in *After the Death of God*, ed. Jeffrey W. Robbins (New York: Columbia University Press, 2007), 108.

6   Dabashi, *Islamic Liberation Theology*, 35, 157.

7   Dabashi, *Islamic Liberation Theology*, 150.

8   Dabashi, *Islamic Liberation Theology*, 168.

9   Dabashi, *Islamic Liberation Theology*, 158. Cf. Saskia Sassen, *Globalization and Its Discontent: Essays on the New Mobility of People and Money* (New York: The New Press, 1998).

10 He uses the term 'autonormativity' in: Hamid Dabashi, *Brown Skin, White Masks (The Islamic Mediterranean)* (2011); *The Arab Spring: The End of Postcolonialism* (London and New York: Zed Books, 2012); *The World of Persian Literary Humanism* (2012).

11 Carl Schmitt and Ernst Jünger are also the subject of Ali Mirsepassi's criticisms, cf. the pertaining sections below.

12 Giorgio Agamben, *Homo Sacer: Sovereign Power and Bare Life* (Palo Alto: Stanford University Press, 1998); *State of Exception* (Chicago: University of Chicago Press 2005).

13 Dabashi, *Islamic Liberation Theology*, 258–9. Cf. Hannah Arendt, *On Revolution* (London: Penguin Books, 1960).

14 Dabashi, *Islamic Liberation Theology*, 214.

15 Dabashi, *Islamic Liberation Theology*, 22.

16 Dabashi, *Islamic Liberation Theology*, 14.

17 Dabashi, *Islamic Liberation Theology*, 16

18 Dabashi, *Islamic Liberation Theology*, 14–5. Cf. also Gianni Vattimo, *The Adventure of Difference*, trans. Cyprian Blamires with Thomas Harrison (Baltimore: Johns Hopkins University Press, 1993); Gianni Vattimo and Pier Aldo Rovatti, *Weak Thought* (Albany: State University of New York Press, 2012). Although 'weak thought' is primarily associated with the name of Vattimo, it is actually the outcome of a collaborative project with other Italian philosophers.

19 Hans Georg Gadamer, *Truth and Method* (New York: Continuum, 2004).

20 Giovanna Borradori, 'Weak Thought and Postmodernism: The Italian Departure from Deconstruction', *Social Text* 18 (1988): 40.

21 Cf. my analysis of Mohammed Arkoun's 'Applied Anthropology': Carool Kersten, *Cosmopolitans and Heretics: New Muslim Intellectuals and the Study of Islam* (London and New York: Hurst and Oxford University Press, 2011), 201–9; 'From Braudel to Derrida: Mohammed Arkoun's Rethinking of Islam and Religion', *Middle East Journal of Culture and Communication* 4, no. 1 (2011): 23–43.

22 Gianni Vattimo, 'Towards a Nonreligious Christianity', in *After the Death of God*, ed. Jeffrey W. Robbins (New York: Columbia University Press, 2007), 36; *The Transparent Society*, trans. David Webb (Cambridge and Malden, MA: Polity Press, 1992), 86.

23 A succinct rendition of its development can be found in Gianni Vattimo, *Belief*, trans. Luca D'Isanto and David Webb (Stanford: Stanford University Press, 1999). The last point is also in line with Gil Anidjar's conclusion in his inquiry into secularism: Gil Anidjar, 'Secularism', *Critical Inquiry* 33, no. 1 (2006): 52–77.

24 Gianni Vattimo, 'The Age of Interpretation', in *The Future of Religion*, ed. Santiago Zabala (New York: Columbia University Press, 2005), 54.

25 Vattimo, *Belief*, 48–9.

26 Vattimo, 'The Age of Interpretation', 46.

27 John D. Caputo, 'Spectral Hermeneutics', in *After the Death of God*, ed. Jeffrey W. Robbins (New York: Columbia University Press, 2007), 81.

28 Cf. Hamid Dabashi, *Being A Muslim in the World: Rethinking Islam for a Post-Western History*, 87–9.

29 Caputo, 'Spectral Hermeneutics', 74.
30 Caputo, 'Spectral Hermeneutics', 76, 68–9.
31 Richard Rorty, *Achieving Our Country: Leftist Thought in Twentieth-Century America* (Cambridge, MA: Harvard University Press, 1998).
32 Caputo, 'Spectral Hermeneutics', 78.
33 Caputo, 'Spectral Hermeneutics', 79–80.
34 Caputo, 'Spectral Hermeneutics', 85.
35 Caputo, 'Spectral Hermeneutics', 80.
36 Caputo, 'Spectral Hermeneutics', 81; Vattimo, *The Transparent Society*, 46.
37 Caputo, 'Spectral Hermeneutics', 82.
38 Caputo, 'Spectral Hermeneutics', 85.
39 Caputo, 'Spectral Hermeneutics', 84.
40 John D. Caputo, 'The Power of the Powerless', in *After the Death of God*, ed. Jeffrey W. Robbins (New York: Columbia University Press, 2007), 157, also 47 and 182, n. 1; Gilles Deleuze, *The Logic of Sense*, ed. Constantin V. Boundas, trans. Mark Lester with Charles Stivale (New York: Columbia University Press, 1969).
41 Alan D. Schrift, 'French Nietzscheanism', in *Poststructuralism and Critical Theory's Second Generation*, ed. Alan D. Schrift (Durhan: Acumen, 2013), 38; Dabashi, *Islamic Liberation Theology*, 22, 44, 71–2, 80. Cf. also Gilles Deleuze, *Pure Immanence: Essays on a Life* (New York: Urzone, 2001).
42 Dabashi, *Islamic Liberation Theology*, 94. Cf. Gilles Deleuze, *Difference and Repetition* (New York: Columbia University, 1994).
43 Borradori, 'Weak Thought and Postmodernism', 45; quoting Gadamer, *Truth and Method*, 542.
44 Dabashi, *The Arab Spring*, 5, 9, 63, 230.
45 Schrift, 'French Nietzscheanism', 38, 40.
46 Borradori, 'Weak Thought and Postmodernism', 43.
47 Concluded in Ali Mirsepassi and Todd Graham Fernée, *At Home and in the World: Islam, Cosmopolitanism, and Democracy* (New York: Cambridge University Press, 2014).
48 Ali Mirsepassi, *Intellectual Discourse and the Politics of Modernization: Negotiating Modernity in Iran* (Cambridge and New York: Cambridge University Press, 2000), 40–53. Dabashi by contrast traces its origins to Kant and accuses Jürgen Harbermas of ignoring or having a blind spot for Kant's blatant racism that lies at the root of Habermas's own privileging of European Enlightenment modernity, cf. Dabashi, *Islamic Liberation Theology*, 100–8.
49 Ali Mirsepassi, *Democracy in Iran: Islam, Culture and Political Change* (New York: New York University Press, 2010), 49; Schrift, 'French Nietzscheanism', 31. Mirsepassi detects traces of 'Heideggerian dualism' in the writing of Partha Chatterjee and Ashsis Nandy, cf. Ali Mirsepassi, *Political Islam, Iran and the Enlightenment: Philosophies of Hope and Despair* (London and Cambridge, MA: Harvard University Press, 2011), 139.
50 Mirsepassi, *Intellectual Discourse and the Politics of Modernization*, 131, 137.
51 Mirsepassi, *Intellectual Discourse and the Politics of Modernization*, 2–7.
52 Dabashi, *Islamic Liberation Theology*, 43, 249.
53 Mirsepassi, *Political Islam, Iran and the Enlightenment*, 8, 186.
54 Dabashi, *The Arab Spring*, 41–58. On Post-Islamism, cf. Asef Bayat, *Post-Islamism: The Changing Faces of Political Islam* (Oxford and New York: Oxford University Press, 2013).
55 In his very latest book, *Persophilia*, Hamid Dabashi takes issue with Mirsepassi's conflation of the thinking of figures such as Jalal Al-e Ahmad and Ali Shariati with nativism (Dabashi, *Persophilia*, 218–9, 260, n. 25). While Dabashi has a point in flagging up the interpretative liberties taken with what Al-e Ahmad and Shariati actually wrote,

he does not do so in regard to Ernst Jünger, whose writings have been equally used and abused, and whose later thinking shows a marked departure from his earlier ideas (Dabashi, *Persophilia*, 208–9).

56 Mirsepassi, *Intellectual Discourse and the Politics of Modernization*, 53. Cf. also Mirsepassi, *Political Islam, Iran and the Enlightenment*, 75.

57 Mirsepassi, *Political Islam, Iran and the Enlightenment*, 26, 129.

58 Mirsepassi, *Political Islam, Iran and the Enlightenment*, 141–2, 160–5; cf. also Mirsepassi's reliance on Hannah Arendt's distinction between the French and American Revolutions: Mirsepassi, *Political Islam, Iran and the Enlightenment*, 9ff.

59 Mirsepassi, *Political Islam, Iran and the Enlightenment*, 71. In his book *A Common Faith* (New Haven: Yale University Press, 1960), Dewey unpacks 'conceptual pluralism' in relation to religion.

60 Mirsepassi, *Political Islam, Iran and the Enlightenment*, 10, 140ff.

61 Mirsepassi, *Political Islam, Iran and the Enlightenment*, 17.

62 Mirsepassi, *Intellectual Discourse and the Politics of Modernization*, 147.

63 David Hiley, 'Rorty among the Continentals', in *Poststructuralism and Critical Theory's Second Generation*, ed. Alan D. Schrift (Durham: Acumen, 2013), 406.

64 Hilary Putnam, *Ethics without Ontology* (Cambridge, MA: Harvard University Press, 2004).

65 Mirsepassi, *Political Islam, Iran and the Enlightenment*, 17; Borradori, 'Weak Thought and Postmodernism', 41.

66 Mirsepassi, *Political Islam, Iran and the Enlightenment*, 17.

67 Mirsepassi, *Political Islam, Iran and the Enlightenment*, 18–9, 130.

68 Mirsepassi, *Political Islam, Iran and the Enlightenment*, 137.

69 Mirsepassi, *Political Islam, Iran and the Enlightenment*, 78.

70 For the problematics of 'primordiality', cf. Mirsepassi, *Political Islam, Iran and the Enlightenment*, 100ff.

References

Agamben, Giorgio. *Homo Sacer: Sovereign Power and Bare Life*. Palo Alto: Stanford University Press, 1998.

Agamben, Giorgio. *State of Exception*. Chicago: University of Chicago Press, 2008.

Anidjar, Gil. 'Secularism'. *Critical Inquiry* 33, no. 1 (2006): 52–77.

Arendt, Hannah. *On Revolution*. London: Penguin Books, 1960.

Arkoun, Mohammed. *L'Humanisme Arabe au IVe/Xe Siécle: Miskaway, Philosophe et Historien*. Paris: Librarie Philosophique J. Vrin, 1982.

Bamyeh, Mohammed. 'Anarchist Method, Liberal Intention, Authoritarian Lesson: The Arab Spring between Three Enlightenments'. *Constellations* 20, no. 2 (2013): 188–202.

Bayat, Asef. *Post-Islamism: The Changing Faces of Political Islam*. Oxford and New York: Oxford University Press, 2013.

Borradori, Giovanna. 'Weak Thought and Postmodernism: The Italian Departure from Deconstruction'. *Social Text* 18 (1988): 39–49.

Caputo, John D. 'The Power of the Powerless'. In *After the Death of God*, edited by Jeffrey W. Robbins, 113–60. New York: Columbia University Press, 2007.

Caputo, John D. 'Spectral Hermeneutics'. In *After the Death of God*, edited by Jeffrey W. Robbins, 47–85. New York: Columbia University Press, 2007.

Dabashi, Hamid. *The Arab Spring: The End of Postcolonialism*. London and New York: Zed Books, 2012.

Dabashi, Hamid. *Being a Muslim in the World: Rethinking Islam for a Post-Western History*. London: Palgrave Macmillan, 2013.

Dabashi, Hamid. *Brown Skin, White Masks (The Islamic Mediterranean)*. London: Pluto Press, 2011.

Dabashi, Hamid. *Iran: A People Interrupted*. London and New York: The New Press, 2007.

Dabashi, Hamid. *Islamic Liberation Theology: Resisting the Empire*. London and New York: Routledge, 2008.

Dabashi, Hamid. *Persophilia: Persian Culture on the Global Scene*. Cambridge, MA: Harvard University Press, 2015.

Dabashi, Hamid. *Post-Orientalism: Knowledge and Power in a Time of Terror*. New Brunswick, N: Transaction Publishers, 2009.

Dabashi, Hamid. *Shi'ism: A Religion of Protest*. Cambridge, MA and London: Belknap, 2011.

Dabashi, Hamid. *Theology of Discontent: The Ideological Foundation of the Islamic Revolution in Iran*. New Brunswick, N: Transaction Publishers, 2006.

Dabashi, Hamid. *The World of Persian Literary Humanism*. Cambridge, MA: Harvard University Press, 2012.

Deleuze, Gilles. *Difference and Repetition*. New York: Columbia University, 1994.

Deleuze, Gilles. *The Logic of Sense*. Edited by Constantin V. Boundas, translated by Mark Lester, with Charles Stivale. New York: Columbia University Press, 1969.

Deleuze, Gilles. *Pure Immanence: Essays on a Life*. New York: Urzone, 2001.

Dewey, John. *A Common Faith*. New Haven: Yale University Press, 1960.

Gabrieli, F. 'Adab'. In *Encyclopaedia of Islam*, edited by P. Bearman, Zh. Bianquis, C.E. Bosworth, E. van Donzel, W.P. Heinrichs. 2nd ed. Leiden: Brill, 1960–2007. Brill Online, 2015. Accessed 7 September 2015. http://referenceworks.brillonline.com/entries/encyclopaedia-of-islam-2/adab-SIM_0293.

Gadamer, Hans-Georg. *Truth and Method*. New York: Continuum, 2004.

Hiley, David. 'Rorty among the Continentals'. In *Poststructuralism and Critical Theory's Second Generation*, edited by Alan D. Schrift, 401–21. Durham: Acumen, 2013.

Kersten, Carool. *Cosmopolitans and Heretics: New Muslim Intellectuals and the Study of Islam*. London and New York: Hurst and Oxford University Press, 2011.

Kersten, Carool. 'From Braudel to Derrida: Mohammed Arkoun's Rethinking of Islam and Religion'. *Middle East Journal of Culture and Communication* 4, no. 1 (2011): 23–43.

Mirsepassi, Ali. *Democracy in Iran: Islam, Culture and Political Change*. New York: New York University Press, 2010.

Mirsepassi, Ali. *Intellectual Discourse and the Politics of Modernization: Negotiating Modernity in Iran*. Cambridge and New York: Cambridge University Press, 2000.

Mirsepassi, Ali. *Political Islam, Iran and the Enlightenment: Philosophies of Hope and Despair*. London and Cambridge, MA: Harvard University Press, 2011.

Mirsepassi, Ali and Todd Graham Fernée. *At Home and in the World: Islam, Cosmopolitanism, and Democracy*. New York: Cambridge University Press, 2014.

Putnam, Hilary. *Ethics without Ontology*. Cambridge, MA: Harvard University Press, 2004.

Rorty, Richard. *Achieving Our Country: Leftist Thought in Twentieth-Century America*. Cambridge, MA: Harvard University Press, 1998.

Sassen, Saskia. *Globalization and Its Discontent: Essays on the New Mobility of People and Money*. New York: The New Press, 1998.

Schrift, Alan D. 'French Nietzscheanism'. In *Poststructuralism and Critical Theory's Second Generation*, edited by Alan D. Schrift, 19–46. Durhan: Acumen, 2013.

Vattimo, Gianni. *The Adventure of Difference: Philosophy after Nietzsche and Heidegger*. Translated by Cyprian Blamires with the assistance of Thomas Harrison. Baltimore: Johns Hopkins University Press, 1993.

Vattimo, Gianni. 'The Age of Interpretation'. In *The Future of Religion*, edited by Santiago Zabala, 43–54. New York: Columbia University Press, 2005.

Vattimo, Gianni. *Belief*. Translated by Luca D'Isanto and David Webb. Stanford: Stanford University Press, 1999.

Vattimo, Gianni. 'A Prayer for Silence'. In *After the Death of God*, edited by Jeffrey W. Robbins, 89–113. New York: Columbia University Press, 2007.

Vattimo, Gianni. 'Towards a Nonreligious Christianity'. In *After the Death of God*, edited by Jeffrey W. Robbins, 27–46. New York: Columbia University Press, 2007.

Vattimo, Gianni. *The Transparent Society*. Translated by David Webb. Cambridge and Malden, MA: Polity Press, 1992.

Vattimo, Gianni and Pier Aldo Rovatti. *Weak Thought*. Translated and with an introduction by Peter Carravetta. Albany: State University of New York Press, 2012.

7 Lanza del Vasto

A Doctrine of Just and Non-Violent Conflict

Klaus-Gerd Giesen

Introduction

Giuseppe Giovanni Luigi Maria Enrico Lanza di Trabia-Branciforte (Italy, 1901 – Spain, 1981) – commonly called Lanza del Vasto – was a French-Italian philosopher, theologian, poet, artist, musician, and non-violent activist. In 1928 he received his PhD in philosophy from the University of Pisa, Italy. In December 1936, Lanza del Vasto travelled to India, joining the movement for Indian independence led by Gandhi. He spent six months with the Mahatma, and then decided to found a Catholic Gandhian movement in Europe. From his experience with Gandhi he drew his most famous book: *Le pèlerinage aux sources.*[1] In 1954 he returned to India and spent five months with Vinoba, Gandhi's successor in the Indian non-violent movement.[2]

Considered to be the first Western disciple of Gandhi, Lanza del Vasto worked for inter-religious dialogue, spiritual renewal, ecology and especially non-violence activism. In 1948 he founded the Community of the Ark in Southern France, which still exists today. Nowadays there are also several community groups in Germany, Canada, Belgium, Spain and Mexico.

Lanza del Vasto's published works include approximately 30 books, many of them being situated in the philosophical and theological realm. Most are written in French. Only four volumes have actually been translated into English. There are a dozen books on Lanza del Vasto, all in French or Italian, but by far not all academic and/or relevant to his doctrine of non-violence.

The originality of Lanza del Vasto's thought lies in his attempt to formally introduce Gandhi's *ahimsa* concept into Catholicism. In this text it will be argued that Lanza del Vasto goes far beyond the classical reference to the Sermon on the Mount,[3] and is more sophisticated than, and actually subverts and deeply transforms, the traditional just war thought of the Catholic church. Indeed, trying to establish a religious Catholic 'Order of the Western Gandhians'[4] he had no choice but to deal with the attempted doctrine of the Church as far as peace and war are concerned. It will be tempting to demonstrate that the philosopher closely examines all aspects of the just war doctrine, enlarges it in order to *formally* include a Kantian *post bellum* perspective, and transforms it into a doctrine of just and non-violent conflict, as a 'complement to the Christ's teaching'.[5] In other words: he applied non-violence to the classical just war criteria.

The focus of the analysis will be limited to interstate war, and leave aside many other important aspects of Lanza del Vasto's thought, such as ecologism, his critique of the machine, and conscientious objection.

From Aquinas to Kant to Lanza del Vasto

In his work, Lanza del Vasto tries to transform just war theory – which is the official doctrine of the Catholic Church since Augustinus – into a theory of just and non-violent conflict. He selects a few formal just war criteria which appear relevant to him, and extracts, so to speak, all violence from them. He writes: 'How is it possible that the Church blesses the canons, that it advocates a theory of just war which can be used to justify all wars? … What I am looking for is a doctrine of just peace'.[6]

Lanza del Vasto needs such a doctrine because non-violent resistance definitely remains in a state of deep conflict with the aggressor. It is quite the opposite of passivity, as emphasized many times both by Gandhi and by Lanza del Vasto.[7] The latter states that 'taking flight is neither a solution nor a victory',[8] celebrates 'the weapon of non-violence to achieve victory',[9] which 'excludes neutrality, flight, and capitulation',[10] and praises even 'the aggressive, provocative, vehement side of non-violence'.[11] 'There is force', he emphasizes,[12] as non-violence is for him 'a method to defend, without offending',[13] 'to liberate [a territory] from foreign occupation'.[14] He insists many times that the main aim is to *resist* foreign domination, instead of staying passive: 'If there is only the choice between violence and cowardice, violence is the better option'.[15] However, he immediately adds a famous quotation of Gandhi: 'Nevertheless, I believe that non-violence is infinitely superior to violence'.[16] Thus, a coherent doctrine is needed to frame such a non-violent resistance in inter-state conflict.

Just war theory is, historically speaking, part of natural law. It stems from a more than two thousand years old tradition (from pre-Christian Cicero to today). Gradually, over the centuries, just war theory has been able to adapt to all technological revolutions in warfare.[17] For instance, Vitoria introduced in the sixteenth century the important distinction between combatants and civilians, with the concomitant notion of collateral damage, as the result of the emergence of artillery technology on the battlefields. Or in the 1940s and 1950s, the Christian theologians and political scientists John Ford, Paul Ramsey and James Turner Johnson, among others, discussed the highly relevant question: can a defensive nuclear war be just? Just war theory is thus very flexible – almost a casuistry – and adaptable to all kind of new experiences and possibilities in warfare.[18]

However, it seems that Lanza del Vasto amended the classical just war theory (especially by Aquinas, one of Lanza del Vasto's main inspirations) by *implicit* reference to Immanuel Kant, in the sense that the latter added to the traditional *jus ad bellum* and *jus in bello* a Kantian *jus post bellum*.[19] It seems that Lanza del Vasto found it important to add this dimension to *any* thought about conflict. Thus, it is an extension of the just war doctrine of the Church.

As I have tried to demonstrate elsewhere,[20] Immanuel Kant was himself not only a philosopher of peace, reputated for his seminal writing on *Perpetual Peace*, but also a philosopher of war, developing in the *Metaphysics of Morals* a theory of just war, except that his ultimate philosophical foundation is provided by the subject and not by a metaphysical natural order. The metaphysicist Lanza del Vasto can definitely not agree with the outlined philosophical foundations, but he seems nevertheless be interested in the Kantian extension to the *jus post bellum*, without, however, making any *explicit* reference to it.

As he did already in *Perpetual Peace*, but contrary to what he had noticed a few years earlier in his *Idee zu einer Geschichte in allgemeiner weltbürgerlicher Absicht*, Kant states in the *Doctrine of Law* that, ultimately, 'perpetual peace … is obviously an impossible idea',[21] especially because the gradual extension of the *foedus pacificum* to the entire surface of the earth appears to be a too optimistic perspective. The problem of the moral status of war remains, therefore, unsolved, since it concerns the conflicting relations among states that historically remain still outside the republican *foedus pacificum*, as well as the relationships of republican states with one or more non-republican states. Paragraphs 56–60 of the *Doctrine of Law* are devoted to define the criteria for determining the justice or injustice of such wars.

From the outset, Kant distinguishes the doctrine of just war from his predecessors. Firstly by the structure of his argument: to the traditional *jus ad bellum*[22] and *jus in bello*[23] he adds, as already mentioned, a surprising *jus post bellum*.[24] Secondly, by the content of the criteria developed. Here Kant goes back to the norms used by Aquinas. Indeed, the four thomistic *jus ad bellum* criteria are found, albeit grouped in a different order than in the *Summa Theologica*, in paragraphs 56 and 57: (1) the purpose of war is a more perfect peace[25] (in the words of Kant's paragraph 57: '… to conduct war according to principles that it is still possible to leave the state of nature of states … and to enter into a legal state'); (2) the formal declaration of war must be declared by the competent authority;[26] (3) the war must have a just cause, i.e. 'it is required that the attack on the enemy is due to some fault'[27] (Kant specifies that it must be either following a first assault, or a threat, or an offense);[28] and (4) 'the right intention by those who make war':[29] for Kant this precept refers to a formal prohibition of punitive wars and wars of extermination which may lead the prince to wage war for 'impure' reasons.[30] In Aquinas, as much as in Kant, the other three criteria of the usual catalogue of *jus ad bellum* are missing; they had been added in between the two authors by Vitoria and Suarez, namely: (1) war must be the last resort to resolve a dispute; (2) there must be a reasonable prospect of success before declaring war; and (3) there must be some proportionality in the relation of misconduct and punishment.[31]

We will now go through all seven *jus ad bellum* criteria (thus including the three Kant did not include) and try to assess how Lanza del Vasto dealt with them. The catalogue is cumulative, which means that all *adopted* criteria must be met if a given conflict is to be considered as a just conflict. The main point lies in the fact that Lanza del Vasto takes almost all just war criteria developed by Aquinas and by

Kant. The *jus ad bellum* is not as much about violent war itself as about the right to *wage* any kind of conflict (violent or not). Therefore, Lanza del Vasto can here almost entirely adhere to Aquinas and Kant. The main transformation of his just war doctrine occurs in the *jus in bello* and *jus post bellum*.

Jus ad bellum

The Ultimate Aim of War (Conflict): A More Perfect Peace (Than before the War)

Here we find one of the main advantages of the non-violent stance: it clearly aims at establishing a better quality of peace after the end of the conflict. Lanza del Vasto writes: 'Non-violence is a combat for peace'.[32] In his book *L'Arche avait pour voilure une vigne* he defines the aim as follows: 'Resolving conflicts in order to reconcile, not to dominate, but to conquer peace'.[33] Therefore, a non-violent conflict seems in any case to be more promising for a 'more perfect peace' than any form of violence. In other words: the doctrine of *jus ad bellum* provides actually a valuable justification for non-violent methods of conflict resolution. As the author notes, 'in [violent] war, peace is not desired'.[34]

The Authority of the Prince: The Declaration of War

For Lanza del Vasto sovereignty ultimately stems from the people, not from the state. However, state authorities are necessary: 'The laws of war and justice are the privilege ... of [state] power'.[35] All other cases, such as the Indian independence movement or civil wars, are not covered by the just war doctrine and must be dealt with on different moral grounds.

A Just Cause

According to Lanza del Vasto, one can never be sure to be in a 'just position'. Contrary to Kant and Aquinas, he believes that there should always remain a doubt. That is the reason why the philosopher adopts Gandhi's imperative: 'Before taking action Gandhi asks his followers to scrutinize themselves and to fully grasp what can be their part of fault in the upcoming conflict ... to offer reparation and public penance'.[36] Nevertheless, Lanza del Vasto maintains this (weakened) *jus ad bellum* norm: the just cause means 'fighting against the bad combat, in favour of the good, through the good, in favour of justice with justice weapons which are offense to nobody'.[37]

A Right Intention

The non-violent activist, as much as Kant, warns about the possible misuse of the just war doctrine by state authorities. Their motivation may be impure: 'One rushes [to war] with furious ambitions, following devious calculations. The gamblers do the same, not by generosity, but by mad lust for gain'.[38] Thus, a right intention to wage conflict is morally absolutely required, but may be difficult to prove. No war profit should be aimed at. Otherwise, the conflict will be considered as unjust. Ultimately, the sole right intention of non-violence 'is to place the culprit in front of his own judgement',[39] because 'my enemy is a human being'.[40]

The Proportionality of Fault and Punishment

Kant, as much as Aquinas, dismisses this criterion, because he wrote his texts at the beginning of the era of mass warfare through the introduction of general conscription:[41] mass warfare makes it almost impossible to tune, so to speak, the counterattack. However, to Lanza del Vasto the standard seems to be essential: non-violent resistance *automatically* remains at the lowest possible level of proportionality. The non-violent army – with its 'masters and soldiers of non-violence'[42] – needs 'years of preparation'[43] in order to limit its actions to exclusively seek 'punishments without violence'.[44] Such an automatic proportionality contributes to the 'humanization of justice'.[45]

War as Last Resort

Immanuel Kant did not adopt this traditional *jus ad bellum* standard, probably because he found it hypocritical. Lanza del Vasto seems to think the same way. However, like Gandhi he makes clear that violent defensive war remains a possibility if (and only if) non-violent means cannot be used, for instance if people are not trained for it. Nevertheless, in his view, 'justice will not come out of it'.[46]

A Reasonable Hope of Success

This last *jus ad bellum* criterion has also been discarded by Kant (and Aquinas), since it requires a considerable capacity of foresight analysis. There is no evidence that Lanza del Vasto uses it. It is true that non-violence strategy can never be sure to fully succeed, even in the long term. It stays fragile, but proves to be morally superior. It can be inferred that according to the French philosopher non-violent resistance should at least be tempted, even if there is no reasonable hope of success.

Jus in bello

In the *Metaphysics of Morals*, Immanuel Kant seems to go back to Aquinas, i.e. to the days prior to Francisco de Vitoria, to formulate the *jus in bello*. First, he develops in paragraph 57 the thomistic notion of permissive and non-permissive tricks: spies, ambush assassins, poisoners, snipers and rumours are explicitly classified as illegal means, because they destroy the trust necessary for the development of a future (perpetual) peace.[47] Second, there is a (weak) proportionality norm in the *jus in bello* which states – just as in Aquinas – that looting is prohibited.

However, the major issue in this parallel between Kant and Aquinas lies in the 'missing' element of the *jus in bello*: the discrimination between combatants and non-combatants, as well as the concomitant notion of collateral damage. Kant makes no mention of this criterion introduced by Vitoria, which underpins the assumption that he adopts a more traditional view.

The absence of the criterion of discrimination between combatants and non-combatants clearly tells us that Kant had detected something in this concept which he deems inappropriate. Francisco de Vitoria introduced it in *De Indis*: 'By accident, it is sometimes permissible to kill innocent people, even voluntarily, for example when you justly attack a fortress or a city, in which we know that there are many innocent people'.[48] The reason for the introduction lies in the technical change that occurred in the art of war between Aquinas and Vitoria: '… and when you can use war machines, sending projectiles or burn buildings without also hitting the innocent along with the guilty'.[49] He refers to the massive introduction of artillery on the battlefields of Asia Minor in the fourteenth and fifteenth centuries, particularly during the fall of Constantinople in 1453 under Mohammed II. The new technology adds a new dimension to existing weapon systems since it introduces the spatial distancing of the hostile combatants from each other, as well as the absolute anonymity of the opponent, and since it has the inevitable effect of possibly affecting a large number of non-combatants.[50] Hence the need felt by Vitoria to clearly distinguish between combatants and non-combatants, while allowing killing the latter by accident only ('collateral damage').

In the *Doctrine of Law*, Kant makes no mention of this important norm. My hypothesis is that he does not see the relevance of making such a discrimination, because of the discontinuity in the art of war which he himself witnessed. Indeed, Immanuel Kant was contemporary to the massification of war. He observes that revolutionary France, as well as Prussia in the late eighteenth century, established the general mobilization of the population for military purposes.[51] The philosopher of Königsberg understands that the nature of warfare has radically been modified: it now embraces the entire social sphere. He draws – this is my hypothesis – an important conclusion: how can we possibly keep the criterion of discrimination between combatants and non-combatants of the *jus in bello*, if the entire society is now involved, in one way or another, in the war effort?

It seems that his silence on this traditionally significant criterion for Vitoria – and therefore his return to the thomistic doctrine – can be interpreted as if Kant connoted that the discrimination between combatants and non-combatants became actually irrelevant. Mass warfare makes such a differentiation impractical. Lanza del Vasto goes into the same direction as Kant. However, contrary to the latter, he also rejects one other *jus in bello* criterion and develops much further the second norm. The three mentioned standards will now be analyzed one after the other.

The Authorization of Tricks and Ruses

This norm is about deceiving the enemy by false appearances. It is already mentioned by Aquinas in his *Summa Theologica*. One could imagine that in order to deter the enemy a state somehow makes it believe that it has far-reaching abilities, which is, however, not true. Such a behaviour seems morally permissible as much as propaganda in times of warfare. For Lanza del Vasto such a stance is not acceptable. Here he clearly opposes Kant and Aquinas: 'Non-violence is [not to] oppose a ruse'.[52] He firmly believes that in any given conflict the belligerents should not cheat, as he notes in the first and second volumes of *Les quatre fléaux*.[53] It is of outmost importance to him that all trust is preserved between the opposing nations in order to prepare the future peace.

The Proportionality of Means

Within this context an approach by successive levels is needed. For instance, a military attack causing a dozen deaths should, of course, legitimate a less severe response than the bombardment with chemical weapons causing thousands of deaths. The second *jus in bello* norm is therefore in its structure almost utilitarian: a true calculation of consequences appears to be essential. To a certain extent Lanza del Vasto adopts such an utilitarian method. Indeed, in his publications he outlines a large framework for proportional, non-violent responses: mass hunger strikes, demonstrations, non-cooperation, general strikes, marches, etc. However, there definitely is an absolutist limit to it: 'One of the strongest points of the Gandhian teaching is the refutation of that adage saying that the end justifies the means'.[54] The absolute limit goes as follows: 'Thou shall not kill, since death is the ultimate and irreparable affliction'.[55] Hence, by introducing a limit, Lanza del Vasto considerably modifies Kant's and Aquinas' proportionality standard.

The Discrimination between Combatants and Non-Combatants

The standard appears to operate the distinction in the conventional battlefield. Fortunately, Vitoria provided us the already mentioned casuistic concept *par excellence*: the 'collateral damage', which is authorized if it is not directly intentioned. This means for instance that the army general supervising a military response and perfectly knowing that it will also affect civilian populations remains morally 'clean' if his action targets first and foremost a military objective. In other words, 'only weaponry capable of discrimination (i.e., directed against legitimate targets) can be used. However, strategists should know that legitimate targets can include civilian objects ... [with] dual military and civilian use'.[56] The ethics of just war requires that targeteers 'do everything possible' to ensure the target is a proper military objective. The Kantian reservation vis-à-vis the concept of collateral damage stems from his point of view that in mass warfare it is actually not possible to clearly distinguish between civilian population and soldiers, as the mass mobilization includes literally everybody. Therefore, he drops the norm and goes back to Aquinas' position. Lanza del Vasto abandons the criterion as well. He doesn't need it, since non-violent resistance targets the entire adverse population until all unjust adverse military action is given up. The non-violent battle takes place in order to make the enemy (its entire population, not just the soldiers) understand that it is doing something wrong. Therefore, civilians are a legitimate 'target' of non-violent action.

Jus post bellum

In order to fully grasp Lanza del Vasto's doctrine it seems necessary to amend the traditional just war theory, which is limited to *jus in bello* and *jus ad bellum*, by adding the Kantian *jus post bellum*. Here, Kant was concerned – at a rather abstract level – about the consequences of a particular war act for *all* or most countries of the international system of his time.[57] We can draw two criteria.

Firstly, Kant is very much preoccupied by the 'violation of [international] public agreements, which presumably are of interest to all peoples, since their freedom is threatened'.[58] Secondly, Kant provides us with an even more far reaching *jus post bellum* norm: an unjust enemy is 'one whose publicly expressed will ... reflects a maxim according to which, if it were a universal rule, no peace is possible between peoples, while on the contrary the state of nature becomes eternal'.[59] Here we recognize easily one form of the categorical imperative. The two Kantian *jus post bellum* criteria of paragraph 60 of the *Metaphysics of Morals* may raise concern for instance about a possible nuclear Armageddon.

Lanza del Vasto very much shares this concern. He writes in 1971: 'We must prevent at all costs that the world war, bringing about economic and social ruins, aberration and moral disorder, sweeps for the third time humanity'.[60] He worries that a nuclear war 'would make the Earth a dead star',[61] and regrets that in Aquinas, 'there is no argument whatsoever which could oppose nuclear armament, and bring forward objection to the just war doctrine'.[62] In other words, Lanza del Vasto here takes an anti-thomistic stance.

Any military defence, including non-violent defence, can take place only if there is no risk of escalation towards a nuclear war, because 'to die in nuclear war is to die three times: to die oneself, to die within our children, to die with the entire nature'.[63] These quotations demonstrate how close Lanza del Vasto actually is with Kant (and takes distance from Aquinas). The *jus post bellum* becomes an important aspect of his doctrine of just and non-violent conflict.

Conclusion

In the foregoing it has been attempted to superficially clear the ground. All the different just war norms deserve further and considerably deeper discussion. It seems that: (1) Lanza del Vasto frequently makes explicit or implicit reference to just war criteria, and expels the violence from them and (2) his just conflict ethics is *formally* closer to Kant than to Aquinas, notably as it includes a *jus post bellum* perspective.

However that may be, as in the writings of many authors praising non-violence, the work of Lanza del Vasto lacks an important dimension: he doesn't make any statement about the *threshold* beyond which violence may be used in defence. That is the essential question Martin Buber raised in his letter to Gandhi of February 24, 1939:[64] should an aggressor aiming at physically eliminating parts of the population be opposed only or mainly by non-violent means? Non-violent resistance may be both useful and efficient when it comes to stop a conquering nation occupying territory and possibly exploiting its natural or industrial resources. It seems to be counterproductive in case of mass persecution and planned genocides.

Notes

1 Giuseppe G. Lanza del Vasto, *Le pèlerinage aux sources* (Paris: Denoël, 1943).
2 Giuseppe G. Lanza del Vasto, *Vinôba ou Le nouveau pèlerinage* (Paris: Denoël, 1954).
3 Giuseppe G. Lanza del Vasto, *L'Arche avait pour voilure une vigne* (Paris: Denoël/Gonthier, 1978), 67.
4 Lanza del Vasto, *L'Arche avait pour voilure une vigne*, 16.
5 Lanza del Vasto, *L'Arche avait pour voilure une vigne*, 12.
6 Lanza del Vasto, *L'Arche avait pour voilure une vigne*, 12.
7 See Lanza del Vasto, *Le pèlerinage aux sources*, 155; Lanza del Vasto, *Vinôba ou Le nouveau pèlerinage*, 305.
8 Lanza del Vasto, *L'Arche avait pour voilure une vigne*, 11.
9 Giuseppe G. Lanza del Vasto, *Dialogues avec Lanza del Vasto (par René Doumerc)* (Paris: Albin Michel, 1980), 217.
10 Giuseppe G. Lanza del Vasto, *Technique de la non-violence* (Paris: Denoël/Gonthier, 1971), 12.
11 Lanza del Vasto, *Technique de la non-violence*, 208.
12 Giuseppe G. Lanza del Vasto, *La roue des révolutions. Les quatre fléaux, Vol. II* (Paris: Denoël/Gonthier, 1959), 202.
13 Lanza del Vasto, *L'Arche avait pour voilure une vigne*, 12.
14 Lanza del Vasto, *L'Arche avait pour voilure une vigne*, 14.
15 Lanza del Vasto, *Le diable dans le jeu, Les quatre fléaux*, vol. I (Paris: Denoël/Gonthier, 1959), 199.
16 Lanza del Vasto, *Dialogues avec Lanza del Vasto*, 47.
17 Michael Walzer, *Just and Unjust Wars* (New York: Basic Books, 1977).
18 Klaus-Gerd Giesen, *L'éthique des relations internationales* (Brussels: Bruylant, 1992), 123–50, 267–77.
19 Immanuel Kant, *Metaphysik der Sitten* (Berlin: Akademie-Ausgabe, 1797), §§58–60.
20 Klaus-Gerd Giesen, 'Kant et la guerre de masse', in *Droit et vertu chez Kant*, ed. Union scientifique franco-hellénique (Athens: Société hellénique d'études philosophiques, 1997), 331–41.
21 Kant, *Metaphysik der Sitten*, §61.
22 Kant, *Metaphysik der Sitten*, §56, §57.
23 Kant, *Metaphysik der Sitten*, §57.
24 Kant, *Metaphysik der Sitten*, §58, §60.
25 Thomas d'Aquin, *Somme théologique* (Paris: Le Cerf, 1985), 219.
26 Kant, *Metaphysik der Sitten*, §55; d'Aquin, *Somme théologique*, 280.
27 d'Aquin, *Somme théologique*, 280.
28 Kant, *Metaphysik der Sitten*, §56.
29 d'Aquin, *Somme théologique*, 280.
30 Kant, *Metaphysik der Sitten*, §56.
31 On these missing criteria see Robert L. Phillips, *War and Justice* (Norman: University of Oklahoma Press, 1984), 12–134.
32 Lanza del Vasto, *Technique de la non-violence*, 50.
33 Lanza del Vasto, *L'Arche avait pour voilure une vigne*, 115.
34 Giuseppe G. Lanza del Vasto, *La roue des revolutions: Les quatre fléaux*, vol. 2 (Paris: Denoël/Gonthier, 1959), 124.
35 Lanza del Vasto, *La roue des revolutions*, 125.
36 Lanza del Vasto, *La roue des revolutions*, 202.

37   Lanza del Vasto, *L'Arche avait pour voilure une vigne*, 99.
38   Lanza del Vasto, *La roue des revolutions*, 67.
39   Lanza del Vasto, *L'Arche avait pour voilure une vigne*, 144.
40   Lanza del Vasto, *Technique de la non-violence*, 14.
41   Giesen, 'Kant et la guerre de masse'.
42   Lanza del Vasto, *La roue des revolutions*, 226.
43   Lanza del Vasto, *Technique de la non-violence*, 55.
44   Lanza del Vasto, *L'Arche avait pour voilure une vigne*, 143.
45   Lanza del Vasto, *L'Arche avait pour voilure une vigne*, 147.
46   Lanza del Vasto, *La roue des revolutions*, 107.
47   Thomas d'Aquin, *Somme théologique*, 282–3.
48   Franciso Vitoria, *De Indis* (Genève: Droz, 1966), 140.
49   Franciso Vitoria, *De Indis*, 140.
50   James Turner Johnson, *Just War and the Restraint of War: A Moral and Historical Inquiry* (Princeton: Princeton University Press, 1981), 175–6.
51   André Corvisier, *La guerre: Essais historiques* (Paris: Presses Universitaires de France, 1995), 162–3.
52   Lanza del Vasto, *L'Arche avait pour voilure une vigne*, 183.
53   Lanza del Vasto, *La roue des revolutions*, 69, 192.
54   Lanza del Vasto, *La roue des revolutions*, 192.
55   Lanza del Vasto, *L'Arche avait pour voilure une vigne*, 174.
56   Charles J. Dunlap Jr., 'Perspectives for Cyber Strategists on Law of Cyberwar', *Strategic Studies Quaterly* 5, no. 1 (2011): 89.
57   Brian Orend, *War and International Justice: A Kantian Perspective* (Waterloo: Wilfried Laurier University Press, 2000); Brian Orend, 'War Effective Justice', *Ethics & International Affairs* 16, no. 1 (2005): 43–56.
58   Kant, *Metaphysik der Sitten*, §60.
59   Kant, *Metaphysik der Sitten*, §60.
60   Lanza del Vasto, *Technique de la non-violence*, 183.
61   Lanza del Vasto, *Technique de la non-violence*, 102.
62   Lanza del Vasto, *Technique de la non-violence*, 101.
63   Lanza del Vasto, *Technique de la non-violence*, 110.
64   Martin Buber, *Letters of Martin Buber: A Life of Dialogue* (Syracuse: Syracuse University Press, 1996), 476–86.

References

Buber, Martin. *Letters of Martin Buber: A Life of Dialogue*. Syracuse: Syracuse University Press, 1996.

Corvisier, André. *La guerre: Essais historiques*. Paris: Presses Universitaires de France, 1995.

d'Aquin, Thomas. *Somme théologique*. Paris: Le Cerf, 1985.

Dunlap Jr., Charles J. 'Perspectives for Cyber Strategists on Law of Cyberwar'. *Strategic Studies Quaterly* 5, no. 1 (2011): 81–99.

Giesen, Klaus-Gerd. *L'éthique des relations internationales*. Brussels: Bruylant, 1992.

Giesen, Klaus-Gerd. 'Kant et la guerre de masse'. In *Droit et vertu chez Kant*, edited by Union scientifique franco-hellénique, 331–41. Athens: Société hellénique d'études philosophiques, 1997.

Johnson, James Turner. *Just War and the Restraint of War: A Moral and Historical Inquiry*. Princeton: Princeton University Press, 1981.

Kant, Immanuel. *Metaphysik der Sitten*. Berlin: Akademie-Ausgabe, 1797.

Lanza del Vasto, Giuseppe G. *L'Arche avait pour voilure une vigne*. Paris: Denoël/ Gonthier, 1978.

Lanza del Vasto, Giuseppe G. *Le diable dans le jeu: Les quatre fléaux*. Vol. 1. Paris: Denoël/Gonthier, 1959a.

Lanza del Vasto, Giuseppe G. *Dialogues avec Lanza del Vasto (par René Doumerc)*. Paris: Albin Michel, 1980.

Lanza del Vasto, Giuseppe G. *Le pèlerinage aux sources*. Paris: Denoël, 1943.

Lanza del Vasto, Giuseppe G. *La roue des revolutions: Les quatre fléaux*. Vol. 2. Paris: Denoël/Gonthier, 1959b.

Lanza del Vasto, Giuseppe G. *Technique de la non-violence*. Paris: Denoël/Gonthier, 1971.

Lanza del Vasto, Giuseppe G. *Vinôba ou Le nouveau pèlerinage*. Paris: Denoël, 1954.

Orend, Brian. *War and International Justice: A Kantian Perspective*. Waterloo: Wilfried Laurier University Press, 2000.

Orend, Brian. 'War Effective Justice'. *Ethics & International Affairs* 16, no. 1 (2005): 43–56.

Phillips, Robert L. *War and Justice*. Norman: University of Oklahoma Press, 1984.

Vitoria, Franciso. *De Indis*. Genève: Droz, 1966. Originally published in 1532.

Walzer, Michael. *Just and Unjust Wars*. New York: Basic Books, 1977.

8 'Woman Under a Roof'

Peace as Ethical Spatiality in Classical Chinese Philosophy

Helena Motoh

Whenever we start with the discussion of the understanding of peace in Chinese contexts, one obvious etymological detail comes to mind, being so graphic and blunt it can not be overlooked. The term *an* (安), that is often understood as an equivalent of 'peace' in European varieties, is up until the present day still written by an ancient pictogram that combines two meaningful parts: first, a 'roof' above, and underneath it, a 'woman'.

Many kinds of potentially amusing interpretations can be drawn from that, spanning from the male chauvinist (women are better locked inside houses if we want to have peace) to the more traditionalist (a woman in the house is a guarantee for a peaceful happy home). Interestingly enough, perhaps because the pictograms are of too ancient a date, the classical Chinese sources do not help much with deciding which of these interpretations is closest to the earliest connotation. *Shuo wen jie zi* (说文解字), a late Han dynasty dictionary, contains the word *an* but gives a surprisingly dry explanation:

静也, 从女, 在宀下。
(Motionless; from a woman, under a roof.)[1]

While it is unclear what this 'woman under a roof' signifies, what can be deciphered from this dictionary explanation is, firstly, that *an* means something that is not moving, that it is contrary to motion, and – secondly – that a certain spatial disposition is required for that to be realised. A woman under a roof is a woman not moving. We would, however, most probably be wrong if we wanted to read this as a sort of a straightforward linguistic reflection of general disrespect of women that are to be 'kept inside'. The original meanings of these earliest written symbols can, for obvious logical reasons, not be proven by any substantial textual evidence.

In the present paper I will attempt to approach this issue from a different perspective. First, I will reflect upon the most elementary problem of intercultural translation: can a classical term, such as *an*, be translated with the European concept of 'peace' at all – and what are the limitations of such a translation? I will introduce the concept of 'thick translation', introduced by Appiah,[2] to provide a framework for our reflection on possible explanations of the term *an* in

Chinese contexts. As for those, the problem of the translation of a given term is necessarily even more complex, because it has to take into consideration the multilayered historical traditions, 'traditions of tradition' and the discrepancies between the Zhou dynasty classical Chinese and the following development stages of the language. Based on this reflection, I will try to identify the possible equivalents of the notion of 'peace' in classical and partly traditional Chinese contexts. I will especially focus on one of them, the term *an*, in order to explore an extremely interesting semantic distinction that the classical uses of this term indicate. Therefore one – and definitely not the only possible – line of interpretation will be followed through the examples of the classical use of *an* in order to show a prevailing understanding of *an* as 'home', a place of temporal and spatial stability and a particular symbolic place. Finally, this exact connotation will be analysed through the idea of the 'geography of peace' and the work of the humanist geographer Duan Yifu (段义孚, Yi-fu Tuan) in order to reflect on the hermeneutic characteristics of *an* and the potential of such an understanding for spatio-temporal humanistic understanding of peace.

I

The notion of peace – expressed in any language – is a very nuanced idea with many different connotations. Therefore when we search for the most suitable Chinese translation for the term 'peace', we should bear in mind that even within Euro-American contexts, the term 'peace' can be understood in many different ways and for many different reasons. The absence of war or disagreement (e.g. *War and Peace*), the overcoming of conflict (e.g. Peace of Augsburg) or a tranquil stable inner state (e.g. peace of mind) and many other meanings all contribute to the general idea of peace which encompasses all these nuances, one being often a prerequisite of another. In his seminal text on the conception of peace in different cultures, Takeshi Ishida[3] points at the multifaceted variety of interpretations of this term, especially when observed from an intercultural perspective. Motivated by the after-war reflection on Japanese militarism, his research of the Japanese perception of peace and his attempt to advocate for a new Japanese pacifism undertakes a comparative study of different perceptions of peace in the world. His key examples are *shalom* of Ancient Judaism, *eirene* of Ancient Greece, *pax* of Ancient Rome, the Chinese notion of *heping* (*pinghe*) with its Japanese interpretation *heiwa* and the Indian concept of *shanti*. What he claims is they express different semantic aspects in different extents. He explained this by arranging them in a table (Table 8.1).

Although the point that Ishida tries to make is extremely interesting, the simplifications he resorts to are perhaps too numerous and extreme to enable a solid argument. The idea of several different views on what peace means and how it fits within the religious, cosmological and social scheme of things is also relevant for the present discussion. The problem with this analysis, however, is first of all, that it presupposes a perennial view on conceptual systems, while at the same time mixing ancient concepts with those of a more recent date.

Table 8.1 Takeshi Ishida's Different Perceptions of Peace[4]

Emphasis Culture	The Will of God, Justice	Prosperity	Order	Tranquillity of Mind
Ancient Judaism	shālōm			
Greece			eirene	
Rome				pax
China (Japan)			ho p'ing or p'ing ho (heiwa)	
India				śānti

Furthermore, what is completely overlooked is the problem of translation. Not just that 'peace' is understood differently in different cultural contexts and different textual and philosophical traditions, but an even more radical question: why would we even use the same term (in translation) for all those differing concepts. Are we dealing with 'peace' understood in many ways or just many different notions, wrongly subsumed under one (English) translation? Is there necessarily the idea of peace expressed in every language? Does there have to be only one?

When translating a concept from one language to the other, one has to take into account both the complexity of a web of different meanings of a term in the original language and another comparatively complex web of meanings that exists in the language of translation. The matching of the two webs, however, even if they do overlap, never tells the whole story. On every further level of explanation we fall into the same semantic trap, not being ever able to discern what the language speaker meant by one abstract term. The problem is even worse with old classical languages and the correspondence between them or between those languages and European languages. When we analyse the contemporary usages and present-day semantic matches, we have certain textual evidence that provides a bridge between the term in a European language and the potential Chinese equivalent – dictionaries, other translations etc. On the other hand, no Latin-Chinese dictionary exists for the Han period, and no substantially long text was translated from Chinese to any European language at the time, so searching for semantic correspondence is unavoidably mere speculation.

In a brilliant analysis on the problem of conceptual translation between different languages and different cultural backgrounds, Wang Hui analyses the translations of the classical text *Zhong yong* (中庸, *Doctrine of the Mean*) made by a nineteenth-century missionary and a famous early sinologist, James Legge. Wang wants to show that Legge's translation strategies and choices show traces of what he calls 'missionary orientalism',[5] a particular ideological and utilitarian context which defines the way certain translation equivalents are chosen. Most notably, he focuses on Legge's choice of a sterile term 'sincerity' as the translation for a much more religious term *cheng* (诚). Pure translation, a search for equivalent terms in both languages, is an impossible task, implies Wang:

> Concepts are rooted in culture and have a history of their own. Seemingly corresponding concepts between languages are rarely, if ever, truly equivalent. When a Chinese concept is translated into an English 'equivalent' and transplanted into foreign soil, miscomprehension often arises, because the history and association of the English word easily gets imposed on the Chinese concept under the illusion of 'equivalence'.[6]

Alleged semantic equivalence, Wang implies, can sometimes mask the fact that we arbitrarily choose a certain translation of a Chinese term, while our decision really relies on other personal motives or beliefs. Instead of looking for one semantic equivalent, a better solution would therefore be to aim for what Kwame Anthony Appiah calls a 'thick translation'. Appiah's idea is based on a very simple yet far-reaching fundamental question:

> To focus on the issue whether a reading is *correct* is to invite the question, 'What is it that a reading is supposed to give a correct account *of?*' The quick answer – one that, as we shall immediately see, tells us less than it pretends to – is, of course, 'the text'. But the text exists as linguistic, as historical, as commercial, as political event ...[7]

Texts are not independent entities and no text can exist in isolation from other texts and contexts. What interests us in the translation, according to Appiah, is therefore not how to convey an isolated correct meaning of a text. What is translated is always the context. Even more, the contexts and not the isolated pieces of text are the main reason *why* we translate texts in the first place. Therefore, what he suggests, especially for texts whose intentions go beyond literal meanings, is to aim for a 'thick translation', a translation that tries to 'locate the text in a rich cultural and linguistic context'.[8]

II

Present day Chinese language gives several translations for 'peace' (和平, 平安, 太平, 平静, 安静, 和谐 ...)[9] and it is evident that most of these stem from four classical Chinese terms (Figure 8.1).

We can therefore retrospectively claim that these four concepts are close to what could be considered an equivalent of 'peace' in classical Chinese context, with the necessary awareness, however, that no such thing as the 'true equivalent' can exist. Although the four concepts semantically overlap to a considerable degree and are meaningfully interrelated, in the present paper we will focus only on one of them, the term *an* (安) and the corresponding meanings. The overlapping of the four different concepts of peace can be seen already from the descriptions given for *an* in the lexical references and this leads to circular definitions and cross-references. One of the first

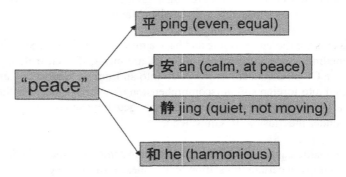

Figure 8.1 Four possible equivalents of 'peace'.[10]

systematic descriptions of the term *an* is given in the Han dynasty *Shi ming* (释名) dictionary, written most probably shortly after the already quoted *Shuo wen jie zi*:

> 安, 晏也。晏晏然和喜, 无动惧也。
> (*An* means quiet. Quietly and in happy harmony, without movement and fear.)[11]

The *Shi ming* definition summarizes very well what this aspect of *an* is all about. The three most important elements of this interpretation can be detected in this short expression: quietude, stillness and comfort. A much more extensive explanation is given by a later Northern Song dynasty *Guang yun* (广韵) dictionary, which gives a series of synonyms:

> 安徐也, 宁也, 止也, 平也 …
> (*An* means going slowly, being peaceful, stopping, being equal.)[12]

When we match the synonyms with the corresponding sub-entries from the same dictionary, we get an interesting semantic scheme (Figure 8.2).

Interestingly, what these definitions have in common is a sort of spatial and temporal balance, limitation or constraint, which is – and this is very important – perceived as good, useful or comforting.

However, in order to give a more substantial 'thick translation' of the term *an* in classical times, we obviously have to reach beyond the lexical definitions. *An* is a term used widely in the classical texts and most of the uses fall into the scope of meaning indicated by the two dictionaries quoted above, although there are also other, especially grammatical uses. In the oldest classical text, the *Book of Changes* (Yi jing 易经), we already find a very interesting use of the term *an* right at the very beginning, in the text that accompanies the second hexagram, *kun*.

> 君子有攸往, 先迷后得主, 利西南得朋, 东北丧朋。安贞, 吉。
> (A noble man starts movement, if he will go ahead, he will get lost, if he follows, he will find leadership, he will benefit by finding friends in the west and in the south, and lose friends in the east and in the north. If he <u>rests in</u> virtue, he will be lucky.)[13]

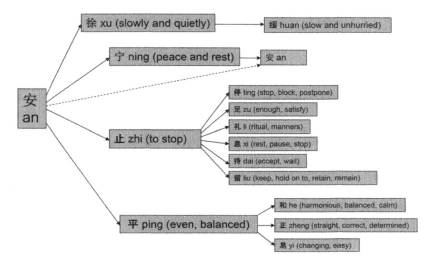

Figure 8.2 Notions of 'peace' – semantic scheme.

Another interesting example can be found in the 'Xi ci' commentary of the *Book of Changes*, where the proper attitude towards the hexagrams, divination and the whole cosmological system is being discussed. The changes that take place according to the course of transformation are conditions which a noble man is supposed to reflect upon and act accordingly. Beneficial effects are brought about by behaving according to the current phase in the process of change and unfavourable effects are triggered by not responding properly to it. The proper relationship between a noble man and the position that he finds himself in within the course of change is interestingly described by the very term *an*:

> 是故, 君子所居而安者, 易之序也。
> (Therefore, what the noble man dwells in and is <u>at peace with</u>, is the order of Change.)[14]

Still within the scope of the Five Classics we can also find that this notion of comfort and being in peace with the course of change has a more outward correlate in the political life. In a description of the proper conduct of a ruler, which 'lies in knowing men and giving repose to the people' (在知人, 在安民。),[15] the historiography classic *Book of Documents* (Shu jing 书经) acknowledges *an* as the best possible state that a ruler can make his people enjoy. There is a link between *an* and the experience of bodily enjoyment, comfort or ease. This is also expressed in a passage from Confucius' *Analects* (Lun yu 论语):

> 君子食无求饱, 居无求安…
> (When a noble man eats, he does not seek to be full, where he resides, he does not seek <u>comfort</u>.)[16]

This particular sentence is a good example of the problem with translation. The only way to get closer to what is meant by *an* in this case is from the context. First of all, the *an* that is spoken about here is a correlate of fullness after a meal, a satisfying bodily experience that a noble man, however, can consciously give up for a more important goal. It could be guessed that a comparable satisfaction with a dwelling place probably signifies a comfortable and/or peaceful feeling. The *an* in this case is a physical and a personal experience, but it is comparable with comfort on other levels. We find another interesting use of the term *an* to describe a psychological equivalent of a satisfying physical experience in a debate between Confucius and his disciple Zai Wo. They discuss the proper mourning time for one's parents and Zai Wo suggests the customary three-year period to be too long and suggests that the mourning should stop after one year. Confucius, dissatisfied with the idea of his student, provokes Zi Wo by saying: 'If you feel at ease doing it, do it!' (安则为之!) and then continues:

夫君子之居丧，食旨不甘，闻乐不乐，居处不安，故不为也。今女安，则为之！

(The noble man, however, during the time he spends mourning, does not enjoy food even if he eats well, he is not happy when listening to music, and in his residing place he does not find comfort, that's why he doesn't do all those. But if you feel at ease, do it!)[17]

This passage is particularly interesting, because we find the term *an* used twice, first as an expression of a comfortable feeling one has in his dwelling place, and another *an* which is used to signify the psychological feeling of ease at having a certain physical feeling. This aspect goes beyond bodily comfort and enjoyment. Confucius seems – perhaps deliberately – to play with words in order to show that there are different levels of *an*, ease, comfort or feeling at peace, and although structurally similar, they mark different stages in the cultivation process of a noble man.

Confucius goes even further with this argument. The *an* of a man tells us about his level of self-cultivation. Finding peace and comfort in something is what describes a person in his most essential characteristics; a person can be best understood by what he finds comfort and ease in:

视其所以，观其所由，察其所安。人焉廋哉？人焉廋哉？"

(See how a person does things, observe his motives, examine where he finds peace. How can a person hide? How can a person hide?)[18]

This again is a case of a difficult translation for *an*. However, as Appiah would say, what we look for is the contextual meaning. *An* in this case could be translated as 'peace', 'ease', 'comfort', 'rest', even 'shelter' or many more. But the contextual idea of this sentence is that a noble man 'finds peace' in benevolence, *ren*, the highest of Confucian virtues and the basis of all ethical human relationships:

不仁者不可以久处约, 不可以长处乐。<u>仁者安仁</u>, 知者利仁。

(Those who are not benevolent, can not endure long in scarcity, and can not endure long in happiness either. <u>The benevolent find peace in benevolence</u>, for the wise benevolence is favourable.)[19]

We could continue with many more examples of the same type, and also many more that show other, different understandings of the term *an*. The choice, however, to stay within the domain of the Classics and the earliest Confucian texts was deliberate. Namely, the intention of this text is not to find the most appropriate or the best translation for the term *an*, because for the reasons mentioned above, there can hardly be such a thing. It is also not an attempt to find the one most common use of the term in classical period, because the uses varied too greatly from passage to passage, author to author, school to school and from one historical period to the other. This particular semantic nuance of *an* was chosen to explore a very interesting aspect of early Chinese philosophy. That is to say, what these uses of *an* show us is an incredibly intriguing vision of 'peace'. On one side *an* describes a place of stillness and quietude, and on the other, a place that is comfortable (and provides comfort), where we feel at ease or – we could dare to say – 'at home' in. In any case, *an* is *a place*, a spatially understood concept. It is not just a place as such, but a fundamentally *symbolic* or symbolically structured place. When we talk about *an* as 'comfort' on the level of physiology, the understanding of *an* as *place* is fairly evident. The connection becomes seemingly more abstract when the psychological aspect of *an* is addressed. It becomes even one step more abstract with the ethical and the political dimension of *an* as a *place of peace* that is to be given or kept within the proper relationship among people and/or peoples.

III

Peace as place is not such a surprising concept after all. Even on an intuitive level it is clear that 'giving' and 'taking' somebody's *place* is closely correlated with the notions of war and peacemaking. The first systematic reflections of this connection can be found within the domain of political geography. The discipline which focuses more precisely on the spatiality of peace within the peace studies calls itself the 'geography of peace'. The relationship between geographical elements (e.g. the division of territory), and peace/war was recognized by several authors from various aspects.[20] But from a reflection of the war as a question for geographers (studying conflict patterns, geopolitics etc.) this line of thought in political geography developed into a more structured field and started to focus on the notion of peace as well. A great conceptual span is to be recognized between the early books on the topic, such as the wartime *The Geography of the Peace* by Spykman and Nicholl[21] and the more recent views in books such as the edited volumes *The Geography of War and Peace*[22] (2005) and *The Geographies of Peace*[23] (2014). In these past decades a new view on the relationship between peace and space/place was introduced, based on a more complex concept of peace, which not only means the absence, overcoming or negation of war, but understands peace as a process, determined by political and social relationships of power. Although very heterogeneous in content and multidisciplinary in approaches it is still based upon key central reflections that are relevant for our present topic: that peace is intrinsically a spatial notion, that spatial relationships determine how peace is introduced, maintained and perceived, and that the politics of peace are necessarily also politics of place. A classical Chinese view on this connection can be found in another Confucian text, Meng Zi. In the beginning of the first debate in the book, where master Meng gives advice to King Hui of Liang, we first read the king's complaints. Although he takes all possible measures, he says, to provide grains for the population in bad seasons, he is disappointed with the fact that the population in his country is still not increasing and the population in neighbouring countries is not decreasing. It is obvious from many classical texts of the period that the phenomenon of populations moving across long distances in search for a better ruler or a more stable country was common in the Warring States' time. We can therefore speak of a classical Chinese version of geography of peace. Many further debates like this take place in the following chapters of the same book and Meng Zi shows a largely pragmatic attitude in his views on what the benevolent ruler should and should not do. First of all, what the ruler is supposed to guarantee is 'peace for the people' (百姓安)[24] and quite literally this includes also and very importantly, that they have 'a place to rest in peace' (所安息).[25] In Meng Zi's description of all that went wrong after the death of Yao and Shun, what we are presented with is very close to what today would be called a speculation in the field of the geography of peace:

> 尧、舜既没，圣人之道衰。暴君代作，坏宫室以为污池，民无所安息；弃田以为园囿，使民不得衣食。邪说暴行又作，园囿、污池、沛泽多而禽兽至。
>
> (After the death of Yao and Shun, the way of the noble men was in decline. One tyrant followed another, they pulled down houses and mansions to make lakes and ponds, and the people had no place to <u>rest in peace</u>; they abandoned the cultivation of fields and converted them into parks and gardens, so people could not get clothing or food. Harmful doctrines and evil acts became universal; gardens and parks, lakes and ponds, thickets and marches became more numerous and birds and beasts would come to live there.)[26]

In this passage we see that for a Confucian thinker of the Warring States period such as Meng Zi, the idea of cultivation (of nature and man) was very close to the idea of peace as a social or even personal state. Nature has to be cultivated so that people have a place of peaceful rest, a ruler has to cultivate himself to give peace to the people, keep the country cultivated and refrain from war, and a noble man has to cultivate himself to find a symbolic resting place in benevolence, *ren*.

In Meng Zi, war and unrest are understood as a problem of spatiality. A clear preference is made for a stable, settled agricultural lifestyle and a good ruler is supposed to let people have a steady home and a safe lifestyle by not engaging them in war. He gives a counterexample of kings in two other, more warlike kingdoms, Qin and Chu:

彼夺其民时, 使不得耕耨以养其父母, 父母冻饿, 兄弟妻子离散。
(Other [rulers] steal the time of their people, so that they cannot plough and weed their fields to take care of their parents, their parents are freezing and hungry, brothers, wives and children depart and separate.)[27]

War is an interruption of the normal cycles of cultivation and prevents people from establishing a home, from having their own place. This idea seems to be what the word *an* is closest to, a symbolic personal space guaranteed by an uninterrupted cycle of cultivation. Stability and ease are necessary preconditions of *an*, and when war prevails, both home and cultivated space disintegrate.

When space is cultivated, organised and given symbolic meaning, it becomes a *place*. The difference between space and place and the symbolic quality of that difference was explored very interestingly by another geographer, Yi-fu Tuan (or Duan Yifu), who introduces a 'humanistic perspective' in geography, creating what is called a 'humanistic geography'. In this line of thought, phenomenology of space and place is taken into account and a clear division is suggested between the two. We will focus especially on Tuan's vision of place because it resonates very much with the particular semantic nuance of *an* that we're trying to present. For Tuan, one of the key elements of 'place' is stability:

A place is the compelling focus of a field; it is a small world, the node at which activities converge.[28]

He distinguishes between two types of places: 'public symbols', recognizable common places of symbolic identification, and 'fields of care', special nodes of symbolic identity, that function as material objects that give 'anchorage' and 'expression' to human feelings,[29] thereby sustaining a person and providing him/her with a stable reference place to depend on. Very simply, as Tuan puts it: 'Place is a centre of meaning constructed by experience'.[30]

In his further exploration of *home* as a paradigmatic *place*, Tuan's phenomenological analysis comes very close to what we find in various descriptions of *an* in the quoted classical texts. Home not only protects and provides shelter, but it is also perceived as a place to *return* to and – in general – a place to *stop* in. Tuan did not deal with the idea of peace as a spatial notion, but if we base our speculation on his thought about place as symbolically constructed space, we can explore these ideas a step further. Giving a meaning and symbolic structure is similar to the process that we will call 'cultivation'. Cultivation takes place on different levels, but is an important central motif in Chinese classical thought, especially in the works of Confucian writers. *An*, we will try to show, is the result of this process.

Three levels of cultivation can therefore be distinguished, that have as their result three different aspects of *an*. As we see from this scheme, *an* functions as a spatial metaphor on three different, but interrelated levels, signifying home, benevolence and peace (Figure 8.3).

On the level of nature, the wilderness has to be cultivated, the fields ploughed and weeded to provide nourishment and safe, favourable conditions for people to live in. It is only in a cultivated nature, in a place that is symbolically structured, that people can settle, stop, and have a home. A similar process is repeated on the level of a person. Cultivation of personality, the Confucian *xiu shen* (修身), is what makes a nobleman, a person who can surpass immediate needs and egotistic satisfaction and achieve the supreme Confucian virtue, benevolence (仁 *ren*). Benevolence, allegorically speaking, is what a noble man 'finds home' in and it is also the virtue that helps him surpass the level of his individual cultivation and reach out to the people and society in general. The third level, achieved by a nobleman engaging in the affairs of a state, is therefore the cultivation of state politics. The aim of such a leader is to lead a state in the name of peace and stability and to protect people from war or from constant struggle. The ruler is supposed to 'give peace' to its people by not interfering with their everyday continuous routines and the agricultural cycle of seasons. This is where we make a full circle and where finally *an*, perceived as ethical spatiality, takes its full scope. A woman under a roof, understood as signifying home, shelter and stability, includes and presupposes efficient peacemaking on all three levels. It is not one of the three levels that can fulfil the desired

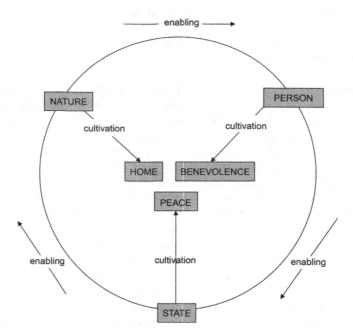

Figure 8.3 An as spatial metaphor – three levels.

scope of *an*. Even a high Confucian value such as benevolence needs to have its outward manifestation. In the last instance, what a benevolent ruler is supposed to achieve is to let his people cultivate their land in peace and have stable homes that they don't need to run away from.

Notes

1 *Shuo wen jie zi* 说文解字, chapter 8. Original text quoted from *Chinese Text Project*, accessed 20 September 2015, http://ctext.org/shuo-wen-jie-zi. All quotations from classical Chinese texts in the present paper are taken from the collection on the *Chinese Text Project* online database (www.ctext.org). The chapter-paragraph-line reference is given at each quote. Translations are made by the author of this paper, unless noted otherwise.
2 Kwame Anthony Appiah, 'Thick Translation', in *Translation Studies Reader*, ed. Lawrence Venuti (London and New York: Routledge, 2012), 417–29.
3 Takeshi Ishida, 'Beyond the Traditional Concepts of Peace in Different Cultures', *Journal of Peace Research* 6, no. 2 (1969): 133–45.
4 Ishida, 'Beyond the Traditional Concepts of Peace in Different Cultures', 135.
5 Hui Wang, *Translating Chinese Classics in a Colonial Context: James Legge and His Two Versions of the Zhongyong* (Bern: Peter Lang, 2008), 143.
6 Wang, *Translating Chinese Classics in a Colonial Context*, 197.
7 Appiah, 'Thick Translation', 426.
8 Cf. for example Appiah, 'Thick Translation', 427.
9 Cf. for example *Oxford Advanced Learner's English-Chinese Dictionary*, 6th ed. (N.p.: The Commercial Press/Oxford University Press, 2004).
10 The author of figures 8.1–8.3 is Helena Motoh.
11 *Shi ming* 释名, chap. 'Shi yan yu' 释言语, line 129. Original text quoted from *Chinese Text Project*, accessed 20 September 2015, http://ctext.org/shi-ming.
12 *Guang yun* 广韵, s.v. 'an'. Original text quoted from *Chinese Text Project*, accessed 20 September 2015, http://ctext.org/guangyun.
13 *Yi jing* 易经, hexagram 2, paragraph 1. Original text quoted from *Chinese Text Project*, accessed 20 September 2015, http://ctext.org/book-of-changes/yi-jing.
14 *Yi jing* 易经, chap. 'Xi ci', line 2. Original text quoted from *Chinese Text Project*, accessed 20 September 2015, http://ctext.org/book-of-changes/yi-jing.
15 *Shu jing* 书经, tr. James Legge, chap. 'Yu shu', section 'Counsels of Gao yao', line 1. Original text quoted from *Chinese Text Project*, accessed 20 September 2015, http://ctext.org/shang-shu/counsels-of-gao-yao/.
16 Confucius, *Lun yu* 论语, chap. 1, paragraph 14. Original text quoted from *Chinese Text Project*, accessed 20 September 2015, http://ctext.org/analects/xue-er/.
17 Confucius, *Lun yu* 论语, chap. 17, paragraph 21.
18 Confucius, *Lun yu* 论语, chap. 2, paragraph 10.
19 Confucius, *Lun yu* 论语, chap. 4, paragraph 2.
20 E.g. Kenneth Hewitt, ed., *Interpretations of Calamity from the Viewpoint of Human Ecology* (Winchester, MA: Allen & Unwin, 1983); Robert David Sack, *Human Territoriality: Its Theory and History* (Cambridge: Cambridge University Press, 1986), etc.
21 Nicholas John Spykman and Helen R. Nicholl, *The Geography of the Peace* (New York: Harcourt Brace and Company, 1944).
22 Colin Flint, ed., *The Geography of War and Peace: From Death Camps to Diplomats* (Oxford and New York: Oxford University Press, 2005).
23 Fiona McConnell, Nick Solly Megoran and Philippa Williams, eds., *Geographies of Peace* (London and New York: I.B. Tauris, 2014).
24 Meng Zi, *Meng Zi*, chap. 9, paragraph 5. Original text quoted from *Chinese Text Project*, accessed 20 September 2015, http://ctext.org/mengzi.
25 Meng Zi, *Meng Zi*, chap. 6, paragraph 14.

26 Meng Zi, *Meng Zi*, chap. 6, paragraph 14.
27 Meng Zi, *Meng Zi*, chap. 1, paragraph 5.
28 Yi-fu Tuan, 'Space and Place: Humanistic Perspective', in *Philosophy in Geography*, ed. Stephen Gale and Gunnar Olsson (Dordrecht, Boston and London: Springer, 1979), 411.
29 Tuan, 'Space and Place: Humanistic Perspective', 417–9.
30 Yi-fu Tuan, 'Place: An Experiential Perspective', *Geographical Review* 65, no. 2 (1975): 152.

References

Appiah, Kwame Anthony. 'Thick Translation'. In *Translation Studies Reader*, edited by Lawrence Venuti, 417–29. London and New York: Routledge, 2012.

Confucius. *Lun yu* 论语. Original text quoted from *Chinese Text Project*. Accessed 20 September 2015. http://ctext.org/analects/.

Flint, Colin, ed. *The Geography of War and Peace: From Death Camps to Diplomats*. Oxford and New York: Oxford University Press, 2005.

Guang yun 广韵. Original text quoted from *Chinese Text Project*. Accessed 20 September 2015. http://ctext.org/guangyun.

Hewitt, Kenneth, ed. *Interpretations of Calamity from the Viewpoint of Human Ecology*. Winchester, MA: Allen & Unwin, 1983.

Ishida, Takeshi. 'Beyond the Traditional Concepts of Peace in Different Cultures'. *Journal of Peace Research* 6, no. 2 (1969): 133–45.

McConnell, Fiona, Nick Solly Megoran and Philippa Williams, eds. *Geographies of Peace*. London and New York: I.B. Tauris & Co, 2014.

Meng Zi. *Meng Zi* 孟子. Original text quoted from *Chinese Text Project*. Accessed 20 September 2015. http://ctext.org/mengzi.

Oxford Advanced Learner's English-Chinese Dictionary. 6th ed. N.p.: The Commercial Press/Oxford University Press, 2004.

Sack, Robert David. *Human Territoriality: Its Theory and History*. Cambridge: Cambridge University Press, 1986.

Shi ming 释名. Original text quoted from *Chinese Text Project*. Accessed 20 September 2015. http://ctext.org/shi-ming.

Shu jing 书经. Translated by James Legge. Original text quoted from *Chinese Text Project*. Accessed 20 September 2015. http://ctext.org/shang-shu/.

Shuo wen jie zi 说文解字. Original text quoted from *Chinese Text Project*. Accessed 20 September 2015. http://ctext.org/shuo-wen-jie-zi.

Spykman, Nicholas John and Helen R. Nicholl. *The Geography of the Peace*. New York: Harcourt Brace and Company, 1944.

Tuan, Yi-fu. 'Place: An Experiential Perspective'. *Geographical Review* 65, no. 2 (1975): 151–65.

Tuan, Yi-fu. 'Space and Place: Humanistic Perspective'. In *Philosophy in Geography*, edited by Stephen Gale and Gunnar Olsson, 387–427. Dordrecht, Boston and London: Springer, 1979.

Wang, Hui. *Translating Chinese Classics in a Colonial Context: James Legge and His Two Versions of the Zhongyong*. Bern: Peter Lang, 2008.

Yi jing 易经. Original text quoted from *Chinese Text Project*. Accessed 20 September 2015. http://ctext.org/book-of-changes/yi-jing.

9 Making Mettā

The Poesis of Wholesome States among Homeleavers in Pāli Buddhism

Victor Forte

Introduction

Pāli Buddhism[1] provides contemporary scholarship with unique challenges and possibilities regarding the meaning of a *poesis* of peace, due to the great value the tradition has placed on renunciation. While a lack of certainty plagues the academic study of the historical Buddha and the formation of the original Buddhist community, there is little doubt that homeleaving was the most essential component of this movement.[2] The traditional biographies of Gautama Buddha for example, are styled primarily as heroic legends, yet the story of his great renunciation, the dramatic discarding of his life of elite pleasure and an ideal family of loving wife and newborn male heir, functions primarilwy as an imperative to disown familial identity. The canon of the tradition, the Pāli *Tipiṭika*, is comprised of three divisions, and two of these collections, the *Vinayapiṭika* and *Abhidhammapiṭika*,[3] were constructed exclusively by, and for, a monastic community. The third division, the *Suttapiṭika*, a nineteen-volume collection of over twelve thousand discourses attributed to the historical Buddha and his original disciples, is overwhelmingly concerned with providing a systematic pedagogy for members of the monastic community. While teachings and references are made to Buddhist laypersons as well, these comprise only a fraction of the total number of discourses. In order to examine the possible meanings of *poesis* in Pāli Buddhism, we must therefore begin with a renunciate context.

Two problems arise however, in an attempt to clarify the meaning of *poesis* in the life of Buddhist homeleavers. First, the Pāli texts indicate that Buddhist renunciation means to both renounce family *and* work. While there are Buddhist sects that arose during the Common Era in East Asia and Tibet emphasizing labor as a central element of monastic practice,[4] the Pāli *Nikāyas* indicate a clear admonition against monastic practitioners engaging in labor of any kind.[5] Notions of *poesis* associated with labor, or the production of works that arise from labor, are not applicable to the earliest known forms of Buddhist monasticism. Second, the social meaning of renunciation as described in the Pāli Canon has become a subject of great interest in contemporary Buddhist discourse due to a lack of clarity in these materials regarding the responsibilities of monastic practitioners for the larger social good. How can a Buddhist monastic community actively generate a *poesis* of peace in response to the social ills of violence, poverty, political injustice, or care for the sick and elderly, while maintaining a renunciate autonomy? In response to this provocative question, movements of 'Socially Engaged Buddhism' have arisen throughout the contemporary Buddhist world, resulting in the formation of organizations of social activism within contemporary Theravada.[6] The primary aim of this chapter is to examine the extent to which the Pāli Discourses provide a basis for *poesis* within the renunciate life, and how such a notion of *poesis* may contribute to a meaningful vision for a *poesis* of peace.

Cultivation of Wholesome States

While the ultimate purpose of the Buddha's prescribed path for the homeleaver is the achievement of liberation from rebirth, the proximate goal is the cultivation of wholesome states of mind (*kusala*). The often-quoted verse 183 from the early Buddhist text, the *Dhammapada*,[7] reveals that the primary good of 'the teaching of all the Buddhas' is acquiring wholesome states (*kusalassa upasampadā*), while the main evil to be avoided is the production of negative karma (*sabbapāpassa akaranam*).

The Pāli term *pāpa*, commonly translated as 'evil', is the antonym of *puñña*, a good associated mainly with the accumulation of positive karmic merit necessary for auspicious rebirths. Householders (i.e. laypersons) accomplish *puñña* through the material support of the monastic community, and by keeping the five precepts. For homeleavers, *puñña* is expanded to include ten precepts as well as obedience to the monastic rules. The five precepts are presented in the Pāli Canon as a set of abstentions,[8] namely not to kill, lie, steal, engage in sexual misconduct, or take intoxicants. In contemporary Western Buddhism positive formulations of the precepts are commonly offered, however the Pāli Discourses overwhelmingly present the precepts as abstentions, actions to be fully avoided due to their association with negative karma and inauspicious rebirths. There are examples in the Pāli Canon where the abstentions are expanded to provide more liberal prohibitions.[9] In addition, the precept against false speech is expanded in a number of discourses to elaborate on other harmful forms of speech, as well as positive counterparts. For example, the following pericope[10] from the *Sāmaññaphala Sutta* in the *Dīgha Nikāya*, or *Collection of Long Discourses*, can be found in other Pāli discourses as well:[11]

> Abandoning false speech, [the monk] dwells refraining from false speech, a truth-speaker, one to be relied on, trustworthy, dependable, not a deceiver of the world. Abandoning malicious speech, he does not repeat there what he heard here to the detriment of these, or repeat here what he heard there to the detriment of those. Thus he is a reconciler of those at variance and an encourager of those at one, rejoicing in peace, loving it, delighting in it, one who speaks up for peace. Abandoning harsh speech, he refrains from it. He speaks whatever is blameless, pleasing to the ear, agreeable, reaching the heart, urbane, pleasing and attractive to the multitude. Abandoning

idle chatter, he speaks at the right time, what is correct and to the point, of Dhamma and discipline. He is a speaker whose words are to be treasured, seasonable, reasoned, well–defined and connected with the goal.[12]

The emphasis placed on the positive dimensions of moral speech is much related to the great importance of spreading the *Buddhadhamma* through the spoken word. Unless the teachings of the Buddha are presented with these positive attributes their dissemination may be resisted by the larger populace. This is of special concern given the reliance of monks on the generosity of laypersons for food and other material needs.[13]

As the primary good of the Buddhadhamma, the great value placed on wholesome states in the Pāli Discourses cannot be underestimated. Throughout these texts there is the repeated association of the Buddha's path with the achievement of wholesome states. It is the promise of this achievement in fact that distinguishes the way of the Buddha from the ways of the Brahmins, as well as the competing heterodox systems of fifth-century BCE Northeast India.[14] The primacy of wholesome states is found, first of all, in the formulations of the Buddha's Noble Eightfold path, namely in Right Intention (*sammā saṅkapa*), and Right Effort (*sammā vāyāma*). The placement of these two portions in the path is of primary significance as well. Right Intention is the second portion of the Eightfold Path, following Right View (*sammā diṭṭhi*), and directly preceding the ethical portions of Right Speech (*sammā vaca*), Right Action (*sammā kammanta*), and Right Livelihood (*sammā ājīva*). Right View is mainly the necessity of entering the Buddhist path through the recognition that the Four Noble Truths are in fact true. So once one has actually entered the path, one begins one's actual practice with Right Intention, described in 'The Exposition of the Truths' (*Saccavibhaṅga Sutta*) as 'Intention of renunciation (*nekkhammasaṅkappo*), intention of non-ill will (*avyāpādasaṅkappo*), and intention of non-cruelty (*avihiṃsāsaṅkappo*)'.[15] What is evident from this formulation of right intention is that first, the path begins with renunciation. Second, the beginning of the cultivation of wholesome states is understood as a negation of the unwholesome,[16] thus mirroring the negative structure of the precepts. Third, the two wholesome states presented are causally related; intention of non-ill will is the intention to negate a negative internal state of mind towards others, while intention of non-cruelty is the wholesome intention not to act outwardly upon feelings of ill will. In directly preceding the ethical portions of the Eightfold Path, the wholesome states that define Right Intention are understood as beneficial for the proper adherence to Buddhist ethical imperatives.

Right Effort is the sixth portion of the path, following the ethical portions of three through five, and placed first in the meditation portions of six through eight. Right Effort has an explicit, straightforward, meaning, described throughout the Discourses with the following pericope:

Here a bhikkhu awakens zeal for the non-arising of unarisen evil unwholesome states, and he makes an effort, arouses energy, exerts his mind, and strives. He awakens zeal for the abandoning of arisen evil unwholesome states, and makes an effort, arouses energy, exerts his mind, and strives. He awakens zeal for the arising of unarisen wholesome states, and he makes an effort, arouses energy, exerts his mind, and strives. He awakens zeal for the continuance, non-disappearance, strengthening, increase, and fulfillment by development of arisen wholesome states and he makes an effort, arouses energy, exerts his mind, and strives.[17]

This effort to limit and remove unwholesome states (*akusala*), while adding and increasing wholesome states (*kusala*), prepares the mind for the meditational portions of the path that follow, Right Mindfulness (*sammā sāti*) and Right Concentration (*sammā samādhi*). Without a mind that has been thoroughly fashioned by wholesome states the achievements of mindfulness and concentration are not possible. The *jhānas*,[18] recognized throughout the Pāli Canon as the highest meditational states of concentration, are commonly presented as a precursor to the attainment of liberation as *nibbāna*:

> Just as bhikkhus, much grass, firewood, and water are stored up in the king's fortress for the delight, relief, and comfort of its inhabitants and for warding off outsiders, so too, secluded from sensual pleasures, secluded from unwholesome states, a noble disciple enters and dwells in the first jhāna, which consists of rapture and pleasure born of seclusion, accompanied by thought and examination – for his own delight, relief, and comfort, and for entering upon nibbāna.[19]

This rendering of liberation as *nibbāna* is itself associated with absolute freedom from unwholesome states, namely the complete eradication of the three taints (*kilesas*): greed or lust (*lobha*), anger or hatred (*dosa*) and delusion (mōha):

> the wanderer Jambukhādaka approached the Venerable Sāriputta and exchanged greetings with him … he sat down to one side and said to the Venerable Sāriputta: 'Friend Sāriputta, it is said, "Nibbāna, Nibbāna". What now is Nibbāna?'
>
> 'The destruction of lust, the destruction of hatred, the destruction of delusion: this, friend is called Nibbāna'.[20]

What makes the value for wholesome states most difficult to interpret for the modern western scholar is the relation between the early Buddhist value for wholesome states and the meaning of positive ethical actions. We have already seen that it is the practice of the precepts that grounds the ethical life of the practicing Buddhist, and that these precepts are presented in a negative structure as admonitions to 'not do'. It is in the non-doing of killing, stealing, and lying for example, that the ethical life of the Buddhist is upheld. Non-doing of evil acts, as we have also seen, results in future auspicious rebirths. In addition, the non-doing of evil limits the arising of unwholesome states, given that the mind is left agitated and anxious when engaging in actions that break the precepts, while bringing about the unwholesome impurities of greed, anger and delusion.

Wholesome states, in contrast to unwholesome states, would seem to have a positive structure, especially in regards to the *Brahmaviharas* or 'divine abidings',[21] of loving-kindness (*mettā*), compassion (*karuṇā*), sympathetic joy (*muditā*), and equanimity (*upekkhā*). However, what is revealed in the Discourses is that like the precepts, wholesome states have a negative structure. The Pāli for the primary unwholesome states (akusala) of greed, anger and delusion is *dosa, lobha* and *mōha*. The corresponding wholesome states (kusala) are linguistically rendered as the negation of these same unwholesome states – *adosa, alobha* and *amōha*, or non-lust, non-hatred and non-delusion. While the *brahmavihāras* of loving kindness and compassion can be clearly understood as positive expressions of wholesome states, they primarily function to negate unwholesome states. In his fifth-century authoritative commentary on the Pāli Discourses, the *Vissudhimagga* (*The Path of Purification*), the author Buddhagosha states,

> The general purpose of these four divine abidings is the bliss of insight and an excellent (form of future) existence. That peculiar to each is respectively the warding off of ill will, and so on. For here loving kindness has the purpose of warding off ill will, while the others have the respective purposes of warding off cruelty, aversion (boredom), and greed or resentment.[22]

The Priority of Wholesome States in the *Kakacūpama Sutta*

There may be no example from the Pāli *Discourses* that better illustrates the negative structure of wholesome states than the *Kakacūpama Sutta* from the *Middle Length Discourses*. It would be hard to imagine anyone who has read this text not being struck by the ethical implications of its message. Yet, this text has been all but ignored by Western interpreters of the Pāli Canon.[23] The discourse begins with a *bhikkhu*[24] who is being admonished by the Buddha for becoming angry when any dispraise is directed towards the *bhikkhunīs*. The *bhikkhu*, Phagguna Moliya, is first told by the Buddha that such responses are not acceptable for homeleavers, stating, 'Phagguna, it is not proper for you, a clansman gone forth out of faith from the home life into homelessness, to associate overmuch with *bhikkhunīs*. Therefore, if anyone speaks dispraise of those *bhikkhunīs* in your presence, you should abandon any desires and any thoughts based on the household life'.[25]

Phagguna's anger is associated here with the protective ways of householders who naturally defend the lives and reputations of relatives and other loved ones. Instead of turning to anger when someone speaks dispraise of a *bhikkhunī*, the Buddha instructs Phagguna to extend thoughts of loving kindness, compassionate for the welfare of the one who speaks dispraise. If there is any doubt of the extent to which the Buddha expects such a practice to be upheld by homeleavers, he states,

> If anyone gives those *bhikkhunīs* a blow with his hand (*pāṇinā pahāraṃ dadeyya*), with a clod (*leḍḍu*), with a stick (*daṇḍa*), or with a knife (*sattha*) in your presence, you should abandon any desires and any thoughts based

on the household life. And herein you should train thus: 'My mind will be unaffected, and I shall utter no evil words; I shall abide compassionate for his welfare, with a mind of loving–kindness, without inner hate'.[26]

The primary concern in this response is to negate the arising of the unwholesome states of anger and hatred, by replacing them with thoughts of loving kindness and compassion. There is no indication that the *bhikkhu* is expected to come to the defense of the victim even in the case of a violent attack. Within the context of the exchange, there is the sense that the *bhikkhu* should, in fact, avoid coming to the defense of the victim, and to instead concentrate on maintaining wholesome states of mind. Of course one could argue that the Buddha never explicitly states not to come to the defense of the victim, but even so, it remains clear that the primary concern in this context is to negate the arising of unwholesome states, regardless of any actions the *bhikkhu* might take.

Furthermore, the Buddha does not only expect the avoidance of unwholesome states when one witnesses an attack, but also when oneself is being attacked. The Buddha continues his corrections of Phagguna by stating,

If anyone should give you a blow with his hand, with a clod, with a stick, or with a knife in your presence, you should abandon any desires and any thoughts based on the household life. And herein you should train thus: 'My mind will be unaffected, and I shall utter no evil words; I shall abide compassionate for his welfare, with a mind of loving-kindness, without inner hate'. That is how you should train Phagguna.[27]

Given that the maintaining of wholesome states is required in both cases, we cannot conclude that this is simply a matter of Pāli Buddhism lacking a commitment to social justice. Rather, it implies a full commitment to the purification of the mind, regardless of the circumstances. There is further support for this argument due to similar instructions given in a separate sutta found in *The Connected Discourses* (SN IV 60–3),[28] which refers to the same kinds of weapons, and demands the same dedication to passivism. Here, a monk named Puṇṇa is planning to travel to the country of Sunāparanta, and meets with the Buddha for a brief teaching. After the Buddha concludes his discourse, he observes, 'Puṇṇa, the people of Sunāparanta are wild and rough, if they abuse and revile you, what will you think about that?' Puṇṇa responds that he will think the people of Sunāparanta are, '…truly excellent, in that they do not give me a blow with the fist [hand] (*pāṇi*)'. This line of questioning continues with the Buddha asking Puṇṇa what he would think if he were in fact, to be struck with a fist. Puṇṇa responds in kind, and continues to do so for the same list of weapons provided in *Kakacūpama Sutta*: a clod (*leḍḍu*), a rod [stick] (*daṇḍa*), and a knife (*sattha*). Finally, in response to the possibility of being stabbed with a knife, Puṇṇa responds, 'There have been disciples of the Blessed One who, being repelled, humiliated, and disgusted by the body and by life, sought for an assailant. But I have come upon this assailant without a search'.[29] The Buddha immediately replies, 'Good, good Puṇṇa! Endowed with such self-control and peacefulness, you will be able to dwell in the Sunāparanta country'.[30]

The *Kakacūpama Sutta* continues with further teachings to the community of bhikkhus. The Buddha reminds them that it is easy to be good-natured when one is not facing adversity, but one's true inner state is only revealed when events take a turn for the worse. In addition, he provides a number of metaphors to clarify the power of wholesome states of mind when one is facing adversity, stating that it is like an adversary attempting to apply paint to empty space, or digging up the earth to find its end, or burning the Ganges River with a torch. Regardless of the situation, if one trains to maintain wholesome states, the mind will remain unaffected by the actions of others. Finally, as the discourse closes, the Buddha leaves his bhikkhus with 'the simile of the saw', stating,

> Bhikkhus, even if bandits were to sever you savagely limb by limb with a two-handled saw, he who gave rise to a mind of hate towards them would not be carrying out my teaching. Herein, bhikkhus, you should train thus: 'Our minds will remain unaffected, and we shall utter no evil words; we shall abide compassionate for their welfare, with a mind of loving-kindness, without inner hate'.[31]

Pāli Buddhist Ethics as Internal Consequentialism

Given the central practice of achieving and maintaining wholesome states in Pāli Buddhism, how are we to characterize the ethical meaning of homeleaving? Over the past twenty-three years, Western scholars have presented a number of contrasting arguments regarding the meaning of Pāli Buddhist ethics. This debate was initiated by Damien Keown's publication of *The Nature of Buddhist Ethics* in 1992. Keown argued that our understanding of Pāli Buddhist ethics would best be served through comparisons with Western ethics in order to determine what system is most similar. He concluded that Aristotelian virtue ethics shares the greatest similarities with Pāli Buddhism, primarily because both are teleological, and both emphasize the cultivation of the virtues in reaching ultimate goals.[32] A number of scholars have responded to Keown's thesis, offering their own hermeneutical positions. In most cases, these studies have argued that multiple systems of Western ethics can be found in the Pāli Canon, rather than a single system, as Keown maintained. Abraham Velez de Cea, for example, argues that the Pāli Discourses indicate both utilitarian ethics and moral realism along with virtue ethics.[33] Mark Sederits characterizes Pāli Buddhism as an *aretaic* consequentialism, recognizing both virtue and consequentialist ethics at work.[34] Peter Harvey finds a range of Western systems evident in the Pāli Discourses, including realist ethics, utilitarianism, Kantian ethics, and Aristotelian virtue ethics.[35] Because there is evidence for multiple Western ethical systems in Pāli Buddhism, both de Cea and Harvey maintain that Pāli Buddhist ethics is therefore *sui generis*, a unique system of ethics not found in the West.

If Pāli Buddhist ethics is truly *sui generis*, rather than equating it with either single or multiple forms of Western ethics, a more idiosyncratic category needs to be formulated. Based upon the evidence that the proximate goal of Buddhist practice is achieving and maintaining wholesome states of mind, it is argued here that a more accurate and succinct category of Pāli Buddhist ethics is *internal consequentialism*. By assigning this category, we are using Western language, while at the same time, identifying a single form of ethics that cannot be equated with any known Western system. This language allows for a clearer distinction between Pāli Buddhist and Western ethics, while identifying the former as *sui generis*.

The category of *internal consequentialism* contrasts with Western systems of ethics in a number of ways. First, while virtue ethics has an internal structure, based upon the formation of personal character through the practice of the virtues, it lacks the consequentialist dimensions of Buddhist practice that are concerned with karmic results. Furthermore, Aristotelian virtue ethics functions as the skillful application of virtue according to the particular socio-political circumstances in which one finds oneself. For this reason, virtue is understood as a mean, while Buddhist ethics is not based in achieving a mean, but in adhering to prescribed abstentions regardless of circumstances. Moral abstentions, according to Aristotle, are not virtues, because they have no mean.[36]

Utilitarian ethics does have a consequentialist structure, but it is based solely upon an assessment of how one's actions affect collective levels of pleasure and pain. While it is clear that Pāli Buddhism recognizes how one's actions affect the pain, pleasures and happiness of other beings, we cannot equate its ethical system with Western notions of utilitarianism, given the role that both karma and wholesome states play in the early Buddhist understanding of consequences. The precepts, for example, are centered on eliminating actions that cause harm to others, but the concept of *puñña*, auspicious karmic results, adds another dimension to consequence that is not included in Western consequentialist ethics. We have also noted from both the *Kakacūpama Sutta* and the *Puṇṇa Sutta* that the internal effects of unwholesome states of mind are given greater weight than consequences of pain for both oneself and others. If one begins with the premise that the proximate goal of Buddhist practice is wholesome states and the ultimate goal is freedom as *nibbāna*, equating Buddhist ethics with Western utilitarianism is not tenable.

This can also be said in regards to moral realism. One cannot separate notions of karmic debt from objective moral truth. Because Buddhist notions of moral truth are inextricably tied to karma, an action is *ipso facto* morally right or wrong based on karmic law, not on the powers of human objectivity. There is, however, Buddhist moral guidance based upon subjective truth, namely in the argument that one directly knows the pain of suffering from one's own experience, and in recognizing this truth, would avoid bringing the same kinds of harm and suffering to others.[37] Harvey identifies this universal subjective knowledge of suffering, as an indication of Kantian deontological ethics. But Kant structures his ethics on the application of an action to universal law in order to objectively determine whether or not one should avoid the action. In Pāli Buddhism the universal law of moral action is given in the traditional notions of karma. Second, in this case the Buddha is actually bypassing objective knowledge, and turning to *internal* subjective experience in order to engender empathy in the practitioner.

It is for these reasons that categorizing Pāli Buddhist ethics as a *sui generis* system of *internal consequentialism*, rather than equating it with either single or multiple forms of Western ethics, allows for greater intelligibility and context. This category underscores the early Buddhist values for the proximate goal of wholesome states, and the ultimate goal of *nibbāna*. It is also allows for the inclusion of early Buddhist notions of karmic law to be retained within the assigned ethical category. In addition, Western language is employed here by identifying Pāli Buddhist ethics as a form of consequentialism, while distinguishing this system from other known Western forms in its emphasis on internal states of mind. Pāli Buddhist ethics would therefore be recognized as a unique system of ethics, and as such, an alternative way of living, a vision of human being that cannot be reduced to Occidental models.

Conclusions: Buddhist Renunciates as Makers of Mettā

If we accept the categorization of Pāli Buddhist ethics as an *internal consequentialism*, how might we consider the possible contributions to social justice and a *poesis* of peace that such an ethics could afford? If we begin with the recognition that the primary values of Pāli Buddhism lie in the cultivation of wholesome states and the ultimate goal of human freedom, then the meaning of social justice would be structured according to these values. The principal social provision for these values is centered in the institution of homeleaving, which allows for a way of life that best sustains the cultivation of wholesome states.[38] The textual records of Pāli Buddhism indicate that one of the historical Buddha's main convictions was in making homeleaving accessible to a wide range of social strata, including both men and women, high and low caste, slaves and criminals. If we were to assess the contributions of the early Buddhist movement to social justice, the inclusivity of the monastic community may be its greatest accomplishment.[39]

This community of homeleavers was, from the beginning, supported by lay Buddhists with the material needs necessary to relieve the former from the requirements of labor. In so doing, those who chose to remain in the world of family and labor contributed to the social good, not only in terms of childrearing and industry, but also in supporting the homeleaver's cultivation of wholesome states. In turn, the opportunity to give to the monks (*dāna*) was understood as bringing about wholesome states of loving-kindness for the layperson. These practices, along with the social elevation of the precepts, were designed to limit unwholesome states of greed, anger and delusion, while increasing wholesome states. Social justice, from this perspective, is most clearly served by providing persons with opportunities to foster an internal mental environment of calm and contentment.

Given the institutional structures of early Buddhist homeleaving, monks and nuns were not expected to develop the skills of farming, trade or craft. Their lives were formed to refrain from work of any kind, from both the production of crops or material goods. Instead, homeleavers were trained to make *mettā*, to bring wholesome states like loving-kindness, into the world. The social value of a renunciate's life is in this higher-order capacity to produce wholesome states. We can understand their place in Buddhist societies as skilled producers of loving kindness, compassion, sympathetic joy, and equanimity. But what is the social cost of this support system for wholesome states? We have examined the example of the *Kakacūpama Sutta* to consider the complexities of the meaning of social justice when the great value for wholesome states requires their precedence in all circumstances, and have found that a committed intervention against unjust violent actions is not given priority, whether it is to intervene for oneself or for another. However, if we begin with the recognition that Buddhist renunciates are charged with, and supported for, the production of wholesome states, then their contribution to society is not a matter of meting out the terms of justice, but in creating a mind of peace that is made available to walk among us.

Notes

1 I.e. contemporary Theravada ('The School of the Elders'), which is based upon the only remaining complete canon of early Buddhism, written in the ancient Indic language of Pāli.
2 While there has always been an essential community of lay Buddhists since the earliest founding of the tradition, the Buddhist Sangha, or community, has been understood specifically as the community of renunciates, practitioners in the fullest extent, who are supported by laypersons in their pursuits of the path.
3 The *Vinayapiṭika* make up the monastic rules, and the *Abhidhammapiṭika* provide sophisticated analyses of mental and physical phenomena.
4 The Tang dynasty Chan master Baizhang (Pai-chang), for example, is attributed with an early formulation of Chan monastic rules, and is famous for stating, 'A day without work is a day without food'. See Steven Heine and Dale S. Wright, eds., *Zen Masters* (New York: Oxford University Press, 2010), 16.
5 See, for example, AN III 171 and AN III 173 in Bhikkhu Bodhi, trans., *The Numerical Discourses of the Buddha: A Translation of the Aṅguttara Nikāya* (Boston: Wisdom Publications, 2012), 762, 764.
6 Notable examples have been the Sri Lanka *Sarvodaya Shramadana* movement, founded by A.T. Ariyaratne in 1958, the late 1960s Dhammic Socialism movement initiated by Bhikkhu Buddhadāsa in Thailand, the 2007 'Saffron Revolution' in Myanmar, and Buddhist Global Relief founded in the U.S. by Bhikkhu Bodhi in 2007.
7 See Sarvepalli Radhakrishnan, ed., *The Dhammapada* (New Delhi: Oxford University Press, 1950), 120.
8 See, for example, AN I 297 in Bodhi, *The Numerical Discourses of the Buddha*, 374–5.
9 For example, not taking women from their families, not accepting slaves, not committing fraud. See Bhikkhu Ñāṇamoli and Bhikkhu Bodhi, trans., *The Middle Length Discourses of the Buddha: A New Translation of the Majjhima Nikāya* (Boston: Wisdom Publications, 1995), 273.
10 A hermeneutical category for language that is repeated across a religious canon.
11 Also see for example, DN i 4, MN i 180, MN i 345.
12 SN i 64 in Maurice Walshe, trans., *The Long Discourses of the Buddha: A Translation of the Dīgha Nikāya* (Boston: Wisdom Publications, 1995), 100.
13 This is not to imply, however, that wholesome forms of speech are only to be valued for the benefits of public reputation. There are obvious benefits for both parties in reducing

conflict, anger and confusion. But the contrast between the positive dimensions of speech and the lack of positive dimensions in the remaining moral precepts is striking.

14 Competing systems of practice focused to a much greater extent on the meaning of action, rather than the internal state of the agent. Brahmanism emphasized the precision of action in ritual, and the necessity of acting according to caste-based notions of Dharmic duty. Jains saw action itself as an impediment to liberation, and so progressively limited action ultimately towards total cessation of physical movement and eating unto death. The *Ajivikas* professed a deterministic view of karma, so that one could not achieve liberation through action, but could only wait out the natural process of karmic law in order to be finally released from rebirth.

15 MN iii 251 in Ñāṇamoli and Bodhi, *The Middle Length Discourses of the Buddha*, 1100.

16 I.e. non-ill will, and non-cruelty.

17 MN iii 252 in Ñāṇamoli and Bodhi, *The Middle Length Discourses of the Buddha*, 1100.

18 The *jhānas* (Sk. *dhyānas*) are categorized according to eight progressive attainments of concentration, further divided in to four *jhānas* of form (*rūpajhanā*) and four formless *jhānas* (*arūpajhanā*). The four *jhānas* of form are much more prevalent in the Canon as precursors to liberation. See for example, in DN i 73–6, MN i 181–3, AN IV 291. The four *jhānas* of form are commonly described in the *Numerical Discourses* as, 'pleasant dwellings in this very life' (*diṭṭhadhammasukhavihārānaṃ*), connoting an interior state that serves as the 'home' of the renunciate.

19 AN IV 111 in Bodhi, *The Numerical Discourses of the Buddha*, 1079.

20 SN IV 251 in Bhikkhu Bodhi, trans., *The Connected Discourses of the Buddha: A New Translation of the Saṃyutta Nikāya* (Boston: Wisdom Publications, 2000), 1294.

21 Like the *jhānas*, providing a 'pleasant dwelling' (*sukhavihārānaṃ*) for the renunciate, the *Brahmavihāras* provide a safe inner-dwelling, protecting the mind from unwholesome states.

22 Vism 318 in Bandantācariya Buddhaghosa, *Visuddhimagga: The Path of Purification*, trans. Bhikkhu Ñāṇamoli (Onalaska, WA: Paryatti Publishing, 1991), 311.

23 For a fuller exegesis of this text see Victor Forte, 'Finding Peace in the Simile of the Saw', in *Mediators and Meditators: Buddhism and Peacemaking*, ed. Chanju Mun (Honolulu: Blue Pine Books, 2007), 259–77.

24 The identity given to Buddhist monks; *Bhikkhu* means 'beggar' or 'mendicant'. *Bhikkhunis* are female renunciates within the monastic community (*Sangha*).

25 MN i 123 in Ñāṇamoli and Bodhi, *The Middle Length Discourses of the Buddha*, 218.

26 MN i 123 in Ñāṇamoli and Bodhi, *The Middle Length Discourses of the Buddha*, 218.

27 MN i 124 in Ñāṇamoli and Bodhi, *The Middle Length Discourses of the Buddha*, 218.

28 See Bodhi, The *Puṇṇa Sutta* in *The Connected Discourses of the Buddha*, 1167–9.

29 This statement makes a reference to another discourse in *The Connected Discourses* (SN V 320–2). The Buddha had given a talk to the bhikkhus on the foulness of the body, and then left for a half-month solitary retreat. When the Buddha returned his attendant monk, Ānanda, informed him that after hearing his talk on the foulness of the body, several monks were so 'repelled, humiliated, and disgusted' with their bodies that they 'sought for an assailant' and 'used the knife'. Ānanda requests the Buddha talk about another method, and the Buddha obliges by teaching the bhikkhus mindfulness of breathing that, 'when developed and cultivated, is peaceful and sublime, an ambrosial pleasant dwelling, and it disperses and quells on the spot evil unwholesome states whenever they arise'. See Bodhi, *The Connected Discourses of the Buddha*, 1773–4.

30 See Bodhi, *The Connected Discourses of the Buddha*, 1167–9.

31 MN i 129 in Ñāṇamoli and Bodhi, *The Middle Length Discourses of the Buddha*, 223.

32 Damien Keown, *The Nature of Buddhist Ethics* (New York: Palgrave, 2001), 21–3.

33 Abraham Velez de Cea, 'The Criteria of Goodness in the Pāli Nikāyas and the Nature of Buddhist Ethics', *Journal of Buddhist Ethics* 11 (2004): 138, http://blogs.dickinson.edu/

buddhistethics/2010/04/27/the-criteria-of-goodness-in-the-pali-nikayas-and-the-
nature-of-buddhist-ethics/.

34 Mark Sederits, 'Buddhist Reductionism and the Structure of Buddhist Ethics', in
    Indian Ethics: Classical Traditions and Contemporary Challenges, ed. Purushottama
    Bilimoria, Joseph Prabhu and Renuka Sharma (Burlington VT: Ashgate Publishing
    Company, 2007), 292.

35 Peter Harvey, 'An Analysis of Factors Related to the Kusala/Akusala Quality of Actions
    in the Pāli Tradition', *Journal of the International Association of Buddhist Studies* 33,
    no. 1–2 (2011): 205–6.

36 'Virtue then, is a state of character concerned with choice, lying in a mean, i.e. the
    mean relative to us, this being determined by a rational principle, and by that princi-
    ple by which the man of practical wisdom would determine it ... not every action nor
    every passion admits of a mean; for some have names that already imply badness, e.g.
    spite, shamelessness, envy and in the case of actions adultery, theft, murder; for all of
    these and suchlike things imply by their names that they are themselves bad, and not
    the excesses or deficiencies of them'. See Aristotle, *Ethica Nicomachea*, in *The Basic
    Works of Aristotle*, ed. Richard McKeon (New York: Random House, 2001), 959.

37 See Dh 129, 'All [beings] tremble at punishment, all [beings] fear death. Likening
    others to oneself, one should neither slay nor cause to slay', in Radhakrishnan, *The
    Dhammapada*, 102.

38 Similar conclusions can be found in Mudagamuwe Maithrimurthi, 'The Buddha's
    Attitude to Social Concerns as Depicted in the Pāli Canon', *Buddhist Studies Review*
    22 (2005): 40.

39 See the following for examples of arguments against caste identity and slavery, and the
    inclusion of socially oppressed groups: Sn 116–42, AN IV 274–9, MN ii 97–105, MN ii
    147–58, DN i 111–26, DN i 141. While the Buddha did agree to restrict certain groups
    from the Sangha like debtors, and those employed by the court, these exclusions mainly
    resulted from the requests of the monarchy in Magadha, and the Buddha complied in
    order to keep the Sangha in good standing with the court. It also needs to be recognized
    that although the Buddha admitted women into the Sangha, the 'eight principles of
    respect' (AN IV 276–8) placed all of them in lower standing than the men, regardless of
    their years of experience or attainments.

Abbreviations

All references to the *Nikāyas* are based on Pāli Text Society notation.

AN	*Aṅguttara Nikāya*
DN	*Dīgha Nikāya*
Dh	*Dhammapada*
MN	*Majjhima Nikāya*
SN	*Samyutta Nikāya*
Sn	*The Sutta-Nipāta*
Vism	*Vissudhimagga*

References

Aristotle. *Ethica Nicomachea*. In *The Basic Works of Aristotle*, edited by Richard McKeon,
    935–1112. New York: Random House, 2001.
Bodhi, Bhikkhu, trans. *The Connected Discourses of the Buddha: A New Translation of the
    Samyutta Nikāya*. Boston: Wisdom Publications, 2000.

Bodhi, Bhikkhu, trans. *The Numerical Discourses of the Buddha: A Translation of the Aṅguttara Nikāya*. Boston: Wisdom Publications, 2012.

Buddhaghosa, Bandantācariya. *Visuddhimagga: The Path of Purification*. Translated by Bhikkhu Ñāṇamoli. Onalaska, WA: Paryatti Publishing, 1991.

de Cea, Abraham Velez. 'The Criteria of Goodness in the Pāli Nikāyas and the Nature of Buddhist Ethics'. *Journal of Buddhist Ethics* 11 (2004): 123–42. http://blogs.dickinson.edu/buddhistethics/2010/04/27/the-criteria-of-goodness-in-the-pali-nikayas-and-the-nature-of-buddhist-ethics/.

Forte, Victor. 'Finding Peace in the Simile of the Saw'. In *Mediators and Meditators: Buddhism and Peacemaking*, edited by Chanju Mun, 259–77. Honolulu: Blue Pine Books, 2007.

Harvey, Peter. 'An Analysis of Factors Related to the Kusala/Akusala Quality of Actions in the Pāli Tradition'. *Journal of the International Association of Buddhist Studies* 33, no. 1–2 (2011): 175–237.

Heine, Steven, and Dale S. Wright, eds. *Zen Masters*. New York: Oxford University Press, 2010.

Keown, Damien. *The Nature of Buddhist Ethics*. New York: Palgrave, 2001.

Maithrimurthi, Mudagamuwe. 'The Buddha's Attitude to Social Concerns as Depicted in the Pali Canon'. *Buddhist Studies Review* 22 (2005): 27–43.

Ñāṇamoli, Bhikkhu, and Bhikkhu Bodhi, trans. *The Middle Length Discourses of the Buddha: A New Translation of the Majjhima Nikāya*. Boston: Wisdom Publications, 1995.

Radhakrishnan, Sarvepalli, ed. *The Dhammapada*. New Delhi: Oxford University Press, 1950.

Saddhatissa H., trans. *The Sutta-Nipāta*. London: Curzon Press, 1994.

Sederits, Mark. 'Buddhist Reductionism and the Structure of Buddhist Ethics'. In *Indian Ethics: Classical Traditions and Contemporary Challenges*, edited by Purushottama Bilimoria, Joseph Prabhu and Renuka Sharma, 283–95. Burlington, VT: Ashgate Publishing Company, 2007.

Walshe, Maurice, trans. *The Long Discourses of the Buddha: A Translation of the Dīgha Nikāya*. Boston: Wisdom Publications, 1995.

10 Peace in Abhinavagupta's Poetics

The Curious Case of *Śānta Rasa*

Tina Košir

The aim of this chapter is to engage somewhat differently the concept of *śānta rasa*, the aesthetic experience of peace, which has occupied an important place in Indian aesthetics since Abhinavagupta's persuasive elaboration of it. The topic itself has engaged any number of scholars: *śānta rasa* was thoroughly dealt with, for example, by Jeffrey Lloyd [Moussaieff] Masson and Madhav V. Patwardhan in their *Śāntarasa and Abhinavagupta's Philosophy of Aesthetics*.[1] Important further contribution came from Edwin Gerow, who first co-authored (with Ashok Aklujkar) a review article of Masson's and Patwardhan's book from the perspective of aesthetic theory,[2] and then proceeded with his own English translation of Abhinavagupta's *śāntarasaprakaraṇa*, to which he wrote an informative introduction, propounding 'to examine the main theses of Abhinava's metaphysics in the light of his aesthetics'[3] and not (only) vice-versa, as had been done before. In terms of understanding Abhinavagupta's argumentation and the place of the concept of *śānta rasa* in the wider context of his philosophy, this paper draws, in large part, on the work of those scholars. However, it is unfortunate that the findings of extant scholarship dealing with premodern Indian thought are too often viewed only as providing a better understanding of historical developments rather than contributing valuable perspectives to contemporary debates. Therefore, I wish to proceed from the assumption that although concepts and ideas discussed are of course to be regarded with due respect of the historical and cultural contexts in which they originated, their scope should not be limited to those contexts alone. On the contrary, I suggest that Abhinavagupta's treatment of *śānta rasa* is a unique mode of argumentation offering elegant solutions to the ontological tensions, such as the relation between unity and multiplicity, transcendence and immanence, immutability and transformation. Abhinavagupta's profound insights will be seen as building blocks in an attempt to develop an understanding of peace as essentially poetic. A subjective experience of peace will be examined as an aesthetic experience *par excellence*, a disinterested perception of an object thereby endowed with non-instrumental value.

Śāntarasaprakaraṇa, discussion of *śānta rasa*, is part of *Abhinavabhāratī*, Abhinavagupta's extensive commentary on the *Nāṭyaśāstra*, the fundamental treatise on the classical Indian performing arts, traditionally attributed to sage Bharata, but in fact very likely a compilation composed by several authors between the second century BC and second century AD. *Nāṭyaśāstra* is a normative text, covering every aspect of theatrical performance, but the most interesting part of it, at least from the point of view of theoretical aesthetics, is the chapter devoted to *rasa*, the essence of aesthetic experience. Though the opinions of the most outstanding theoreticians preceding Abhinavagupta on how exactly the *rasas* are produced were varied, it was axiomatically believed that each of the eight *rasas* is based on one of the permanent mental states (*sthāyibhāvas*) common to human nature: erotic delight (*rati*), laughter (*hāsa*), sorrow (*śoka*), anger (*krodha*), hero-ism (*utsāha*), fear (*bhaya*), disgust (*jugupsā*) and astonishment (*vismaya*). While all these emotions are common to everyday human experience, in a play they are mysteriously transformed so that they (even the commonly unpleasant ones) are enjoyed aesthetically as *rasas*: the erotic (*śṛṅgāra*), the comic (*hāsya*), the sor-rowful (*karuṇa*), the furious (*raudra*), the heroic (*vīra*), the terrible (*bhayānaka*), the odious (*bībhatsa*) and the marvellous (*adbhuta*). Abhinavagupta's defence of *śānta rasa*, the peaceful, tranquil *rasa* as the ninth (and most important) *rasa* is closely linked to his understanding of the phenomenology of *rasa* as such. His most influential interlocutor on the subject was Bhaṭṭa Nāyaka, who thoroughly reformulated what had previously been believed about how *rasa* is born.

What is known of Bhaṭṭa Nāyaka for certain amounts to not much more than that he 'wrote in Kashmir sometime between Ānandavardhana (c. 850), whom he critiques, and Abhinavagupta (c. 1000), who critiques him',[4] but his original work was lost and hence his doctrine could only be reconstructed from the surviv-ing texts by other authors who referred to it. Abhinavagupta, for example, sum-marises Nāyaka's view – alongside a brief treatment of the opinions of Lollaṭa (who taught *rasa* is simply the intensified form of the corresponding permanent mental state) and Śaṅkuka (who understood *rasa* as the imitation of the perma-nent mental state of the imitated character) – to then proceed to form his own both on the basis of Nāyaka's and in opposition to it. The essence of Nāyaka's paradigmatic shift, according to Sheldon Pollock, 'was the concern with redirect-ing attention away from the process by which emotion is engendered in and made accessible through the literary work, and toward the spectator's or reader's own subjective experience of this emotion'.[5] *Rasa*, argued Bhaṭṭa Nāyaka (as reported by Abhinavagupta), cannot be perceived as something external to the perceiving subject, for if that were the case, then 'it could not be a "taste" (that is, something experienced), but an object, like a pot, toward which one would be emotionally indifferent'.[6] Hence *rasa* takes place in the consciousness of the perceiving sub-ject. The question, however, is how. Nāyaka is clear that this is not in any way that would resemble other ways of perception relating to the subject's personal experience – for if the sorrowful *rasa* was perceived as the subject's own sorrow, he would refuse to be exposed to the tragic performances. *Rasa*, according to Bhaṭṭa Nāyaka, is 'revealed (*bhāvyamāna*) by a special power assumed by words in poetry and drama, the power of revelation (*bhāvanā*)'.[7] The function of this power is two-fold: it generalises the particular causes (such as loss of a loved one) and effects (such as crying) that take place in a literary work in relation to the emotional states of the characters and it does that in such a way that 'the thick pall of mental stupor (*moha*) which cloaks one's own consciousness'[8] is suppressed. What is thus revealed to the spectator is *rasa*, ready to be 'enjoyed (*bhuj*) with a kind of enjoyment (*bhoga*),[9] different from direct experience, memory, etc.'[10] This enjoyment is characterised by resting (*viśrānti*) on one's own consciousness, an aesthetic absorption full of bliss (*ānanda*) and light (*prakāśa*) akin to the highest mystical state of savouring (*āsvāda*) the Absolute, the supreme *brahman*.

Abhinavagupta adopts Bhaṭṭa Nāyaka's focus on *rasa* as something pertaining to the consciousness of the spectator, but he disagrees with Nāyaka's view that it is neither perceived nor produced nor manifested: '... if we do not admit that Rasa is produced or manifested, we shall be forced to conclude that it is either eternal or non-existent: no third possibility exists. A thing which cannot be perceived cannot be said to exist at all'.[11] But as he proceeds to probe the 'true nature of *rasa*', his analysis is indeed deeply influenced by Bhaṭṭa Nāyaka's. In this respect, Abhinavagupta also speaks of a special function of poetry that transcends the literal meaning. Immediately after the perception of the literal sense of drama (or poetry), a different perception takes place: it is an inner (*mānasī*) perception 'devoid of its particularity (*viśeṣa*)'[12] – all the particularities of an event in a performance, such as time and place, are eliminated in a way to enable the perceiver to taste the flavour of the emotion as such. As a spectator of a terrifying scene, I am neither really afraid for my own life nor for the life of the actual actor, so what I experience is, according to Abhinavagupta, fear as such – the terrible *rasa*. Because aesthetic experience is disinterested, it is devoid of the obstacles (*vighna*), such as desire of pleasure and fear of pain, by which consciousness is contracted and clouded in everyday ordinary experience. It is a state of delightful wonder (*camatkāra*), not only abstract but also physical (the physical effects of aesthetic wonder are, among others, trembling, horripilation and vibrations of joy).[13]

> That is to say, what is called *camatkāra* is an uninterrupted (*acchina*) state of immersion (*āveśa*) in an Enjoyment, characterized by the presence of a sensation of inner fullness. It might be said indeed that *camatkāra* is an action proper to a tasting (*cam*) or enjoying subject, i.e., to a person immersed in the inner movement (*spanda*) of a magic (*adbhuta*) enjoyment.[14]

Navjivan Rastogi puts it thus:

> The credit for the technical development of the notion of *camatkāra* and its theoretical exploitation will have to be accorded to Abhinavagupta. It appears that Abhinava has deliberately employed the idea of *camatkāra* and injected doctrinal nuances into its treatment for providing an answer to several unsolved questions with regard to the art-experience. Prior to Abhinavagupta, *camatkāra* had been discussed rather superficially.[15]

It is one of the essential concepts in his metaphysics but Abhinavagupta nevertheless draws a clear line between the aesthetic and the mystical/yogic experience. If aesthetic experience is dependent on the aesthetic stimuli and thus cannot be everlasting, the yogic cognition is seen to be deprived of beauty (*saundarya-virahāt*).

However, the limit between the aesthetic and the mystical appears to be particularly blurry in the case of *śānta rasa* as Abhinavagupta defines it. Prior to his defence of *śānta* (peace, tranquillity) not only as rasa, but as the highest form of rasa, tranquillity was generally considered a rather poor choice in terms of the effect a theatrical performance should aim to achieve. A comparatively simplistic description of *śānta rasa*, which Abhinavagupta summarises at the beginning of his discussion on the subject, claimed *śānta rasa* was grounded in the stable emotional basis (*sthāyibhāva*) of peace (*śama*). In a play, it was understood as produced by factors such as ascetic practice or association with ascetics, and manifested in a character as absence of desire and anger. The opponents of this view were quick to point out the shortcomings of such a view: association with ascetics, they said, cannot be considered to be a direct cause of peace, while absence of desire can be attributed to states that are exactly the opposite to *śānta*. But the strongest argument against *śānta* was probably this: '… it is not something that can be suitably represented on the stage (*prayogāsamvāyitvāt*). For the cessation of activity is not a suitable subject for stage presentation'.[16]

Abhinavagupta begins his argument to the contrary by confirming that peace is intimately connected with spiritual liberation (*mokṣa*), as was widely accepted within the culture of his time (hence the attempt to define *śānta rasa* as connected to ascetic practices portrayed in a play). His crucial question is: '[W]hy may not the state of mind (*cittavṛtti*) conducive to "liberation", the highest human goal, not also be capable of transformation into rasa (*kimiti rasatvaṃ nānīyate*)?'[17] This implies the first task at hand is hence to establish which 'state of mind' is a direct cause of liberation.

The first possible candidate is indifference (*nirveda*), believed to be a consequence of the ultimate *gnosis*: 'Now the "indifference" which arises from knowledge of truth supresses all other stable emotions'.[18] Indifference might cancel out all emotions, but since it is itself only a consequence, its true cause should be examined as the one by which *śānta rasa* is directly produced: the knowledge of the ultimate truth (*tattvajñāna*). So the next step Abhinavagupta takes by way of defining *śānta rasa* is to explain the ultimate realisation from the perspective of his metaphysics.

> What then is the stable (emotional basis of *śānta* rasa)? It is said: to the extent that knowledge of the truth is a means to the (accomplishment of) liberation, it is that alone that ought to be stable where liberation (is concerned). But 'knowledge of truth' is nothing but knowledge of the Self – knowledge of a Self, as it were, an object apart (from mundane objects)…. It follows then that the Self – possessed of untainted qualities such as knowledge and joy, and untouched by affections for presumptive objects – is the stable (basis for *śānta* rasa).[19]

Its stability is actually of the highest order – all other emotive states are in comparison only relatively stable, 'to the extent that they attach themselves for a time to the wall of the Self, whose nature it is to be "stable"'.[20] It is not 'associated with any separable bliss',[21] as is the case with other *rasas*, but is bliss as such, untainted delight of consciousness savouring its own supreme taste. '[T]his form of the Self we have described is not, in its unalloyed form (*asaṃpṛktena vapuṣā*), within the province of the ordinary understanding'.[22] Its nature is, indeed, peace.

> Devoid of all the complex of sufferings that derive from looking away (from it), it shines out from both poetic and practical works generally as the single consciousness through which is attained supreme delight – and, by distinguishing (itself) in the interior condition (of the spectator), effects a sensibility of the same sort, which leads to (the experience of) a transcendental joy.[23]

Such vision of the Self is in accordance with the teachings of the non-dual Kashmir Śaivism. The name designates various schools and practices that flourished in Kashmir from the latter centuries of the first millennium AD through the early centuries of the second. Though origin of the schools is tantric, the (most) transgressive rites were gradually domesticated through Brahmanic appropriation. The key feature of the non-dual Kashmir Śaivism is its integral monism, the belief in ontological unity between the transcendent (in the form of the god Śiva) and the immanent (goddess Śakti). They are ontologically inseparable, although Śiva, who is of the nature of absolute consciousness, is understood as the primal principle, the possessor of Śakti (*śaktiman*), the primordial absolute power manifested as the cosmic theatre of diverse phenomena. There is no essential divide between the immanent (*viśvamaya*) and the transcendent (*viśvottīrna*), although the transcendent is not at all fully manifested in the immanent alone. The phenomenal manifestation is not illusionary, it is fully pervaded by the absolute consciousness – through the immanent, the transcendent is indicated.

The most philosophical among the branches of the non-dual Kashmir Śaivism is the *Pratyabhijñā* (Recognition) system, the aim of which is to logically prove the validity of the monistic Śaiva ontotheology, both in order to defeat rival doctrines as well as to help a spiritual aspirant reach liberation through the act of divine self-recognition. The seminal work of the system is Somānanda's (c. 900–950 AD) *Śivadṛṣṭi* (Cognition of Śiva), though the main concepts concerning here were formulated by Utpaladeva in his *Īśvarapratyabhijñā-kārikā* (Verses on the Recognition of the Lord) with auto-commentaries and further developed by Abhinavagupta in his extensive commentaries on Utpaladeva's work (*Īśvarapratjabhijñā-vimarśinī* and *Īśvarapratjabhijñā-vivṛti-vimarśinī*).

The main opponents, against whom Utpaladeva set to establish his *Pratyabhijñā* doctrine, were the proponents of the Buddhist logico-epistemological school, who thoroughly deconstructed the notions of (individual) self (*ātman*) and God. In Utpaladeva's reformulation, God (*Īśvara*) is the ultimate Self, the self of all selves, the only truly existent Subject of any cognition or action:

> The Self of all beings, the substratum of the establishment of all objects, who embraces the establishment of himself – since otherwise it would be impossible to establish all the various objects – self-luminous, whose nature is uniquely that of cognizer, formerly established, 'ancient', possesses

knowledge and action. Sovereignty (*aiśvaryam*) is established through inner awareness.[24]

He is actually 'directly perceived (*dṛṣṭe'pi*)' but 'not discerned for what He is because of delusion'.[25] The Self is directly perceived as 'I', pure subjectivity, the inner core of any cognition, unrecognised due to the fact that ordinary perception is too engrossed in the vision of perceived objects to be aware of itself as its foundation. Against the Buddhist argument that no permanent self is necessary in order to explain the flux of cognitions, Utpaladeva first explores the fact of memory and concludes that remembering would be impossible without a stable unificatory principle that underlines various cognitions: 'The mutual unification of all cognitions of things is [constituted by] the consciousness principle (*cittatvam*) whose form is all, since nothing distinct from it is admissible'.[26] He continues to define memory: 'The Free One (*svairī*), the perceiver of the object formerly perceived, continuing also to exist later, has the reflective awareness: "that". This is what is called "remembering"'.[27] In memory, the perception is not manifested in a form of an external object, but 'appears as resting on the self'.[28] In the reflective awareness (for instance: 'I saw that'), two elements are manifested within the cogniser: the perceiving subject and the perceived object.

The analysis of reflective awareness (*vimarśa*) makes for Utpaladeva's vital contribution and is of no lesser importance also to Abhinavagupta's aesthetics. Utpaladeva understands reflective awareness as the essential nature of the light (*prakāśa*)[29] of consciousness, on account of which consciousness can be called sentient. 'In the absence of this reflective awareness, light, though objects make it assume different forms, would merely be "limpid", but not sentient, since there is no "savouring" (*camatkṛteh*)'.[30] Consciousness (whether individual or absolute) savours itself by nature – in that sense, consciousness as defined by Utpaladeva is essentially aesthetic. It is alive/sentient precisely due to the fact that it is naturally self-aware, constantly relishing itself.

It is this reflective awareness that is transformed into perception of objects ('that'). When an object is perceived, the perceiving consciousness is seemingly perceiving something external, however it is actually perceiving an internal appearance and is hence again only aware of itself (although in a form of a perceived object). But in Utpaladeva's ontotheology this realisation does not lead to a solipsistic conclusion – on the contrary, since the individual consciousness is believed to be of the same essence as the absolute (only in a contracted form), it ultimately illustrates the workings of the mind of the divine Subject. It is through His reflective awareness that the absolute Subject 'transforms his very self, which is not the object of cognition, into cognizable reality'.[31]

By way of a thorough analysis every cognition can thus be traced back to its ultimate source, the subject. The unifying factor behind the multitude of sentient perceivers is pure subjectivity of the absolute Subject: 'The variety of notions such as "I" etc., does not entail diversity in the nature of the self, because a self is created precisely as he who lends himself to being the object of the reflective awareness "I" (*ahaṃmṛśyataiva*)'.[32] The pure reflective awareness of an individual subject, when untainted by anything that would particularise it and objectively define it ('I' without any 'am that'), is no longer individual, since it contains nothing that would make it such. Cognition, traced to its root, recognises itself as the ultimate Cogniser, the Subject of any imaginable cognition. The individual subject is limited through the identification with given objects of perception to which the notion 'I' is attached (a particular body, memories, etc.), but if the self rests in its own self, it is unlimited – to him 'things appear full of his own self, like his own self'.[33] But even if the self is forgetful of its own true nature, this is due to the play of the highest Lord, Parameśvara, and thus nothing is diminished:

> The fact that the various entities existing as subject and object of knowledge are determined as differentiated from each other and from Parameśvara (or from the self), is [due to] the creative power of Parameśvara, who, yet, thus shines in absolute fullness, neither does his own permanent form ever in any way cease to exist as a consequence of this determination.[34]

Thus the *Pratyabhijñā* thinkers built their ontotheology on the assumption of the absolute as Subject, whose reflective awareness serves as a fertile ground for an infinite multiplicity of diverse objects that appear in the mind of the divine Cognisor. Besides being blissful (*ānanda*), absolutely free to create anything (*svātantrya*), Śiva is also described as peaceful (*śānta*). In his commentary of Abhinavagupta's *Paramārthasāra* 10–11, for example, Yogarāja (second half of the eleventh century) explains that the ultimate principle is called serene (*śānta*), because He is 'reposing [ever] in its absolute nature, in unison (*sāmarasya*) with its Śakti, for there is no disturbance (*kṣobha*) arising from the dichotomy between the knower and the known. Yet, it does not at all resemble a piece of stone [as does the *śāntabrahman* of the Advaitins]'.[35]

To return to the topic of *śānta rasa*, several elements of the *Pratyabhijñā* philosophy can be recognised in Abhinavagupta's treatment of an aesthetic experience. Bhaṭṭa Nāyaka's approach towards *rasa* as pertaining to the spectator enables Abhinavagupta to intertwine aesthetics with the *Pratyabhijñā* doctrine to show the essentially recognitive nature of the *rasa* experience.

Among several sorts of cognitions, aesthetic perception holds a particularly esteemed position. A theatrical performance is uniquely tailored to enable the spectator to forget his ordinary identity, the objective limitations of time and place and to thus savour the taste of the emotions as such, or, as in the case of the highest, *śānta rasa*, the taste of consciousness itself. This is no doubt a beautiful theory – but how applicable is it to actual theatrical practice? In their analysis of Abhinavagupta's concept of *śānta rasa*, Masson and Patwardhan are, for example, quite critical in this respect:

> Abhinava's weakest point was that he did not really have any example of a great play in which *śāntarasa* was dominant, to lend credence to his theories.... By seeing beyond literature to the universal experience that lies behind it, Abhinava is undermining the autonomy, the uniqueness of literary experience. He is in danger of turning literature into an icon, a representational object,

an aid to devotion rather than an experience unique and precious for its own sake.... By insisting on putting such significance into poetry Abhinava is in danger of making much of Sanskrit literature top-heavy; one is wary that it simply cannot bear the philosophical burden he places on it.[36]

Nāgānanda, the play Abhinavagupta refers to as an exemplary for producing *śānta rasa*, 'could hardly be considered great literature'.[37]

Although 'the occurrence of *rasa* in poetry is wholly analogous to its occurrence in drama' and 'the same scheme (*saraṇi*) holds for both forms of art',[38] the text to which *śānta rasa* is ascribed in Ānadavardhana's masterpiece on poetics *Dhvanyāloka* (Light on *Dhvani*) and Abhinavagupta's commentary *Locana* (The Eye) is the epic *Mahābhārata*. The choice of *Mahābhārata* as the most representative piece of literature to produce *śānta rasa* seems quite unusual. The genre of epic (*itihāsa*) was traditionally rather strictly differentiated from poetry (*kāvya*), to which (besides drama) the *rasa* theory applies. It was Ānandavardhana's innovation to analyse it as a literary work. 'Before Ānanda nobody ever considered the possibility of looking at a piece of literature as a unified whole, with a single dominant suggestive atmosphere, and certainly not something of such gigantic proportions as the *Mahābhārata*'.[39]

Ānandavardhana's argument in favour of analysing both great epics as poetry is that they embody what he recognised as 'the soul of poetry', the suggestive meaning (*dhvani*). One of the ways to detect the suggestive meaning is to consider whether the words used are primarily meant to carry mere information and thus lose their importance after their meaning is comprehended (in which case there is no suggestive meaning) or there is some additional beauty in the way they are combined, which cannot be expressed in any other way and can hence be enjoyed even if heard/read over and over again. According to Ānandavardhana, this is true of the two great epics: 'And so it is that in such works as the *Rāmāyaṇa* and the *Mahābhārata* the battle scenes, etc., although they occur repeatedly, always appear new. Furthermore, one primary *rasa*, being woven into the work, gives it special meaning and extra beauty'.[40] But there is another reason why the *Mahābhārata* seems an unusual example of a work evoking *śānta rasa* – as an epic portraying rivalry between two clans that culminates in a horrific war of apocalyptic consequences, peace is not a frequent occurrence in the *Mahābhārata*. However, according to Ānandavardhana, that does not mean it is not suggested. On the contrary,

> in the *Mahābhārata* ... the great sage who was its author, by his furnishing a conclusion that dismays our hearts by the miserable end of the Vṛṣṇis and Pāṇḍavas, shows that the primary aim of his work has been to produce disenchantment with the world and that he has intended his primary subject to be liberation (*mokṣa*) from worldly life and the *rasa* of peace.[41]

The inclusion of the *Mahābhārata* notwithstanding, the actual number of literary works recognised to exemplify *śānta rasa* is negligible. To what extent, we might ask, does that diminish the value of Abhinavagupta's theory? To the extent that one would try to apply it specifically to classical Sanskrit poetry and drama, this might indeed turn out to be problematic. Masson and Patwardhan conclude their Introduction into *Śāntarasa and Abhinavagupta's Philosophy of Aesthetics* with an illustratory thought: 'One's mind is irreverently invaded by an image of Kālidāsa sitting politely bored, listening to Abhinavagupta explain to him the deeper significance of his plays, his ears really attuned to the joyous shouts of the spring festival taking place outside'.[42] But the boredom of an imaginary Kālidāsa is perhaps not the ultimate measure of the worth of Abhinavagupta's theoretical insight. Though his analysis of *rasa* takes place within the frame of traditional theory of performative arts (*nāṭyaśāstra*) and poetics (*kāvyaśāstra*) and is further defined by the scope of the original works Abhinavagupta comments upon (as well as the challenges posed by the preceding commentators), the stress of his theory is, nevertheless, placed primarily on the phenomenology of the aesthetic experience as perceived by the spectator/reader. The aesthetic stimulant, whether it comes by way of a play or a poem, is a means (*upāya*) of triggering the experience. It is of course not negligible, defining as it does the experience to some extent, but the essence of the *rasa* experience is nonetheless seen to transcend the domain of what provoked it. The insights of the *rasa* theory may thus prove to be equally, if not more, applicable outside the limited framework within which they were initially developed.

Another interesting question regarding the *rasa* doctrine is to what degree it informs the explication of the integral monistic ontology. As Gerow observed, '[s]ince the publication of K.C. Pandey's pioneering *Indian Aesthetics*, one of the leitmotifs of scholarship on Abhinavagupta's remarkable aesthetic theory has been commentary on its "philosophical" basis'.[43] However, explaining aesthetics via metaphysics does potentially lead to a reductive attitude towards aesthetics – an approach that cannot be traced back to Abhinavagupta. In order to properly honour his endeavours, Gerow proposes the opposite approach: '... we may better appreciate Abhinava's problem by asking how a sovereign aesthetics might help a Śaiva mystic develop a philosophically accountable notion of the Lord, who is, after all, *at play*'.[44] The play of the Lord is enacted within His divine mind as a dynamic dance of the multiplicity of phenomena on the screen of the unitary consciousness. The ultimate ontological ground is the epistemological playground of the absolute reflective awareness. The divine hides itself from itself in a creative act of self-forgetful veiling to perform the cosmic drama, in which an infinite number of individual subjects perceive the world as if it was exterior to their perception and suffer due to their imagined limitations, likes and dislikes. In the diametric move of self-recognition, the divine consciousness follows the stream of multiple perceptions back to their core in its own omnipotent bliss, savouring itself with the aesthetic amazement of the highest order. Since there is nothing outside the divine, the Absolute is poetically auto-poetic. Cosmic manifestation is akin to poetry. As Gerow puts it,

> Many theories of metaphor call attention to its reflexive character. A general view on the subject of poetic diction is that it is self-referential – calls attention

to itself as well as to what it says. If metaphor is the basic formal device of poetry – by which poetry itself is differentiated from non-poetic discourse – it would appear that Abhinava's notion that the absolute reality is reflexive consciousness is a necessarily poetic notion.[45]

It is worth adding here that cosmic manifestation is also poetic in the sense in which 'the soul of poetry' was defined by Ānandavardhana and Abhinavagupta – the immanent can be perceived as suggestive of the transcendent. The experience of *rasa* follows the trajectory of the divine aesthetically savouring itself to the point of all opposites merging in a state of the most potent, inherently dynamic inertness, called peace.

Is the *rasa* doctrine thus acceptable only as far as one is also prepared to adopt the onto-theology of the Pratyabhijñā? Kathleen Marie Higgins writes:

The Western reader might wonder whether Abhinava's theory has much relevance to someone who does not share his spiritual vision or the Indian conviction that *mokṣa* is the supreme end of human life. Abhinava's sugges-tions that aesthetic experience leads to tranquillity, and that this has some significant but complex relationship to equanimity in 'real' life are, however, transposable to Western formulation, regardless of whether we want to con-sider the possibility of a universal consciousness.[46]

In the final part of this chapter, I would therefore like to take Abhinavagupta's notion of *śānta rasa* out of its original context and think about how it might enrich our contemporary discourse on peace.

First, Abhinavagupta's conception inspires us to think of peace as inherently dynamic. It is not peace pertaining to a piece of stone, but rather something at the core of liveliness. Secondly, it is all-encompassing, beyond all opposites and yet embracing them. Such an absolute concept of peace, some might argue, is empty. If peace is axiomatically believed to be at the basis of any subjective experience and is also assumed to be ontologically all-pervasive, such 'peace' is inescapable. If there is no way to think of anything as not being peaceful in its essence, why speak of peace at all? A concept placed in the domain transcending all opposites is at risk of having no actual content. If it is not semantically limited so as to exclude what is non-peace, can it have any meaning at all?

To address this, I wish to draw our attention back to what I will call the aesthetic nature of the subjective experience of peace, not by following Abhinavagupta's argument directly, but rather by starting with a subjective experience of peace regardless of its cause and assume it is, as Abhinavagupta defined it, the resting of the self in itself, consciousness savouring its own taste. As such, it presents a state of intense attentiveness and inherent wonder (*camatkāra*), the bliss of it aligned with a feeling of fulfilment. Such a state may be triggered by a poem or a play, a tune or natural scenery. Or, alternatively, it might be provoked by some-thing seemingly contradictory, like a calamity of sorts. Peace is not only felt by a sensitive reader of the *Mahābhārata*, but is also experienced in everyday life in extraordinary, but not uncommon moments when distress caused by unfortunate circumstances is interrupted by a brief, unexpected flash of tranquillity. A sense of beauty and awe may sometimes occur in the midst of most unlikely circumstances. I believe Abhinavagupta's insights in the nature of *śānta rasa* could help account for what happens in such instances.

In that sense, an aesthetic experience is not defined as an experience of an aesthetic object, but as a specific type of perception by which any object can be experienced aesthetically. Constituent to an aesthetic experience defined thus are the following elements: (a) disinterestedness on the part of the perceiving subject; (b) the object being perceived non-instrumentally; and (c) the blissful (*ānanda*) nature of the experience. The experience of peace can be acknowledged as the peak aesthetic experience because all of the listed factors are experienced to the highest degree: it is the most disinterested of all of the experiences, the perception of the object is absolutely non-instrumental and the experience itself is intensely blissful. When such a perception takes the world as its object, the world is revealed as a place of immense beauty, fullness and aliveness. Thus the answer to the initial criticism regarding the meaninglessness of the concept of all-pervasive peace is that although peaceful does not objectively have an opposite, what could be described as non-peaceful is any perception that is based on personal concern regarding potential gain or loss, that perceives an object (whatever it may be) instrumentally and is therefore lacking in bliss (although it might be pleasurable).

Another argument against such a definition of the peaceful could be ethical. In times when superficial interpretations of 'non-duality' dominate the discourse of new-age commercial pop-spirituality, a concern that non-dual ontological assumptions may lead to a partial or even complete ignorance of ethical issues does seem well grounded. If the state of the world is perceived as ultimately non-problematic, then the suffering of another is not only tolerable, but can easily be explained away as illusionary. However, the conclusion Abhinavagupta draws is exactly the opposite – if I perceive suffering as illusionary, I will not hesitate to do what may bring me discomfort to help alleviate the suffering of those who still experience their pain as real. An experience of *śānta rasa* does not lead to ethical ignorance and insensitivity; on the contrary, it paves the way for the most radical expressions of compassion. 'Since then they who have apprehended the lower and the higher (selves) have nothing left to accomplish in reference to their own Self – their minds now being tranquil – the sacrifice of their own body, or wealth, for the welfare of others, is not incompatible with (their) tranquillity'.[47] Even more, any truly altruistic deed is possible *only* if the disinterested state of mind is achieved – in all other cases, our actions, no matter how non-selfish they may seem, are tainted by egotistic motivations. 'Whatever is done – teaching, giving of gifts, and finally the abandoning of the body – without reference to one's own interest and for the sake of another, is wholly inconceivable on the part of those who have not acquired a knowledge of the truth of the self'.[48]

In Abhinavagupta's view, the primary purpose of poetry or drama is to enable a reader or a spectator to experience bliss and not to provide moral guidance.

However, despite or precisely because of that it can be used to didactically influence those who come in contact with it. 'Princes, who are not educated in scripture ... can be given instruction in the four goals of men only by our entering into their hearts. And what enters into the heart is the relish of rasa ...'.[49] A subjective aesthetic experience of peace may thus also contribute to intersubjective ethical sensitivity that is a *sine qua non* of a more peaceful worldly co-existence.

Notes

1 Jeffrey Lloyd Masson and Madhav V. Patwardhan, *Śāntarasa and Abhinavagupta's Philosophy of Aesthetics* (Poona: Bhandarkar Oriental Research Institute, 1969).

2 Edwin Gerow and Ashok Aklujkar, 'On Śānta Rasa in Sanskrit Poetics', *Journal of the American Oriental Society* 92 (1972): 80–7.

3 Edwin Gerow, 'Abhinavagupta's Aesthetics as a Speculative Paradigm', *Journal of the American Oriental Society* 114, no. 2 (1994): 186.

4 Sheldon Pollock, 'What Was Bhaṭṭa Nāyaka Saying? The Hermeneutical Transformation of Indian Aesthetics', in *Epic and Argument in Sanskrit Literary History: Essays in Honor of Robert P. Goldman*, ed. Sheldon Pollock (Delhi: Manohar, 2010), 144.

5 Pollock, 'What was Bhaṭṭa Nāyaka Saying', 146.

6 Abhinavagupta, *Abhinavabhāratī (ABh)*, in Pollock, 'What Was Bhaṭṭa Nāyaka Saying', 165.

7 Abhinavagupta, *Abhinavabhāratī (ABh)*, trans. Raniero Gnoli, in Raniero Gnoli, *The Aesthetic Experience According to Abhinavagupta* (Rome: Istituto Italiano per il Medio ed Estremo Oriente, 1956), 53.

8 Abhinavagupta, *ABh*, in Gnoli, *Aesthetic Experience*, 53.

9 *Bhoga* is usually translated as 'enjoyment', as in Gnoli's translation of *Abhinavabhāratī* used here. Pollock, however, chose to translate it as 'experience', explaining his choice thus: 'The phenomenon of literary experientialization is far more than "enjoyment", as the usual translation has it. *Bhoga* signifies a complex kind of living-through, of disengaged engagement with, the various emotions'. Pollock, 'What Was Bhaṭṭa Nāyaka Saying',155.

10 Abhinavagupta, *ABh*, in Gnoli, *Aesthetic Experience*, 54.

11 Abhinavagupta, *ABh*, in Gnoli, *Aesthetic Experience*, 58.

12 Abhinavagupta, *ABh*, in Gnoli, *Aesthetic Experience*, 67.

13 Gnoli, *Aesthetic Experience*, 72–3.

14 Abhinavagupta, *ABh*, in Gnoli, *Aesthetic Experience*, 73–4.

15 Navjivan Rastogi, 'Quintessentiality of Camatkāra in Rasa-Experience: Revisiting Abhinavagupta', in *Abhinavā – Perspectives on Abhinavagupta: Studies in Memory of K.C. Pandey on His Centenary*, ed. Navjivan Rastogi and Meera Rastogi (New Delhi: Munshiram Manoharlal Publishers, 2013), 432.

16 Abhinavagupta, *ABh*, in Gerow, 'Abhinavagupta's Aesthetics', 194.

17 Abhinavagupta, *ABh*, in Gerow, 'Abhinavagupta's Aesthetics', 195.

18 Abhinavagupta, *ABh*, in Gerow, 'Abhinavagupta's Aesthetics', 196.

19 Abhinavagupta, *ABh*, in Gerow, 'Abhinavagupta's Aesthetics', 199–200.

20 Abhinavagupta, *ABh*, in Gerow, 'Abhinavagupta's Aesthetics', 200.

21 Abhinavagupta, *ABh*, in Gerow, 'Abhinavagupta's Aesthetics', 200.

22 Abhinavagupta, *ABh*, in Gerow, 'Abhinavagupta's Aesthetics', 200.

23 Abhinavagupta, *ABh*, in Gerow, 'Abhinavagupta's Aesthetics', 208.

24 Utpaladeva, *Īśvarapratyabhijñākārikāvṛtti (ĪPvṛ)*, in Raffaele Torella, trans., *The Īśvarapratyabhijñākārikā of Utpaladeva with the Author's Vṛtti: Critical edition and annotated translation* (Delhi: Motilal Banarsidass, 2002), 86.

25 Utpaladeva, *Īśvarapratyabhijñākārikā (ĪPK)*, in Torella, *Īśvarapratyabhijñākārikā*, 86.

26 Utpaladeva, *ĪPvṛ*, in Torella, *Īśvarapratyabhijñākārikā*, 103.
27 Utpaladeva, *ĪPK*, in Torella, *Īśvarapratyabhijñākārikā*, 104.
28 Utpaladeva, *ĪPK*, in Torella, *Īśvarapratyabhijñākārikā*, 107.
29 In perception, consciousness is 'light' in the absence of which nothing would 'shine' (appear). In the absolute sense, the whole cosmos is believed to appear in the consciousness of the absolute Cogniser (Śiva).
30 Utpaladeva, *ĪPvṛ*, in Torella, *Īśvarapratyabhijñākārikā*, 118.
31 Utpaladeva, *ĪPvṛ*, in Torella, *Īśvarapratyabhijñākārikā*, 122.
32 Utpaladeva, *ĪPK*, in Torella, *Īśvarapratyabhijñākārikā*, 123.
33 Utpaladeva, *ĪPK*, in Torella, *Īśvarapratyabhijñākārikā*, 155.
34 Utpaladeva, *ĪPvṛ*, in Torella, *Īśvarapratyabhijñākārikā*, 156.
35 Yogarāja, *Paramārthasāravivṛtti (PSV)*, in Lyne Bansat-Boudon and Kamaleshadatta Tripathi, trans., *An Introduction to Tantric Philosophy: The* Paramārthasāra *of Abhinavagupta with the Commentary of Yogarāja*, (London: New York: Routledge, 2013), 110.
36 Masson and Patwardhan, *Śāntarasa*, xvi–xvii.
37 Masson and Patwardhan, *Śāntarasa*, xvi.
38 Abhinavagupta, *Locana*, in Daniel H.H. Ingalls, Jeffrey Moussaieff Masson and Madhav V. Patwardhan, trans., *The* Dhvanyāloka *of Ānandavardhana with the* Locana *of Abhinavagupta* (Cambridge, MA and London: Harvard University Press, 1990), 224.
39 Masson and Patwardhan, *Śāntarasa*, ix–x.
40 Ānandavardhana, *Dhvanyāloka (DhĀl)*, in Ingalls, Masson and Patwardhan, *Dhvanyāloka of Ānandavardhana*, 690.
41 Ānandavardhana, *DhĀl*, in Ingalls, Masson and Patwardhan, *Dhvanyāloka of Ānandavardhana*, 690–1.
42 Masson and Patwardhan, *Śāntarasa*, xvii.
43 Gerow, 'Abhinavagupta's Aesthetics', 186.
44 Gerow, 'Abhinavagupta's Aesthetics', 187.
45 Gerow, 'Abhinavagupta's Aesthetics', 192.
46 Kathleen Marie Higgins, 'An Alchemy of Emotion: Rasa and Aesthetic Breakthroughs', *The Journal of Aesthetics and Art Criticism* 65, no. 1 (2007): 50.
47 Abhinavagupta, *ABh*, in Gerow, 'Abhinavagupta's Aesthetics', 203.
48 Abhinavagupta, *ABh*, in Gerow, 'Abhinavagupta's Aesthetics', 203.
49 Abhinavagupta, *Locana*, in Ingalls, Masson and Patwardhan, *Dhvanyāloka of Ānandavardhana*, 437.

References

Bansat-Boudon, Lyne, and Kamaleshadatta Tripathi, trans. *An Introduction to Tantric Philosophy: The Paramārthasāra of Abhinavagupta with the Commentary of Yogarāja*. New York and London: Routledge, 2013.
Gerow, Edwin. 'Abhinavagupta's Aesthetics as a Speculative Paradigm'. *Journal of the American Oriental Society* 114 (1994): 186–208.
Gerow, Edwin and Ashok Aklujkar. 'On Śānta Rasa in Sanskrit Poetics'. *Journal of the American Oriental Society* 92 (1972): 80–7.
Gnoli, Raniero. *The Aesthetic Experience According to Abhinavagupta*. Rome: Istituto Italiano per il Medio ed Estremo Oriente, 1956.
Higgins, Kathleen Marie. 'An Alchemy of Emotion: Rasa and Aesthetic Breakthroughs'. *The Journal of Aesthetics and Art Criticism* 65, no. 1 (2007): 43–54.
Ingalls, Daniel H.H., Jeffrey Moussaieff Masson and Madhav V. Patwardhan. *The* Dhvanyāloka *of Ānandavardhana with the* Locana *of Abhinavagupta*. Cambridge, MA and London: Harvard University Press, 1990.

Masson, Jeffrey Lloyd, and Madhav V. Patwardhan. *Śāntarasa and Abhinavagupta's Philosophy of Aesthetics*. Poona: Bhandarkar Oriental Research Institute, 1969.

Pollock, Sheldon. 'What Was Bhaṭṭa Nāyaka Saying? The Hermeneutical Transformation of Indian Aesthetics'. In *Epic and Argument in Sanskrit Literary History: Essays in Honor of Robert P. Goldman*, edited by Sheldon Pollock, 143–84. Delhi: Manohar, 2010.

Rastogi, Navjivan. 'Quintessentiality of Camatkāra in Rasa-Experience: Revisiting Abhinavagupta'. In *Abhinavā: Perspectives on Abhinavagupta: Studies in Memory of K.C. Pandey on His Centenary*, edited by Navjivan Rastogi and Meera Rastogi, 429–56. New Delhi: Munshiram Manoharlal Publishers, 2013.

Torella, Raffaele, trans. *The Īśvarapratyabhijñākārikā of Utpaladeva with the Author's Vṛtti: Critical edition and annotated translation*. Delhi: Motilal Banarsidass, 2002.

Part III
Poetic Dwellings and Landscapes of Peace

11 Blanchot's Hölderlin

Kevin Hart

Let us assume that we have a body of work – poetry, drama, essays, letters, a novel, and translations – that we call 'Hölderlin', and let us assume also that we can revolve it in our minds. One by one its aspects would come before us, and over time we would view many profiles of these aspects. Some readers might say that Hölderlin is finally given to them in a manifold of profiles, and it is easy to see what they would mean. They would grasp Hölderlin's individual works, of course, but also they would comprehend the work as a whole in terms of the genres he uses, through his characteristic themes, and with respect to his language, his rhythms, and his preferred forms. By way of association, they would see the work now in relation to Pindar and Sophocles or Klopstock and Schiller, and now in relation to George, Rilke, Celan, and René Char, or, in our own day, in conversation with Geoffrey Hill, Gustaf Sobin, or, as surprising as it might seem, John Ashbery.[1] Also by way of association, they would see Hölderlin emerge in his various maturities in an overlapping sequence: the novel *Hyperion* (1792–99), his early odes and epigrams (1797–99), the three versions of *Der Tod des Empedokles* (1798–99), the later odes (1798–1803), the hymns (1799–1805), the elegies (1800–01), *Die Trauerspiele des Sophokles* (1804), the Pindar fragments and commentaries (1805), and the last poems (1807–43). In the same manner, they would see Hölderlin in groups of themes, most likely beginning with 'Poetry and Philosophy', because, after all, the poet is linked from the beginning and forever with Greek thought, with Kant, with Hegel and Schelling, and, since the 1930s, with Heidegger.[2] Needless to say, that last name would also bring in tow the array 'Poetry and Politics', and in parts it would be darkly shaded. Doubtless too our admirers of the poet would see him in another arrangement, 'Poetry and Religion', for Hölderlin, student at the Tübingen *Stift*, has long been regarded as a *poeta theologus* and even a *sacer vates*. Greek and Hebrew elements would come into view, as would the hard words of the 'default of God', and much else besides.

Maurice Blanchot is a thinker, neither a critic nor a philosopher in the strict sense of either word, whose quest as a reader of literature is 'to find out what the fact that the poem, the song, exists really signifies'.[3] He is clear that it does not signify anything in aesthetics. Appeals to the aesthetic, he thinks, conceal the disruptive movement of writing rather than reveal anything telling about it. Instead, he wishes to make us see Hölderlin as surely within the field of 'Poetry and Religion' as within 'Poetry and Philosophy', and this is not because he is an apologist for religion, as other contemporary admirers of Hölderlin are: Hans Urs von Balthasar and Jean-Luc Marion, for example.[4] On the contrary, Blanchot is a radical and consequent atheist, his atheism not revolving around theism like a dark moon but rather preceding the distinction between the two and questioning the unity presumed in both terms ('God' and 'man').[5] Nor does he wish to make a small claim, that some of Hölderlin's poems are religious in one or another sense of the word.[6] Not at all: he makes a big claim, somewhat to the side of the small claim, that all of Hölderlin's poems involve the sacred or the holy. (I shall use both words interchangeably as translations of *das Heilige*.[7]) 'Religion' is bracketed. All literature draws on the sacred, or whatever is left of the sacred, Blanchot argues, although Hölderlin does so in an exemplary manner. So we are not talking about an argument for minor literature ('religious poetry') but about literature as such and its future. At the same time, though, Blanchot dismisses the very idea of there being a wholeness to Hölderlin, in all his works or even in just the one poem, that could be given to us through imaginative variation of the sort I have entertained. No sooner does he name Friedrich Gundolf in his early essay 'La parole "sacrée" de Hölderlin' (1946) than he acidly observes that the critic 'took care to ruin his study from the beginning by recalling that a poem is a whole'.[8] On the contrary, for Blanchot a poem has no unity in which it subsists or that properly supervenes with respect to it; and if he rejects the idea of a whole as early as *Le part du feu* (1949) he will come, by the time of *L'Entretien infini* (1969), to contest in the name of 'writing' all unity, wholeness and totality in whatever guise they assume: 'the idea of God, of the Self, of the Subject, then of Truth and the One, then finally the idea of the Book and the Work'.[9]

Blanchot remains close to Heidegger's reading of Hölderlin both in his selection of poems to discuss and at times in his language that echoes the phrasings of the German thinker in the essays gathered in *Erläuterungen zu Hölderlins Dichtung* (1st ed., 1951) and in courses of the 1930s and 1940s: 'Hölderlins Hymnen ("Der Rhein" und "Germanien")' (Winter, 1934–35) and 'Hölderlins "Andenken"' (Summer, 1942). 'The Sacred is the shining power that opens to the sacred all that its shining attains', Blanchot writes, with Heidegger's ink flowing from his pen.[10] At the same time Blanchot detaches himself from Heidegger: he is alert to the motif of exile in poetry, to poetry as exile, rather than to poetry arising from the *Heimat* and rooting one there.[11] That Heidegger writes of un-truth as wandering is of course true, but the wandering that leads to exile is of another order than the one that Heidegger discusses.[12] It is not a matter of a flight 'from the mystery to what is readily available, onward from one thing to the next' but the very nature of the poetic condition: to write is to be exiled, to belong 'to the outside', a notion that, as we shall see, comes to bear significant conceptual freight.[13] It is in terms of his distance from Heidegger as well as in his closeness to him that Blanchot writes of Hölderlin while drawing on a religious vocabulary. He uses a received lexicon ('the gods', 'revelation', 'sacred', 'sacrifice') that Hölderlin himself takes from Judaism, Paganism, and Christianity, a lexicon that is appropriated by Heidegger and put to his own ends, and one that is redirected by Blanchot to his own ends, which are as unorthodox as Hölderlin's and Heidegger's but in quite other ways.

On four occasions Blanchot writes at length about Hölderlin. First, in conversation with a then recent issue of the review *Fontaine* devoted to French translations of the poet and two of his most eminent critics, he proposes to specify the nature of the poet's '"sacred" speech', the quotation marks indicating his prudential distance from the convictions of both the poet and the thinker.[14] Then, responding to Karl Jaspers's *Strindberg und van Gogh: Versuch einer pathographischen Analyse unter vergleichender Heranziehung von Swedenborg und Hölderlin* (1949), he attends to the question of Hölderlin's madness. Then, in a study of the poet's itinerary, he seeks to discern 'the mystery of the God's departure' in the poetry.[15] And, finally, with a backward glance to his first interest, Blanchot tries to rethink what 'sacred' might mean for literature and for us. This is the sequence from *Le part du feu* (1949) to 'La folie par excellence' (1951) to *L'Espace de littérature* (1955) to *L'Entretien infini* (1969). These essays are not the only places where Blanchot refers to Hölderlin, and not the only occasions when the pressure of the poet can be felt.[16] It is true that René Char becomes increasingly the exemplary poet for Blanchot, yet it is no less true that one or more profiles of Hölderlin stand behind the figure of Char, including the figure of the poet as prophet. And if it is true that Hölderlin marks for Blanchot one vanishing point in poetry, in what poetry can and really must say to us today, it is equally true that Mallarmé marks another.[17]

Blanchot learns slightly different things from Hölderlin and Mallarmé, however, although both occur in the difficult and painful field of modern religious experience. Mallarmé taught Blanchot a great deal about how the felt absence of God could lead one to the 'pure novel', a work of fiction that could come about only through the insights of Mallarmé's atheistic mysticism.[18] Those insights are a counterpart in literature of what St John of the Cross's 'the dark night of the soul' is for Christian spirituality. Blanchot learned from Mallarmé that there is a link between self-sacrifice and literature: for a writer to touch the night may not be the same as for a mystic to lose himself in 'a divine Conception' but it is to reach 'the extreme point of an entirely conscious meditation', one that associates literature and an endless movement of dying that denies any possibility of there being a unified self.[19] From Hölderlin he learned something else, a lesson that comes from another place, that the sacred must be retained if there is to be art, including poetry as art. And yet, against Hölderlin, he also maintained that one may not pass in any direction between 'sacred' and 'whole', and indeed that the sacred – or, better, the 'Sacred' – is what disrupts the whole.

*

Let us take this lesson and counter-lesson as our starting point. 'It is well known', Blanchot says, 'that Hölderlin profoundly linked god and man, each needing the other, with only poetic existence ensuring the truth of their union'.[20] This god, or more properly these gods, do not exist *a se*, as the Christian God does. In the Christian vision, at least according to St Thomas Aquinas, our relations with God are real, *relatio realis*, although God's relations with us are unreal, *relatio rationis tantum*: we depend ontologically on the Creator, but the Creator does not need to have created anything in order to enjoy all possible perfections as God.[21] For Hölderlin, though, the gods are secondary to nature, φύσις: even 'the sacred

Father', the highest of the gods, would languish without the poets and without people reading them. In 'Der Mütter Erde' Hölderlin writes,

> Denn wenn er schon der Zeichen genug
> Und Fluthen in seiner Macht und Wetterflammen
> Wie Gedanken hat der heilige Vater,
>   unaussprechlich wär er wohl
> Und nirgend fänd er wahr sich unter den Lebenden wieder
> Wenn zum Gesange nicht hätt ein Herz die Gemeinde.

> [For though he has tokens enough
> And floods in the power and thunder-flames
> Like thoughts, the holy Father,
>   yet, it seems, he would be unutterable
> And nowhere he would find himself truly again among the living
> If the community had no heart for singing.][22]

It is the poets who enable the Father to be properly praised (that is, celebrated), and so keep him in relation with mortals, and yet the poet requires a community to read and recite his poems. The lines bespeak either a smooth or a vicious circle. If all is well – if the community sings the poet's words, and the gods are one with us – the circle may well continue endlessly, enriching all who participate in it, and, if so, a *Volksreligion* will be founded and elaborated. Yet if the circle breaks, if the people find themselves without gods, the old ones having become incredible and the new ones not yet having revealed themselves, then the community will not sing the poet's words, and the poet cannot praise the gods. This is of course the situation in which Hölderlin found himself: 'in dürftige Zeit', in a thin time, as he says in 'Brod und Wein'; and the only way out of this vicious circle, the sole way for Hölderlin to be a poet, Blanchot argues, is for him to 'exist as a presentiment of himself', to be ahead of himself and his age.

Now we might take this affirmation of the poet to be a doctrine of poetic or even religious genius. Only the poet, the truly creative person, lives prophetically! There is a sense in which Blanchot could subscribe to this proposition, for he considers the poet to speak prophetically of the Outside, the non-place where being passes endlessly into image, which will interest us later.[23] Yet Blanchot prefers another explanation of how the poet can reach into the future, an explanation that is entirely paradoxical. The poet already abides in time to come because the poem not only reaches ahead but also precedes him, and he conforms himself to the poem. One can unravel this paradox by appealing to different Greek sources. One can point to Plato's argument in book ten of *The Republic* (596b) and in *Cratylus* 389b that the craftsman sees the εἶδος of what he creates in his soul, or one can refer to a quite traditional notion of inspiration: the poem is given to the poet, and is unjustified by any principle of sufficient reason, certainly any principle of sufficient *historical* reason. Also, the poem is always ahead of itself insofar as its meanings are never to be unfolded in any present. I may read 'Heimkunft' every year of my life, and each time I may write a commentary on it, one that is each year to be succeeded by a longer account of the subtleties, heights and depths of the elegy. At no time, though, can I say that I have exhausted the poem, for it is always possible that new relations between its figures and tropes can be discerned, new links between this elegy and other poems by Hölderlin, hidden paths from 'Heimkumft' to odes by Pindar, as well as to poems still be to be written that may illuminate facets of the elegy in utterly unexpected ways. Thoroughly reasonable, and completely in tune with contemporary secular criticism, this kind of explanation is precisely *not* what Blanchot offers us. 'Hölderlin's entire work', he tells us, 'bears witness to the awareness of an anterior power surpassing the gods as well as men, the very one that prepares the universe to be "completely whole"'.[24]

So Blanchot allows Hölderlin's commitment to the All, and to the wholeness of the All, to come before us, front and center. 'To be one with all – that is the life of the divinity, that is the heaven of man', Hyperion writes to Bellarmin in the poet's early epistolary novel, but of course Blanchot cannot agree with him or any of the Romantics who yearn for the All or the One.[25] He may acknowledge the 'joyful movement' of inspiration affirmed there and also the 'desire for death' latent in Hyperion's words, yet it is the wholeness of the All, and the possibility of fusion with it, that he seeks to expose as delusive.[26] Before he critically engages with the All, however, Blanchot looks over his shoulder to Heidegger who determines that this prior wholeness is 'das Heilige', the holy or the sacred. Several poems could have served as proof texts – 'Patmos', 'In Lieblicher Bläue...', and even, perhaps, 'Der Einzige' among them – but we are turned to read or re-read some lines in the unfinished Pindaric hymn 'Wie Wenn am Feiertage...' (1799) in the context of Heidegger's elucidation of that poem. This is, Heidegger testifies, 'the purest poem on the essence of poetry', and it is one that in 1946 had just been translated into French by Joseph Rivan.[27] The lines have become well known in discussions of poetry and philosophy as well as in poetry and religion:

Jezt aber tagts! Ich harrt und sah es kommen,
Und was ich sah, das Heilige sei mein Wort.
Denn sie, sie selbst, die älter denn die Zeiten
Und über die Götter des Abends und Orients ist,
Die Natur is jezt mit Waffenklang erwacht,
Und hoch vom Aether bis zum Abgrund nieder
Nach vestem Geseze, wie einst, aus heiligem Chaos gezeugt,
Fühlt neu die Begeisterung sich,
Die Allerschaffende wieder.

[But now day breaks! I waited and saw it come.
And what I saw, the hallowed [Sacred], my word shall convey,
For she, she herself, who is older than the ages
And higher than the gods of Orient and Occident,
Nature has now awoken amid the clang of arms,
And from high Aether down to the low abyss,

According to fixed law, begotten, as in the past, on holy Chaos,
Delight the all-creative,
Delights in self-renewal.][28]

'What is the Sacred?' Blanchot asks, and right away gives Heidegger's answer: 'the immediate that is never communicated but is the principle of all possibility of communication'.[29] No contestation *of* the sacred is considered, only a contestation *within* the sacred.

Blanchot does not disagree with Heidegger when he looks to Hölderlin's commentary on Pindar ('Das Höchste') where we are told that 'The immediate, strictly speaking, is impossible for mortals, as for immortals'.[30] The Sacred is not a property of the gods but precedes them, the gods being, for the Greeks, the highest beings in the cosmos and not beyond it.[31] The Sacred is not Chaos, as Heidegger surmises. Blanchot clearly marks his disagreement with the German thinker, for Chaos is nocturnal, he says, and there is nothing of the night, nothing of Novalis's *Hymnen an die Nacht* (1800), say, in Hölderlin. Mallarmé is Blanchot's poet of the night, the poet of the dark nights of Tournon, and Hölderlin is his poet of the morning. (We might wonder how to square Blanchot's insistence on Hölderlin as a poet of the morning with the German's lines about the 'heiliger Nacht' ['holy night'] in 'Brot und Wein' or the 'heil'ger Nacht' in 'Lebenslauf' and elsewhere.) The Sacred 'is the day', Blanchot adds, 'but anterior to the day, and always anterior to itself'.[32] So we have another paradox, a very important one to Blanchot, one that makes him into who he is, but before I try to make sense of it, I would like to explore an alternate path that could have been followed in explicating these lines from 'Wie Wenn am Feiertage...'.

It is important to recognize, as Heidegger does, that the poem is framed by a holiday: a holy day, feast day, or festival.[33] Just as the countryman sees that his vines are safe the morning after a storm, so too the poets are lightly embraced by nature. When nature seems to be sleeping, in winter for example, the poets may seem sad, yet they are nonetheless divining the presence of the All. Hölderlin, the 'I' of the poem, has been waiting for the daybreak on a holy day, even if it is an ordinary day regarded by virtue of its presence as holy. We remember how in ancient Greece a πόλις would send a man as a representative to a distant festival, and this person, the θεωρός, would witness the event and participate in it. On coming back home, he would tell his people what he had seen, but on returning might find himself changed by what he has seen and done. He would be no longer entirely one with his people. We remember too how Plato in the parable of the Cave in book seven of *The Republic* thought of the philosopher as θεωρός, as a person who, through the practice of dialectic, achieved insight into the forms, saw the truth of being, and returned to tell his countrymen about it only to be rejected by them.[34] Plato has internalized the arduous journey to another place to participate in a festival. In 'Wie Wann am Feiertage...' Holderlin also interiorizes the role of the θεωρός but in terms of the poet, not the philosopher.[35] He waits reverently, perhaps right where he is, for the day to break, sees the holy coming, the light that reaches over the horizon just before the sun appears, and rejoices in its advent.[36] He accepts the role of witnessing it: 'das Heilige sei mein Wort'. The poetry he shall write from now on will not actually say the holy in so many words (he does not write 'das Heilige *ist* mein Wort') but, in adopting the optative mood, he prays that the poetry will preserve the mystery of nature as a mystery, preserve its immediacy, and communicate it indirectly, not translate it into other terms.

For Hölderlin, the poetry to be written by him precedes composition in that it is the silent mystery of nature that shall be artfully gathered in individual poems. At the same time, the poet lives ahead of himself by dint of what he has witnessed. He lives now in order to be the man who will have written those poems and thereby testified to the wordless mystery that has been revealed to him. As Heidegger notes, this poetry will be the 'hymn *of* the holy',[37] and because the holy is the All it can bring forth endless poems if the poet is strong enough to write them. The poet is charged with a hard task: not to speak the holy directly, for it would annul itself in losing its immediacy, but to preserve the unsayable mystery of the holy in his own words that speak of phenomena. In talking of particular, ordinary things – vines and storms, mountains and fields, rivers and the homeland – the poet must also allow the holy immediately to communicate itself beneath, within and around those very words. We can say, as a placing shot, that the poet must sacrifice himself, including his personal themes as poet, in order to allow the sacred to speak silently through his poems. Poetry, then, will be oriented to θεωρία, the rapt contemplation of the All, and will be offered to the community to which the poet belongs.[38] If the community accepts the words of the poet, they will sing his words; if they refuse those words, then the 'tender and infinite relations' of mortals and gods, mediated without mediation by the poet, will be broken.[39] Note that in speaking of holiness, the poet does not necessarily speak of the gods; for the holy is what appears, and not the gods, who remain distant in this meager time.

For Heidegger, 'Wie Wenn am Feiertage...' is pure in that it speaks clearly of the essence of poetry. As Paul de Man rightly observes, Heidegger needs Hölderlin to be a witness to the coming of being. He, the thinker, 'is not so sure that he has seen Being and, in any case', de Man says, then adds a little archly, 'he knows that he has nothing to say about it beyond the fact that it conceals itself. Yet he does not intend to give up discourse since it is still his intention to collect and found Being by means of language'.[40] In other words, Heidegger needs a θεωρός to come home to Germany from Greece to give witness to the coming of Being that he has experienced there. 'There must be someone', de Man continues, 'of unquestionable purity, who can say that he has traveled this route and seen the flash of illumination. One such person is enough, but there must be one. For then, the truth, which is the presence of the present, has entered the work that is language'.[41] Of course, the poetry does not *say* the holy, as Heidegger wishes; it can communicate it only obliquely and silently, and although de Man does not take this path one might argue that this obliqueness justifies in principle Heidegger's exegetical procedures in reading Hölderlin.

It may be that de Man insists overly that Heidegger must *make* Hölderlin declare that poetry *says* the holy. Why? Because if one looks aside, to Heidegger's lecture course in the winter semester of 1942–43, just three years after writing his commentary on 'Wie Wenn am Feiertage...', we find an alternative way of thinking about the matter. Here is Heidegger reflecting on a thought of Parmenides in the following way:

> Sight into the unconcealed transpires first, and only, in the disclosive word. Sight looks, and is the appearing self-showing that it is, only in the disclosive domain of the word and of telling perception. Only if we recognize the original relation between the word and the essence of Being will we be capable of grasping why, for the Greeks and only for them, to the divine (τὸ θεῖον) must correspond the legendary (ὁ μῦθος). This correspondence is indeed the primordial essence of all analogy (homology), the word 'ana-logy' taken essentially and literally.[42]

And, a little later, speaking of the plastic arts, he tells his students,

> The statue and the temple stand in silent dialogue with man in the unconcealed. If there were not the *silent word* [schweigende Wort], then the looking good as sight of the statue and of the features of its figure could never appear.[43]

It is entirely possible that Heidegger credits Hölderlin with saying the 'silent word' in his poems, the word that the words of an ode, elegy or hymn can indicate without actually pronouncing. Heraclitus would have been in the background of Heidegger's thinking here: 'The lord whose oracle is in Delphi neither speaks out nor conceals, but gives a sign'.[44] And of course the idea of poetry speaking a silent word has become familiar in contemporary poetics. Consider Octavio Paz, who states the idea without leaning very heavily on either philosophical or religious language: 'The Word has its roots in a silence *previous* to speech – a presentiment of language. Silence, *after* the Word, is based on a language – it is an embodied silence. The poem is the trajectory between these two silences – between the wish to speak and the silence that fuses the wishing and the speaking'.[45]

*

It is one thing to debate how to read Hölderlin and another to ponder what of Hölderlin to read, indeed what counts as 'Hölderlin'. Heidegger's poet is a man of morning knowledge, and de Man, who stealthily follows the thinker step by step, like a patient hunter walking in the footprints of his prey, does not question this. Certainly Hölderlin speaks of the holy as a gaiety, even if in the midst of our tragedy joy is sometimes expressed by way of mourning. We lament the passing of the gods and anticipate with hope and joy those who will come. Nonetheless, poetry will preserve holiness in this distressed time, and holiness is the very ether of the gods. When they reveal themselves once more, perhaps in an utterly unexpected manner, the poets will have preserved the medium of revelation, and the people will be ready to receive the revelation if they have sung the poems. In more modest ways, both T. S. Eliot and Karl Rahner offer versions of the same position within orthodox Christianity.[46]

Yet is Hölderlin so sanguine, even in his witnessing of the holy? It is significant that Heidegger excludes from the text of the ode the fragmentary lines at the end of the poem as textually established by Friedrich Beißner:

> Des Vaters Stral, der reine versengt es nicht
> Und tierferschüttert, die Leiden des Stärkeren
> Mitleidend, bleibt in den hochherstürzenden Stürmen
> Des Gottes, wenn er nahet, der Herz doch fest.
> Doch weh mir! Wenn von

> Weh mir!

> [The Father's ray, the pure, will not sear our hearts
> And, deeply convulsed, and sharing his sufferings
> Who is stronger than we are, yet in the far-flung down-rushing storms of
> The God, when he draws near, will the heart stand fast.
> But, oh, my shame! When of

> My shame!][47]

The poet as θεωρός is changed by what he experiences, and sometimes finds himself woefully inadequate to what he witnesses. So fully does Hölderlin identify himself with the role of receiving the holy and communicating it in his poems that he sees himself, in the draft's final lines, as 'Den falschen Priester', the false priest, who has been burnt by the divine and can at best sing 'the warning song'.[48] How far we have come from 'Des Morgans' where the approach to the gods is made in all innocence and without the slightest sense of things going awry. 'Komm nun, o komm, und eile mir nicht nicht zu schnell, / De goldner Tagm zum Gipfel des Himmels fort!' ['Now come, O come, and not too impatiently, / You golden day, speed on the peaks of heaven!'],[49] Hölderlin sings, and then, later, says, gloriously, 'Des frohen übermüthigen du, daß er / Dir gleichen möchte' ['But at my happy arrogance now you smile, / That would be like you']. It is that smile at 'frohen übermüthigen' that is severely denied in the last stanzas of 'Wie Wenn am Feiertage...'. And yet we have not come far from *Der Tod des Empedokles*. In the first version of the play we hear Hermokrates talk of Empedokles:

> Es haben ihn die Götter sehr geliebt.
> Doch nicht is er der erste, den sie drauf
> Hinab in sinnenlose Nacht verstoßen
> Vom Gipfel ihres güttigen Vertrauns,
> Weil er des Unterschieds zu sehr vergab
> Im übergroben Glück, und sich allein
> Nur fühlte.

[The gods once loved him overmuch.
Yet he is not the first whom soon enough
They thrust into the senseless night,
Cast down from heights of their familiarity
Because he proved forgetful of the difference
In his extravagant delight, feeling for
Himself alone.][50]

Taken together, *Der Tod des Empedokles* and 'Des Morgans' illustrate the motif from Empedocles with which Hölderlin closely identified, Φιλίαν καὶ Νεῖκος, love and strife.

It is difficult to interpret the final lines of 'Wie Wenn am Feiertage...; with any certainty, not knowing how they would have fitted into the poem were it completed, but once we place them in context we can get some idea of what is being said:

Und sag ich gleich,

Ich sei genaht, die Himmlischen zu schauen,
Sie selbst, sie werfen mich tief unter die Lebenden
Den falschen Priester, ins Dunkel, daß ich
Das warnende Lied den Gelehrigen singe.
Dort

[And let me say at once,

That I approached to see the Heavenly,
And they themselves cast me down, deep down
Below the living, into the dark cast down
The false priest that I am, to sing,
For those who have ears to hear, the warning song.
There].[51]

The poet witnesses the holy and seeks to go further, to approach the gods themselves, but the right time for their self-revelation has not yet come, and the divine beings remain far from all mortals, including poets, and cast Hölderlin down as punishment for his presumption at seeking to see them or even name them. Now he is lower than ordinary mortals. The proper religious role of the poet is that of the participation of the θεωρός; as a self-appointed priest, actively mediating between mortals and gods, he can only be a failure.

Why does the image of the priest even occur to Hölderlin as something he could plausibly adopt as a figure for himself as poet? It follows generally from his understanding of Oedipus. 'The *intelligibility* of the whole', he writes of *Oedipus Tyrannos*, 'rests primarily on one's [ability to] focus on the scene where Oedipus interprets the saying of the oracle *too infinitely*, and is tempted into *nefas*'.[52] And, Hölderlin notes, 'right afterwards [Oedipus] speaks in priestly fashion'.[53]

The idea of the poet as priest also follows, more particularly, from the answer that Heinse, the dedicatee of 'Brot und Wein', supposedly gives to the question 'wosu Dichter in dürftiger Zeit?' ('who wants poets at all in lean years?'):

> Aber sie sind, sagst du, wie des Weingotts heilige Priester,
>   Welche von Lande zu Land zogen in heilige Nacht.

> (But they are, you say, like those holy ones, priests of the wine god
>   Who in holy night roamed from one place to the next.)[54]

I pause to note that Hölderlin says, 'Wie' ('like'): the poets are *like* the priests of Dionysius and are not priests themselves. Still more pressingly, Hölderlin thinks of the figure of the priest because of the lines in 'Wie wenn am Feiertage...' about Semele, the priestess of Zeus.

Ovid beautifully tells the story of Semele in *Metamorphoses* III: 308–12. In Hölderlin's words, 'da sie sichtbar / Den Gott zu sehen begehrte, sein Bliz auf Semeles Haus / Und die göttlichgetroffne gebahr, / Die Frucht des Gewitters, den heiligen Bacchus' ['when she desired to see / The god in person, visible, did his lightning fall / On Semele's house, and the divinely struck gave birth to / The thunder-storm's fruit, to holy Bacchus'].[55] What Hölderlin omits is precisely Juno's plot against Semele, her disguising herself as an old woman and telling the young woman to ask Jove, who had already promised her anything, to appear as he really is, with 'his bright three-forkèd mace'. As Juno well knows, the mere sight of Jove will kill Semele, even if he brings his 'second mace', which has 'less fierceness, lesser might'. Yet it is far more likely that Hölderlin had in mind the opening lines of Dionysus's first speech in Euripides's *The Bacchæ* than the more complete and elegant narrative of Ovid.[56] He is entranced by the rhythm of Euripides's lines. Dionysus begins,

> Ἥκω Διὸς παῖς τήνδε Θηβαίαν χθόνα
> Διόνυσος,ὃν τίκτει ποθ' ἡ Κάδμου κόρη
> Σεμέλη λοχευθεῖσ' ἀστραπηφόρωι πυρί·

In Hölderlin's rendition, we read,

> Ich komme, Jovis Sohn, hier ins Thebanerland,
> Dionysos, den gebar vormals des Kadmos Tochter
> Semele, geschwängert von Gewitterfeur.[57]

> [I am Dionysius, the son of Zeus,
> come back to Thebes, this land where I was born.
> My mother was Cadmus' daughter, Semele by name,
> midwived by fire, delivered by the lightning's
> blast.][58]

And of course Euripides's audience would have known that Semele was the priestess of Zeus.

Even if we prefer Ovid's fuller narrative to Euripides', the outcome is the same. Even Zeus's second mace is too much for Semele. As Arthur Golding renders Ovid's lines:

> She, being mortal, was too weak and feeble to withstand
> Such troublous tumults of the heavens, and therefore out of hand
> Was burnèd in her lover's arms.[59]

There is no trickery for Hölderlin, however; his downfall is brought about purely by hubris. Now he is to warn the people that in this thin time, the late Enlightenment, it is not propitious to approach the gods or to seek to name them. The tryst of Semele and Zeus brings forth wine; the 'fruit' of Hölderlin's misjudged encounter with the gods is the very poem we read, along with other poems by Hölderlin, and its incompleteness is a sign of the damage that too much illumination can make. The most that a poet can do is to preserve the holy in his song; it cannot be rendered as ὁ μῦθος. Of course, it would be difficult for Heidegger to fold these fragmentary lines into his understanding of the hymn. For him, 'being is prior to all beings, for they owe what they are to being. And the gods likewise: to the degree that they *are*, and however they are, they too all stand *under* "being"'.[60] It makes sense for Heidegger for the poet to bespeak the holy, but it would be difficult for him to explain how the gods, beings, are experienced as *higher* than being. Only the Christian God is higher or beyond being, ὑπερουσία, and Hölderlin and Heidegger agree that the Christian God has withdrawn from the Earth.

*

It is hard to see either Semele or Hölderlin as sacrificing themselves according to Christian models of redemptive sacrifice. To understand what is at issue for Hölderlin and Blanchot, we must ponder tragic sacrifice, and keep in mind that neither Aristotelian nor Hegelian notions of tragedy are fitting for the poet. Schelling's concept, as sketched in the tenth of the *Philosophische Briefe über Dogmatismus und Kritizismus* (1795), is closer to Hölderlin. 'Greek tragedy honored human freedom; it was the *honor* due to freedom. Greek tragedy honored human freedom, letting its hero *fight* against the superior power of fate. In order not to go beyond the limits of art, the tragedy had to let him succumb. Nevertheless, in order to make restitution for this humiliation of human freedom extorted by art, it had to let him *atone* even for the crime committed by fate'.[61] In Hölderlin's own terms, as he writes about *Oedipus*: 'Tragedy resides in this: that the immediate God, wholly one with man (for the god of an apostle is less immediate but is the highest the understanding is capable of, in the highest spirit), that an infinite enthusiasm infinitely, which is to say in antithesis, in consciousness that cancels out [*aufhebt*] consciousness, and sacramentally departing from itself, apprehends itself, and the god, in the shape of death, is present'.[62] Tragedy, here, is religious rather than aesthetic or ethical. That the suffering Hölderlin sees himself as an Oedipus figure is clear from his letters to Casimir Ulrich Böhlendorff in December 1802 ('consumed in flames – we expiate the flames which we could not tame', 'I may say that Apollo has struck me').[63] The poet grasps himself as poet, as truly inspired, in drawing close to death.

The motif of this sort of sacrifice surfaces from time to time in Hölderlin's own poems. *Der Tod des Empedokles* offers several instances where one witnesses the mutual engagement of pain and joy.[64] Consider, above all, however, these demanding lines from 'Der Rhein':

> Denn weil
> Die Seeligsten nichts fühlen von selbst,
> Muß wohl, wenn solches zu sagen
> Erlaubt ist, in der Götter Nahmen
> Theilnehmend fühlen ein Andrer,
> Den brauchen sie; jedoch ihr Gericht
> Ist, daß sein eigenes Haus
> Zerbreche der und das Liebste
> Wie den Feind schelt' und sich Vater und Kind
> Begrabe unter den Trümmern,
> Wenn einer, wie sie, seyn will und nicht
> Ungleiches dulden, der Schwärmer.

> [For since
> The most Blessed in themselves feel nothing
> Another, if to say such a thing is
> Permitted, must, I suppose,
> Vicariously feel in the name of the gods,
> And him they need; but their rule is that
> He shall demolish his
> Own house and curse like an enemy
> Those dearest to him and under the rubble
> Shall bury his father and child,
> When one aspires to be like them, refusing
> To bear with inequality, the fantast.][65]

We may well wonder what it means to feel vicariously. Compassion might be an answer, but can one feel compassion for the gods? Could the Greeks? In 'Der Rhein' Hölderlin seems to figure the poet's role by way of empathy, of passing from the inside to the outside, but in his essay on the ground of Empedocles, he says something quite different: 'Precisely because he expresses the deepest inwardness, the tragic poet denies altogether his individuality, his subjectivity, and thus also the object present to him; he conveys them into a foreign personality, into a foreign objectivity'.[66] Could it be that vicarious feeling 'in the name of the gods' is true inwardness? That could at least be an understanding of what the θεωρός takes away from the festival.

We have seen that in 'Wie Wenn am Feiertage...' Hölderlin is punished by the gods for seeking to be a priest, and that the figure of the priest is inappropriate to the poet. Not reading the fragmentary end of the hymn, Blanchot denies that there is a punishment for hubris, and focuses on the sacrifice of Hölderlin as poet. Thus in 'La folie par excellence' we read,

> We must say this once again: it is not excess that the gods punish in the man who becomes the mediator; it is not punishment for an offence that sanctions his ruin, but the poet must be ruined in order that in and through him the measureless excess of the divine might become measure, common measure; this destruction, moreover, this effacement at the heart of language is what makes language speak, and causes it to be the sign *par excellence*. 'That which is without language, in him becomes language; that which is general and remains in the form of the unconscious, in him takes the form of the conscious and concrete, but that which is translated into words is for him what cannot possibly be stated (*Empedocles*)'.[67]

Sacrifice, for Blanchot, is tragic but not punitive; the poet is ruined by having to render the measureless in measure, the ineffable in meter. If one thinks (for Hölderlin) of Kant on the aesthetic idea, one also thinks (for us) of Marion urging us to think of revelation, saturation to the second degree, being received in the mode of counter-experience.[68] Above all, though, sacrifice for Blanchot is not redemptive. The poet is no priest and redeems nothing through his sacrifice, and even his authority as poet is expiated in the writing of the poem. We are used to thinking of redemptive sacrifice rendering something sacred. Here, though, it is tragic sacrifice that brings about the sacred. The poet waits for dawn to break and makes himself available to receive what he cannot bear, and it is that 'beginning, the origin', that is 'the point where the Sacred communicates and founds itself in the firm resolve of language'.[69] That Blanchot passes over the punishment for hubris may make us wonder if his theory of sacrifice is drawn from Hölderlin.

As early as one of his regular columns in *Journal des débats*, 'Oeuvres poétiques' (1942), Blanchot had written, 'The poet, careful as he may be to use a technique for which his most conscious "I" is necessary, tries to sacrifice [*tend à sacrifier*] that which constitutes the limit, boundary, pleasure without risk, consciousness of this "I". By putting into play his personal gifts, he proceeds to an existence in which this word personal no longer has any meaning. "*Je est un autre*", [I is an other] said Rimbaud'.[70] Not that Blanchot draws this theory of sacrifice from Rimbaud rather than Hölderlin. It is grounded, rather, in the speculations of Georges Bataille, specifically in his account of the nexus of communication and sacrifice, and was adapted by Blanchot as a general view, one that he had sufficiently made his own by the time he introduced *Faux pas* (1943): 'The writer is summoned by his anguish to an actual sacrifice of himself' [*L'écrivain est appelé par son angoisse à un réel sacrifice de lui-même*].[71] The theory of sacrifice that Blanchot ventures is articulated in terms of theories of contestation and communication.[72]

Let us interrupt Blanchot meditating on an aspect of Bataille's *L'Expérience intérieure* (1943): 'Contestation, experience, communication are narrowly defined terms – to say no more. Contestation is the calling into question of a particular and limited being, and it is also, consequently, an effort to break this particularity and these limits… Communication thus begins being authentic only when experience has stripped existence'.[73] Communication, here, is neither verbal nor non-verbal; rather, it is fusion with what is, amounting to a loss of self, as in death, and – following Laure's speculations – is held to be sacred.[74] That Bataille's ideas were refined in conversation with Blanchot is evident from reading *L'Expérience intérieure*, where Bataille credits his friend with pointing out that in experience authority must expiate itself.[75] At any rate, for Blanchot we see that the poet, in trying to resolve an intolerable tension, sacrifices or – more accurately – *contests* himself in the writing of a poem. Whatever authority he has been given by the gods is expiated in the writing of the poem, and the poem communicates the holy without recourse to ὁ μῦθος. And so we have 'sacred' speech in Hölderlin's poetry, a speech that is justified not by the poet's authority or his individual concerns but that stands outside all personality and all dialogue; it comes from the anteriority of the holy and points to a time to come in which the gods may reveal themselves, which means that it has no ground in the present.[76]

*

At the time of 'La parole "sacrée" de Hölderlin' (1946) Blanchot figures 'sacred' speech solely by way of contestation and communication. If we move ahead, though, to *L'Espace littéraire* (1955) we hear Blanchot speaking in slightly different terms:

> When art is the language of the gods, when the temple is the house where the god dwells, the work is invisible and art unknown. The poem names the sacred, and men hear the sacred, not the poem. And yet the poem names the sacred as unnamable; in this silence it speaks the unspeakable…. The poem shows, then; it discloses, but by concealing, because it detains in the dark that which can only be revealed in the light of darkness and keeps this mystery dark even in the light which the dark makes the first dawn of all. The poem is effaced before the sacred which it names; it is the silence that brings to the word the god that speaks in silence – but since the divine is unspeakable and ever speechless, the poem, through the silence of the god which it encloses in language, is also that which speaks as poem, and shows itself, as a work, at the same time that it remains hidden.[77]

In hearing Blanchot here we also hear Heidegger, the thinker of 'The Origin of the Work of Art' (1935) and of the 'silent word', and we hear the word 'sacred' pronounced without quotation marks because Blanchot is speaking of the Greeks, and not Hölderlin, of a world in which τὸ θεῖον is indexed to ὁ μῦθος. Notice that there is no talk of sacrifice here, only of the sacred. And yet, as we shall see, sacrifice has not dropped out of the picture altogether. Notice too that the sacred is not held in suspense anymore. If we ask ourselves what happens in the passage from 'sacred' to '"sacred"', we have only to read on for a few more pages for Blanchot to ask the same question in his own way:

> Why is art so intimately allied with the sacred? It is because in the relationship between art and the sacred, between that which shows itself and that which does not ... the work finds the profound *reserve* which it needs.... What will become of art, now that the gods and even their absence are gone, and now that man's presence offers no support? ... And where will art find, *elsewhere than in the divine, elsewhere than in the world* [ailleurs que dans le divin, ailleurs que dans le monde], the space [*l'espace*] in which to base and to withhold itself?[78]

The answer, Blanchot tells us, is 'the experience of the origin';[79] this origin is the 'elsewhere', yet to go there is not to encounter plenitude, the sudden communication of the dawn that is the Sacred as evoked in 'La folie par excellence'. On the contrary, in *L'Espace littéraire*, art 'indicates the menacing proximity of a vague and vacant outside, a neutral existence, nil and limitless; art points into a sordid absence, a suffocating condensation where being ceaselessly perpetuates itself as nothingness'.[80] The poet, in seeking the origin of the poem, grasps image rather than being, not as an accidental mistake but as a constitutive error of writing, for being gives itself in art only as image. Not *an* image, but *image*. Being and truth are withheld, and indeed the desired wholeness of the poem, if there was one to begin with, is shattered by the experience of vacancy rather than fullness.

When Blanchot turns to characterize this situation, he does so in terms taken directly from Hölderlin. 'Do we have art?' Blanchot asks, and then responds to his own question:

> The poet is the one who, through his sacrifice, keeps the question open in his work. At every time he lives the time of distress, and his time is always the empty time when what he must live is the double infidelity: that of men, that of the gods – and also the double absence of the gods who are no longer *and* who are not yet. The poem's space is entirely represented by this *and*, which indicates the double absence, the separation at its most tragic instant. But as for whether it is the *and* that unites and binds together, the pure word in which the void of the past and the void of the future become true presence, the 'now' of dawn – this question is reserved in the work.[81]

These are difficult sentences, and they call for interpretation along two paths.

1   As we know, for Hölderlin the gods have turned away from mortals; it is a hard lesson he learns from Sophocles's tragedy *Oedipus Tyrannos*, namely the teaching of the caesura. In pain, we mortals must also turn away from the gods. 'Nämlich es reichen / Die Sterblichen eh' an den Abgrund', we are told in the second version of 'Mnemosyne': 'Namely mortals / Are closer to

the abyss'.[82] Our touching of the abyss is a mimetic act of infidelity, and is what Hölderlin calls the 'categorical reversal'. The poem abides in a double space, that between mortals and gods, and that between the old gods and the gods that may one day come. With respect to this first space Blanchot says, 'Hölderlin maintains the purity of the sacred realm left empty by the double infidelity of men and gods. For the sacred is this very void, the sheer void of the interval which must be kept pure and empty according to the ultimate requirement "Preserve God with the purity of what distinguishes"'.[83] The Sacred then has passed from immediacy to interval, from the incommunicable allowing communication to take place to the holding apart and together of a space between gods and mortals, an interval that is *neutral* precisely because it is neither that of the gods or mortals.

2   The poem's space, Blanchot tells us, is represented by the 'and' between the gods who are no longer and the gods who are to come. Is this 'the *and* that unites and binds together'? If so, this 'and' would stand for 'religion', which, as Blanchot tells us much later, in *L'Écriture du désastre* (1980), is, as his friend Lévinas says, 'that which binds, that which holds together'.[84] Yet it is possible, he implies, that there is another relation than one that binds, a relation that would not be religious at all: 'a non-bond which disjoins beyond unity – which escapes the synchrony of "holding together", yet does so without breaking all relations or without ceasing, in this break or in this absence of relation, to open yet another relation'.[85] If this is so, the sacrifice of the poet in the writing of a poem, the 'most tragic instant', would open a space that is sacred but not religious, and the sacred for us (though not for the Greeks) would be indexed to the third relation. Would an artist be able to draw on this sense of what remains of the sacred, rather than on religion (even a religion of art), in order to make art? That is exactly the question that Blanchot poses, and the question, he thinks, that abides in the artwork itself. Whether a Romantic or post-Romantic poem can be art, as Pindar's odes are art, turns on the question of the sacred being posed in it, and doubtless not being answered by the poem itself. Art, for us, is not the Jena 'literary absolute' in which philosophy is folded into literature but is rather the question of the sacred that is posed in all rigor but that awaits an answer.[86]

Blanchot's affirmation of the sacred in Hölderlin, centered on tragic sacrifice, makes no reference to the role that Christ plays in the poetry. 'Hölderlin's Christology will not be found where those who squeeze the text look for it; perceivable only as a water-mark, it is dissolved throughout the existential statement as a whole, and can be most powerfully felt when directly contradicted by the framework inside which it is stretched'.[87] Balthasar's assessment is entirely correct. To be sure, Hölderlin is no orthodox Christian: he incorporates the revelation of the Christ into the Greek theophanies that preoccupy him. In 'Der Einzige' he calls Christ 'Mein Meister und Herr!' ['My Master and Lord'] and 'mein Lehrer!' ['my Teacher!']; but in the end Christ remains 'Des Halbgott' ['the demigod'], as Hölderlin says in 'Patmos'. How could one not ascribe Arianism to him? For

Marion, to be sure, there are richer though more elusive Christian resources in Hölderlin's poems. It is in the default of the divine, the Frenchman thinks, that we find the very question of how God manifests Himself. That manifestation turns on distance: the Father must withdraw for us to see Him in and through the incarnation of Christ. We read Hölderlin well, Marion thinks, when we see in his poems that 'withdrawal' is 'the most radical mode of presence for God'.[88] One may or may not agree with Marion. Yet it is plain that Blanchot bypasses 'Der Einzige', 'In Lieblicher Bläue...', and 'Patmos' and the other poems on which Marion draws to make his case.

The poet's sacrifice, for Blanchot, is his act of holding himself between mortals and gods, between the old gods and the new gods, maintaining 'the extreme limit of suffering'.[89] We have art if we can draw upon the Sacred, but we do not have the 'now', the immediate that is the Sacred, only the neutral space that the poet's tragic sacrifice *renders* sacred. Is this sufficient for art? Or do we need the sacred to be folded into religion in order to have art? We do not know. Of course, if we reflect on what Blanchot has said about the Outside and wish to assimilate it to the neutral space of the Sacred, we have a problem, for the language about the one ('sordid absence', 'suffocating condensation') does not square with the language about the other ('purity'). And yet the 'experience of the origin', which generates the dark language about the Outside, seems to be Blanchot's answer to the pressing question as to the relation between art and the sacred. The 'elsewhere' he seeks is the origin of the poem. No satisfactory solution is possible in the terms offered in *L'Espace littéraire*, and so we must pass to Blanchot's last discussion of Hölderlin in *L'Entretien infini*. That occurs in 'Le Grand Refus', Blanchot's long and patient engagement with the great poet Yves Bonnefoy who, like Hölderlin, but in a completely different manner, prizes the relation of poetry and the 'now' in his early essays gathered in *L'Improbable* (1959) and throughout his poetry, beginning with *Du mouvement et de l'immobilité de Douve* (1953).

There can be no dialectical rethinking of immediacy, Blanchot insists, nor can it be thought by way of mystical fusion. He accepts Hölderlin's statement that '*the immediate is for mortals as well as for mortals, strictly speaking, impossible*', and responds by saying that, if this is so, 'it is perhaps because impossibility – a relation escaping power – is the form of relation with the immediate'.[90] Here we find Blanchot shifting the center of gravity of Hölderlin's statement, seeking to make the immediate (and hence the Sacred) into what he calls 'the third relation' or 'the neutral relation'. The only relation one can have with the Outside is neutral; but how can we discover this obscure region, when it is beyond the realm of phenomena? There is an attunement to it, Blanchot suggests, and that is suffering, 'The present of suffering is the abyss of the present, indefinitely hollowed out and in this hollowing indefinitely distended, radically alien to the possibility that one might be present to it through the mastery of presence'.[91] In suffering, 'we are delivered over to another time – to time as other, as absence and neutrality; precisely to a time that can no longer redeem us, that constitutes no recourse'.[92] If the poet sacrifices himself or herself, it is the suffering that comes of this act that leads him or her to the Outside and that stalls one there in fascination, in relation with 'the *ungraspable that one cannot let go of*,[93] that is, being passing endlessly into image. Immediate presence, then, is 'presence as Outside'[94] or, as he glosses the statement (revolving and even reversing 'presence' in order by his lights to be more precise), presence as 'a neutral, an empty or an infinite presence' so that 'The immediate as non-presence, that is to say, the immediately *other*'.[95] Of course, suffering is not the preserve of the poets; and so anyone can pass from the phenomenal world to the non-world of the Outside, and so 'discover the obscure'. Yet we cannot name this obscurity; we can only respond to it. The self-sacrifice of the poet can be saved only if his or her sacrifice, his or her response to the Outside, is regarded as exemplary. The writing of poetry is a model of experience as such.

What remains of the Sacred exists without religion, Blanchot thinks, and it breaks up the unity and wholeness that religion has traditionally offered. Blanchot's Hölderlin has no Christian moment, as we may well have surmised; he has no religious moment, either. Sacrifice for him is entirely tragic which, for Blanchot, means that it is endless contestation with no redemption in play, a contestation that shatters the manifold of profiles that give us the unity of 'Hölderlin'. Heidegger's Hölderlin is the θεωρός of Being. Blanchot's Hölderlin is the θεωρός of the Outside.

Notes

1 See Geoffrey Hill, 'Little Apocalypse: Hölderlin: 1770–1843', *Selected Poems* (London: Penguin, 2006), 18. The impress of Hölderlin on Hill goes far beyond this short lyric, needless to say. Also see Gustaf Sobin, *Collected Poems*, ed. Esther Sobin et al., intro. Andrew Joron and Andrew Zawacki (Greenfield, MA: Talisman House, 2010). John Ashbery's ways of drawing on and displacing Hölderlin in a good many of his poems has not yet been detailed. Two poems in particular that could be approached with Hölderlin in mind are 'Evening in the Country', *The Double Dream of Spring* (New York: Ecco Press, 1976), 33–34, and 'Poem at the New Year', *Hotel Lautréamont* (New York: Alfred A. Knopf, 1992), 83.

2 On the relation of Hölderlin to Kant, less well known than the other philosophical relations, see Jean-Luc Nancy, 'Hyperion's Joy', trans. Christine Laennec and Michael Syrotinski, *The Birth to Presence*, trans. Brian Holmes et al. (Stanford: Stanford University Press, 1993), 58–81.

3 Maurice Blanchot, 'The "Sacred" Speech of Hölderlin', *The Work of Fire*, trans. Charlotte Mandell (New York: Fordham University Press, 1995), 114. Also see, 'Note', *The Infinite Conversation*, trans. Susan Hanson (Minneapolis: The University of Minnesota Press, 1993), xi.

4 See Hans Urs von Balthasar, *The Glory of the Lord: A Theological Aesthetics*, V: *The Realm of Metaphysics in the Modern Age*, trans. Oliver Davies et al. (Edinburgh: T. and T. Clark, 1991), 298–338, and Jean-Luc Marion, *The Idol and Distance: Five Studies*, trans, and intro. Thomas A. Carlson (New York; Fordham University Press, 2001), §§ 8–12.

5 Blanchot observes, 'We carry on about atheism, which has always been a privileged way of talking about God', which may be true of some atheists, but the atheism that he affirms is not merely a denial of theism. See his *The Writing of the Disaster*, trans. Ann Smock (Lincoln: The University of Nebraska Press, 1986), 92.

6 For a study that reads Hölderlin in this way, see Martin F. A. Simon, *Friedrich Hölderlin, The Theory and Practice of Religious Poetry: Studies in the Elegies* (Stuttgart: Hans-Dieter Heniz, Akademischer Verlag Stuttgart, 1988).

7   Needless to say, various distinctions may be drawn between 'sacred' and 'holy' but to impose any one of them here would skew the poems under consideration.

8   Blanchot, 'The "Sacred" Speech of Hölderlin', 111.

9   Blanchot, *The Infinite Conversation*, xii.

10 Blanchot, 'The "Sacred" Speech of Hölderlin', 119.

11 See Blanchot, *The Space of Literature*, trans. Ann Smock (Lincoln: University of Nebraska Press, 1982), 237–9.

12 See Martin Heidegger, 'On the Essence of Truth', *Pathmarks*, ed. William McNeill (Cambridge: Cambridge University Press, 1998), 150–2. Also see his *Introduction to Metaphysics*, trans. Ralph Manheim (New Haven: Yale University Press, 1959), 92.

13 Blanchot, *The Space of Literature*, 237.

14 Blanchot's text is a review essay that refers to four pieces in *Fontaine* 54 (1946): Hölderlin's 'Tel qu'en un jour de fête', trans. Joseph Rivan, 199–205, Heidegger's 'L'hymne "Tel qu'en un jour de fête"', trans. Joseph Rivan, 206–35, Hölderlin, 'Dix letters', trans. Denise Naville, 256–9, and Rainer Maria Rilke, *A Hölderlin*, trans. Jean Wahl, 260–2.

15 See Blanchot, 'Le Tournant', *Nouvelle Nouvelle Revue Française*, 25 (1955), 110–20, and 'L'Itinerarie de Hölderlin' in *L'Espace littéraire* (Paris: Gallimard, 1955), 363–74.

16 See, for example, Blanchot, 'Holderlin', *L'Observateur* 17, 3 August 1950, 19.

17 See my essay, 'Blanchot's Mallarmé', *Southerly*, 68: 3 (2008), 135–58.

18 See Blanchot, 'Le Roman pur', *Chroniques littéraires du 'Journal des débats': Avril 1941–août 1944*, ed. Christophe Bident (Paris: Gallimard, 2007), 506–13.

19 Blanchot, 'The Silence of Mallarmé', *Faux Pas*, trans. Charlotte Mandell (Stanford: Stanford University Press, 2001), 101, 104.

20 Blanchot, 'The "Sacred" Speech of Hölderlin', 116.

21 See Thomas Aquinas, *Summa theologiæ*, I, q. 13 art. 7, c; I, q. 28, art. 1, ad 3; I, q. 45 art. 3, *On the Power of God*, trans. Lawrence Shapcote (1932; rpt. Eugene, OR: Wipf and Stock, 2004), I, q. iii, iii, and *Truth*, I, q. 4 art. 5, reply.

22 Michael Hamburger, trans., *Friedrich Hölderlin: Poems and Fragments* (London: Anvil Press, 1994), 401. All quotations from the poems of Hölderlin, in German and English, will be from this edition (reproduced by kind permission of Carcanet Press Limited, Manchester, UK), except for some lines from the second version of 'Mnemosyne' and translations from *Der Tod des Empedokles,* which will be taken from *The Death of Empedocles: A Mourning Play*, trans., intro. and notes David Farrell Krell (Albany: State University of New York Press, 2008).

23 See Blanchot, 'Prophetic Speech', *The Book to Come*, trans. Charlotte Mandell (Stanford: Stanford University Press, 2003), 79–85. Also see 'The Beast of Lascaux', trans. Leslie Hill, *The Oxford Literary Review* 22 (2000), 12.

24 Blanchot, 'The "Sacred" Speech of Hölderlin', 119.

25 Friedrich Hölderlin, *Hyperion or The Hermit in Greece*, trans. Ross Benjamin (Brooklyn: Archipelago Books, 2008), 12.

26 See Blanchot, 'Hölderlin's Itinerary', *The Space of Literature*, 269.

27 Heidegger, 'Hölderlin and the Essence of Poetry', *Elucidations of Hölderlin's Poetry*, 61. For other French translations of the poet, see Friedrich Hölderlin, *Oeuvres*, trans. Philippe Jaccottet (Paris: Gallimard, 1967).

28 Hamburger, Friedrich Hölderlin, 395.

29 See Heidegger, 'As When on a Holiday...', *Elucidations of Hölderlin's Poetry*, 85, 90, 94. Note that Heidegger observes 'that the holy is entrusted to a mediation by the god and the poets, and is born in song, threatens to invert the essence of the holy into its opposite. The immediate thus becomes something mediated', 94. Blanchot does not cite the second sentence. See Blanchot, 'The "Sacred" Speech of Hölderlin', 120.

30 See Hamburger, *Friedrich Hölderlin*, 639.

31 On this theme, see Robert Sokolowski, *The God of Faith and Reason: Foundations of Christian Theology*, 2nd ed. (Washington, DC: Catholic University of America Press, 1995), esp. ch. 2.

32 Blanchot, 'The "Sacred" Speech of Hölderlin', 121.
33 See Heidegger, 'Remembrance', *Elucidations of Hölderlin's Poetry*, 126–8.
34 See Andrea Wilson Nightingale, *Spectacles of Truth in Classical Greek Philosophy: 'Theoria' in its Cultural Context* (Cambridge: Cambridge University Press, 2004), ch. 2.
35 See Gregory Nagy, 'Early Greek Views of Poets and Poetry', *The Cambridge History of Literary Criticism*, I: *Classical Criticism*, ed. George A. Kennedy (Cambridge: Cambridge University Press, 1989), 28.
36 On the motif of waiting, see Heidegger, *Hölderlin's Hymn 'The Ister'*, trans. William McNeill and Julia Davis (Bloomington: Indiana University Press, 1996), 55.
37 Heidegger, 'As When on a Holiday,' 98.
38 See Heidegger, *Plato's 'Sophist'*, trans. Richard Rojcewicz and André Schuwer (Bloomington: Indiana University Press, 1997), 44. Also see *Parmenides*, 147.
39 Hölderlin, 'On Religion', *Essays and Letters on Theory*, ed. Thomas Pfau (Albany: State University of New York Press, 1988), 92.
40 Paul de Man, 'Heidegger's Exegeses of Hölderlin', *Blindness and Insight: Essays in the Rhetoric of Contemporary Criticism*, 2nd ed. rev. (London: Methuen, 1983), 253.
41 De Man, 'Heidegger's Exegeses of Hölderlin', 253.
42 Heidegger, *Parmenides*, trans. Richard Rojcewicz and André Schuwer (Bloomington: Indiana University Press, 1992), 114.
43 Heidegger, *Parmenides*, 116.
44 G. S. Kirk and J. E. Raven, *The Presocratic Philosophers: A Critical History with a Selection of Texts* (Cambridge: Cambridge University Press, 1962), 211.
45 Octavio Paz, 'Recapitulations', *Alternating Current*, trans. Helen R. Lane (London: Wildwood House, 1974), 69.
46 See T. S. Eliot, 'The Social Function of Poetry', *On Poetry and Poets* (London: Faber and Faber, 1957), esp. 25, and Karl Rahner, 'Poetry and the Christian', *Theological Investigations*, IV: *More Recent Writings*, trans. Kevin Smyth (London: Darton, Longman and Todd, 1974), 357–67.
47 Hamburger, *Friedrich Hölderlin*, 399.
48 On this neglected aspect of the poem, see Jennifer Anna Gosetti-Ferencei, *Heidegger, Hölderlin, and the Subject of Poetic Language: Toward a New Poetics of Dasein* (New York: Fordham University Press, 2004), 101–2.
49 Hamburger, *Friedrich Hölderlin*, 78.
50 Hölderlin, *The Death of Empedocles*, 45.
51 Hamburger, *Friedrich Hölderlin*, 399.
52 Hölderlin, 'Remarks on "Oedipus"', *Essays and Letters on Theory*, 102. Also see on this point Philippe Lacoue-Labarthe, 'The Caesura of the Speculative', *Typography: Mimesis, Philosophy, Politics*, ed. Christopher Fynsk and intro. Jacques Derrida (Cambridge: Harvard University Press, 1989), 233.
53 Hölderlin, 'Remarks on "Oedipus"', 103.
54 Hamburger, *Friedrich Hölderlin*, 271.
55 Hamburger, *Friedrich Hölderlin*, 396.
56 The draft of the poem follows Hölderlin's manuscript translation of the opening of *The Bacchæ*. See David Constantine, *Hölderlin* (Oxford: Clarendon Press, 1988), 119.
57 Hölderlin, *Sämtliche Werke*, ed. Friedrich Beißner, 8 vols (Stuttgard: W. Kohlhammer Verlag, 1952), 5, 41.
58 David Grene and Richard Lattimore, eds., *The Bacchæ*, in *The Complete Greek Tragedies, Euripides* V (Chicago: The University of Chicago Press, 1959), 155.
59 Ovid, *Metamophoses*, trans. Arthur Golding, ed. Madeleine Forey (London: Penguin, 2001), Book III, ll. 387–9.
60 Heidegger, 'On the Essence and Concept of φύσις', *Pathmarks*, 184.
61 F. W. J. Schelling, 'Philosophical Letters on Dogmatism and Criticism', *The Unconditional in Human Knowledge: Four Early Essays; 1794–1796*. trans. Fritz Marti (Lewisburg: Bucknell University Press, 1980), 193.

62 Constantine, trans., 'Notes to *Antigone*', *Hölderlin's Sophocles: Oedipus and Antigone* (Highgreen, Tarset: Bloodaxe Books, 2001), 116.
63 Hölderlin, *Essays and Letters on Theory*, 150, 152. For the idea that the sacrifice is national, a view that goes back to Friedrich Wolters, see Joseph Suglia, *Hölderlin and Blanchot on Self-Sacrifice* (New York: Peter Lang, 2004), 51.
64 See Hölderlin, 'Becoming in Dissolution', *Essays and Letters on Theory*, 98.
65 Hamburger, *Friedrich Hölderlin*, 436–7.
66 Hölderlin, 'The Ground for "Empedocles"', *Essays and Letters on Theory*, 52.
67 Blanchot, 'Madness *par excellence*', trans. Ann Smock, *The Blanchot Reader*, ed. Michael Holland (Oxford: Basil Blackwell, 1995), 124.
68 See Immanuel Kant, *Critique of Judgement*, trans. James Creed Meredith (Oxford: Oxford University Press, 1969), 175–6, and Marion, *Being Given: Toward a Phenomenology of Givenness*, trans. Jeffrey L. Kosky (Stanford: Stanford University Press, 2002), 215–6.
69 Blanchot, 'The "Sacred" Speech of Hölderlin', 123.
70 Blanchot, 'Involuntary Poetry', *Faux Pas*, 133. The passage in question first appeared in 'Oeuvres poétiques', *Journal des débats*, 9 December 1942, 3.
71 Blanchot, 'Author's Introduction', *Faux Pas*, 5.
72 Bataille's understanding of sacrifice was developed over several decades. A signal text is the well known essay 'Hegel, la mort et le sacrifice' (1955), *Oeuvres complètes*, 12 vols (Paris: Gallimard, 1970–88), XII, 326–45, but the theme of sacrifice is announced as early as 'Sacrifices' (1936), the text that accompanies artwork by André Masson. See *Oeuvres complètes* I, 87–96.
73 Blanchot, 'Inner Experience', *Faux Pas*, 40. Trans. modified.
74 See Jeanine Herman, trans., *Laure: The Collected Writings* (San Francisco: City Lights Books, 1995), 37–94.
75 See Georges Bataille, *Inner Experience*, trans. and intro. Leslie Anne Boldt (Albany: State University of New York Press, 1988), 53.
76 Blanchot speaks of René Char in the same terms. See his 'The Beast of Lascaux', 12.
77 Blanchot, *The Space of Literature*, 230.
78 Blanchot, *The Space of Literature*, 233.
79 Blanchot, *The Space of Literature*, 233.
80 Blanchot, *The Space of Literature*, 242–43.
81 Blanchot, *The Space of Literature*, 247.
82 I quote from Anital Ronell's translation as quoted by Jacques Derrida, *Memories: For Paul de Man*, trans. Cecile Lindsay et al. (New York: Columbia University Press, 1986), 4.
83 Also see Blanchot, *The Space of Literature*, 274, 245 n. 7.
84 Blanchot, *The Writing of the Disaster*, 64.
85 Blanchot, *The Writing of the Disaster*, 64.
86 See Blanchot, 'The Athenaeum', *The Infinite Conversation*, 351–9, and Philippe Lacoue-Labarthe and Jean-Luc Nancy, *The Literary Absolute: The Theory of Literature in German Romanticism*, trans. Philip Barnard and Cheryl Lester (Albany: State University of New York Press, 1988).
87 Balthasar, *The Glory of the Lord*, V, 320.
88 Marion, *The Idol and Distance*, 89.
89 Blanchot, *The Space of Literature*, 274.
90 Blanchot, 'The Great Refusal', *The Infinite Conversation*, 39.
91 Blanchot, 'The Great Refusal', 44.
92 Blanchot, 'The Great Refusal', 44.
93 Blanchot, 'The Great Refusal', 45.
94 Blanchot, 'The Great Refusal,' 46.
95 Blanchot, 'The Great Refusal', 440 n. 7.

References

Aquinas, Thomas. *On the Power of God.* Translated by Lawrence Shapcote, 1932. Reprint, Eugene, OR: Wipf and Stock, 2004.

Aquinas, Thomas. *Summa theologiæ.* Cambridge: Blackfriars, 1964–1973.

Aquinas, Thomas. *Truth.* Translated by Robert W. Mulligan, James V. McGlynn and Robert W. Schmidt. 3 vols. 1952–1954. Reprint, Indianapolis: Hackett, 1994.

Ashbery, John. 'Evening in the Country'. In *The Double Dream of Spring*, 33–4. New York: Ecco Press, 1976.

Ashbery, John. 'Poem at the New Year'. In *Hotel Lautréamont*, 83. New York: Alfred A. Knopf, 1992.

Balthasar, Hans Urs von. *The Glory of the Lord: A Theological Aesthetics.* Vol. 5. *The Realm of Metaphysics in the Modern Age.* Translated by Oliver Davies et al. Edinburgh: T. and T. Clark, 1991.

Bataille, Georges. *Inner Experience.* Translated and introduction by Leslie Anne Boldt. Albany: State University of New York Press, 1988.

Bataille, Georges. 'Sacrifices'. In *Oeuvres completes*, 1:87–96. Paris: Gallimard, 1970.

Bataille, Georges. 'Hegel, la mort et le sacrifice'. In *Oeuvres completes*, 12:326–45. Paris: Gallimard, 1988.

Blanchot, Maurice. 'Hölderlin'. *L'Observateur* 17 (3 August 1950): 19.

Blanchot, Maurice. 'Hölderlin's Itinerary'. In *The Space of Literature*, translated by Ann Smock, 269–76. Lincoln: University of Nebraska Press, 1982.

Blanchot, Maurice. 'Inner Experience'. In *Faux Pas*, translated by Charlotte Mandell, 37–41. Stanford: Stanford University Press, 2001.

Blanchot, Maurice. 'Involuntary Poetry'. In *Faux Pas*, translated by Charlotte Mandell, 132–4. Stanford: Stanford University Press, 2001.

Blanchot, Maurice. 'L'Itinerarie de Hölderlin'. In *L'Espace littéraire*, 363–74. Paris: Gallimard, 1955.

Blanchot, Maurice. 'Le Roman pur'. In *Chroniques littéraires du 'Journal des débats': Avril 1941–août 1944*, edited by Christophe Bident, 506–13. Paris: Gallimard, 2007.

Blanchot, Maurice. 'Le Tournant'. *Nouvelle Nouvelle Revue Française* 25 (1955): 110–20.

Blanchot, Maurice. 'Madness *par excellence*'. Translated by Ann Smock. In *The Blanchot Reader*, edited by Michael Holland, 110–28. Oxford: Basil Blackwell, 1995.

Blanchot, Maurice. 'Prophetic Speech'. In *The Book to Come*, translated by Charlotte Mandell, 79–85. Stanford: Stanford University Press, 2003.

Blanchot, Maurice. 'The "Sacred" Speech of Hölderlin'. In *The Work of Fire*, translated by Charlotte Mandell, 111–31. New York: Fordham University Press, 1995.

Blanchot, Maurice. 'The Athenaeum'. In *The Infinite Conversation*, translated by Susan Hanson, 351–9. Minneapolis: The University of Minnesota Press, 1993.

Blanchot, Maurice. 'The Beast of Lascaux'. Translated by Leslie Hill. *The Oxford Literary Review* 22 (2000): 9–18.

Blanchot, Maurice. 'The Great Refusal'. In *The Infinite Conversation*, translated by Susan Hanson, 33–48. Minneapolis: The University of Minnesota Press, 1993.

Blanchot, Maurice. 'The Silence of Mallarmé'. In *Faux Pas*, translated by Charlotte Mandell, 99–106. Stanford: Stanford University Press, 2001.

Blanchot, Maurice. *Faux Pas.* Translated by Charlotte Mandell. Stanford: Stanford University Press, 2001.

Blanchot, Maurice. *The Infinite Conversation.* Translated by Susan Hanson. Minneapolis: The University of Minnesota Press, 1993.

Blanchot, Maurice. *The Space of Literature.* Translated by Ann Smock. Lincoln: University of Nebraska Press, 1982.

Blanchot, Maurice. *The Writing of the Disaster.* Translated by Ann Smock. Lincoln: The University of Nebraska Press, 1986.

Constantine, David, trans. 'Notes to *Antigone*'. In *Hölderlin's Sophocles: Oedipus and Antigone*, 113–18. Highgreen, Tarset: Bloodaxe Books, 2001.

Constantine, David. *Hölderlin*. Oxford: Clarendon Press, 1988.

Derrida, Jacques. *Memories: For Paul de Man*. Translated by Cecile Lindsay et al. New York: Columbia University Press, 1986.

Eliot, Thomas S. 'The Social Function of Poetry'. In *On Poetry and Poets*, 15–25. London: Faber and Faber, 1957.

Gosetti-Ferencei, Jennifer Anna. *Heidegger, Hölderlin, and the Subject of Poetic Language: Toward a New Poetics of Dasein*. New York: Fordham University Press, 2004.

Grene, David and Richard Lattimore, eds. *The Bacchæ*. In *The Complete Greek Tragedies, Euripides V*, 141–220. Chicago: The University of Chicago Press, 1959.

Hamburger, Michael, trans. *Friedrich Hölderlin: Poems and Fragments*. London: Anvil Press, 1994.

Hart, Kevin. 'Blanchot's Mallarmé'. *Southerly* 68, no. 3 (2008): 135–58.

Heidegger, Martin. '"As When on a Holiday …"'. In *Elucidations of Hölderlin's Poetry*, translated and introduction by Keith Hoeller, 67–99. New York: Humanity Books, 2000.

Heidegger, Martin. 'Hölderlin and the Essence of Poetry'. In *Elucidations of Hölderlin's Poetry*, translated and introduction by Keith Hoeller, 51–65. New York: Humanity Books, 2000.

Heidegger, Martin. '"Remembrance"'. In *Elucidations of Hölderlin's Poetry*, translated and introduction by Keith Hoeller, 101–73. New York: Humanity Books, 2000.

Heidegger, Martin. 'L'hymne "Tel qu'en un jour de fête"'. Translated by Joseph Rivan. *Fontaine* 54 (1946): 206–35.

Heidegger, Martin. 'On the Essence and Concept of φύσις'. In *Pathmarks*, edited by William McNeill, 183–230. Cambridge: Cambridge University Press, 1998.

Heidegger, Martin. 'On the Essence of Truth'. In *Pathmarks*, edited by William McNeill, 136–54. Cambridge: Cambridge University Press, 1998.

Heidegger, Martin. *Hölderlin's Hymn 'The Ister'*. Translated by William McNeill and Julia Davis. Bloomington: Indiana University Press, 1996.

Heidegger, Martin. *Introduction to Metaphysics*. Translated by Ralph Manheim. New Haven: Yale University Press, 1959.

Heidegger, Martin. *Parmenides*. Translated by Richard Rojcewicz and André Schuwer. Bloomington: Indiana University Press, 1992.

Heidegger, Martin. *Plato's 'Sophist'*. Translated by Richard Rojcewicz and André Schuwer. Bloomington: Indiana University Press, 1997.

Herman, Jeanine, trans. *Laure: The Collected Writings*. San Francisco: City Lights Books, 1995.

Hill, Geoffrey. 'Little Apocalypse: Hölderlin: 1770–1843'. In *Selected Poems*, 18. London: Penguin, 2006.

Hölderlin, Friedrich. 'Becoming in Dissolution'. In *Essays and Letters on Theory*, edited by Thomas Pfau, 96–100. Albany: State University of New York Press, 1988.

Hölderlin, Friedrich. 'Dix letters'. Translated by Denise Naville. *Fontaine* 54 (1946): 256–9.

Hölderlin, Friedrich. 'On Religion'. In *Essays and Letters on Theory*, edited by Thomas Pfau, 90–5. Albany: State University of New York Press, 1988.

Hölderlin, Friedrich. 'Remarks on "Oedipus"'. In *Essays and Letters on Theory*, edited by Thomas Pfau, 101–8. Albany: State University of New York Press, 1988.

Hölderlin, Friedrich. *Sämtliche Werke*, edited by Friedrich Beißner, 8 vols. Stuttgard: W. Kohlhammer Verlag, 1952.

Hölderlin, Friedrich. 'Tel qu'en un jour de fête'. Translated by Joseph Rivan. *Fontaine* 54 (1946): 199–205.

Hölderlin, Friedrich. 'The Ground for "Empedocles"'. In *Essays and Letters on Theory*, edited by Thomas Pfau, 50–61. Albany: State University of New York Press, 1988.

Hölderlin, Friedrich. *Essays and Letters on Theory*. Edited by Thomas Pfau. Albany: State University of New York Press, 1988.

Hölderlin, Friedrich. *Hyperion or The Hermit in Greece*. Translated by Ross Benjamin. Brooklyn: Archipelago Books, 2008.

Hölderlin, Friedrich. *Oeuvres*. Translated by Philippe Jaccottet. Paris: Gallimard, 1967.

Hölderlin, Friedrich. *The Death of Empedocles: A Mourning Play*. Translated, introduction and notes by David Farrell Krell. Albany: State University of New York Press, 2008.

Kant, Immanuel. *Critique of Judgement*. Translated by James Creed Meredith. Oxford: Oxford University Press, 1969.

Kirk, Geoffrey S. and John E. Raven. *The Presocratic Philosophers: A Critical History with a Selection of Texts*. Cambridge: Cambridge University Press, 1962.

Lacoue-Labarthe, Philippe and Jean-Luc Nancy. *The Literary Absolute: The Theory of Literature in German Romanticism*. Translated by Philip Barnard and Cheryl Lester. Albany: State University of New York Press, 1988.

Lacoue-Labarthe, Philippe. 'The Caesura of the Speculative'. In *Typography: Mimesis, Philosophy, Politics*, edited by Christopher Fynsk and introduction by Jacques Derrida, 208–35. Cambridge: Harvard University Press, 1989.

Man, Paul de. 'Heidegger's Exegeses of Hölderlin'. In *Blindness and Insight: Essays in the Rhetoric of Contemporary Criticism*, 2nd rev. ed., 246–66. London: Methuen, 1983.

Marion, Jean-Luc. *Being Given: Toward a Phenomenology of Givenness*. Translated by Jeffrey L. Kosky. Stanford: Stanford University Press, 2002.

Marion, Jean-Luc. *The Idol and Distance: Five Studies*. Translated and introduction by Thomas A. Carlson. New York: Fordham University Press, 2001.

Nagy, Gregory. 'Early Greek Views of Poets and Poetry'. In *The Cambridge History of Literary Criticism, I: Classical Criticism*, edited by George A. Kennedy, 1–77. Cambridge: Cambridge University Press, 1989.

Nancy, Jean-Luc. 'Hyperion's Joy'. Translated by Christine Laennec and Michael Syrotinski. In *The Birth to Presence*, translated by Brian Holmes et al., 58–81. Stanford: Stanford University Press, 1993.

Nightingale, Andrea Wilson. *Spectacles of Truth in Classical Greek Philosophy: 'Theoria' in its Cultural Context*. Cambridge: Cambridge University Press, 2004.

Ovid. *Metamorphoses*. Translated by Arthur Golding and edited by Madeleine Forey. London: Penguin, 2001.

Paz, Octavio. 'Recapitulations'. In *Alternating Current*, translated by Helen R. Lane, 65–72. London: Wildwood House, 1974.

Rahner, Karl. 'Poetry and the Christian'. In *Theological Investigations, IV: More Recent Writings*, translated by Kevin Smyth, 357–67. London: Darton, Longman and Todd, 1974.

Rilke, Rainer Maria. 'A Hölderlin'. Translated by Jean Wahl. *Fontaine* 54 (1946): 260–2.

Schelling, F.W.J. 'Philosophical Letters on Dogmatism and Criticism'. In *The Unconditional in Human Knowledge: Four Early Essays; 1794–1796*, translated by Fritz Marti, 156–96. Lewisburg: Bucknell University Press, 1980.

Simon, Martin F.A. *Friedrich Hölderlin, The Theory and Practice of Religious Poetry: Studies in the Elegies*. Stuttgart: Hans–Dieter Heniz, Akademischer Verlag Stuttgart, 1988.

Sobin, Gustaf. *Collected Poems*. Edited by Esther Sobin et al., introduction by Andrew Joron and Andrew Zawacki. Greenfield, MA: Talisman House, 2010.

Sokolowski, Robert. *The God of Faith and Reason: Foundations of Christian Theology*. 2nd ed. Washington, DC: Catholic University of America Press, 1995.

Suglia, Joseph. *Hölderlin and Blanchot on Self-Sacrifice*. New York: Peter Lang, 2004.

12 Edgelands

Topographies of Metaphor and the Renewal of Wilderness

Owen Gurrey

> This far: alert, curious, more or less naked, without language, looking out over the green Savannah. Now that was a leap, that's an outlook. You see open space with trees whose branches spread out near the ground and bear fruit. You see a river or path that winds away out of sight, beyond the horizon. You see a few animals, you see changing clouds. You like what you see. Two hundred thousand years later you'll call this outlook 'beautiful' but the word's no use to you now.[1]

Glyn Maxwell's *On Poetry* begins as far back as the archaic half-light with perception of space. The scene he is describing is not a psychoanalytical 'site', a moment or mirror-stage of cognitive development; it is the whole process of becoming homo-sapiens. The genesis of the hominid is an unveiling of the hunting, roaming creature of the lower Palaeolithic age. Maxwell is asking the impossible question: what are they looking at? How do these visions make sense? 'Art, drawing, writing, poetry – are marks made in time by that gazing creature'.[2] Everywhere poets are giving voice to vision; in the process they are testing form as an act of mind to characterise this vision.

We will return to Maxwell's early-man in due course. For now we must leap from this Palaeolithic precipice and descend to the plains of the anthroposcene. Are we capable of attending to the phenomena of simply existing? Is there such a thing as a pure, unadulterated apprehension of things as we find them? The answer for many linguists and philosophers would be a resounding no. How can one think without language? Or has our pre-lapsarian instinct been obfuscated by the resistible rise of man as first-principle, first-cause and first-priority. We must surely have to put a coat on, venture outside and get amongst things.

> The meaning of our experience is finally unfathomable, it reaches in to our toes and back to before we were born and into the atom, with vague shadows and changing features, and elements that no expression of any kind can take hold of.[3]

Ted Hughes here echoes the fate of his famous Crow. It is on the wings of birds that we may begin our descent to the *all-too-human* world of the twenty-first century and start our journey to the edgelands.[4]

The Birds and 'The Big Hum'

> Crow spraddled head-down in the beach-garbage, guzzling a dropped ice-cream.[5]

There's no fanciful romanticising of the Crow, he is the shadow man forever eking a life from the remnants of our human trail. The birds dance and map the world with and beyond our human footprint and occupy our urbane world as well as mystify us. In Hughes' famous collection, stories of apocalypse, divine error, sacrilege and death are played out almost in a free-floating form where the words, complete with their primitive evocations, work off one another to create a vision of Crow as a creature in apprehension, an ambivalent trespasser into the workings of the world, coming to terms with his earthly life and the spaces he finds himself, rather like a poet.

Here is Paul Farley, the poet who will be the main focus of the themes under discussion. His is a poetry in celebration of the piled up wreckage of post-industry. Here, in 'The Big Hum', he is accommodating himself to the world at the city's edge:

> I'm on the edge of a reed bed, just before dawn
> As the birds grow active, I become stock-still
>
> and part of the landscape, which lends my voice
> the furtive veritas of cigarettes[6]

'The Big Hum' from Farley's third collection, *Tramp in Flames*, is a small-hours documentary of the edgelands sound. Farley is bedding himself into the birds' world. The poem is a long sequence of twenty stanzas which sees him in a kind of civic territory. The narrator is here to make some field recordings, 'Miles of tape / wind through the twilight, getting it all down' and it's the site at which he attempts to chart the noise and throb of the edgelands, 'But I don't romanticise the birds, like poets. / Their songs are strictly territorial, / perfumed and glandular, bitter as gall'. 'The Big Hum' becomes the metaphor for 'the room tone of the world, / like an approaching storm' and there is something epochal about the way the poem describes this wash of sound as a new phenomenon, the global timbre of encroaching *24/7*, the backbeat of commerce getting in to things.

The poem is working out a perspective and a reason for this hum. In first-person we are taken right to the heart of nature's audiolab, and the subtlety of the environmental critique is again exposed as the cosmic explaining-away doesn't wash with the narrator. 'The Big Hum' is his metaphor:

> From the damp and dead legs of the first position
> of level meter and boom microphone,
> I've heard the gain cranked up over the years.

The subject here is the development of a language of metaphor, the language of man, the gazing creature naming ground as it transmutes onto our mental universe. Unlike Crow, man is word-hungry, and the slipperiness with which he takes aim at the world is where the poet intervenes to snap-shot this scene of recognition. 'The Big Hum' is threatening the calls and songs of the birds and so a tape from forty springs becomes a celebration and a record, a field guide: poetry as a commemorative act. 'The whole island a bird colony' to be recorded one by one 'into the studio's ark' is a subtle warning of what is creeping-in, Noah before the flood, 'a turbine coming over the earth's curve'. It could be a response to Rachel Carson's *Silent Spring* half a century on as the poet records the songs and calls of birds down the decades 'to see me through / the dark winter ahead'.[7]

'Birders have got to know the edgelands better than most [...] today it would be unbecoming of any birder not to spend at least some time exploring sewage farms, as well as landfill sites and rubbish tips'.[8] Hardly the dramatic scenery of the North York Moors or the Brecon Beacons, yet it is the poetry that gets into these places and reveals these new grazing lands for the keen birder. The significance of these new places as sites for nature seemingly *in absentia* is not lost on the poets and the *Field Guide to the Birds of Britain & Europe* gets updated in *Edgelands*.

As many British sewage-treatment plants are owned by private companies, it would be unbecoming of our poets not to follow this chain of ownership to its source and locate the new territories for the birds and 'The Big Hum'. Their account of what were once local or civic spaces at the edges of cities now reveals the interconnections of decades of privatisation and outsourcing. The piled up urban landscape is a jumble of individually owned freeholds and plots and our authors' observations lend a counterpoint to the birds' wild non-observance to any idea of territory, border or locale:

> Imagine seeing a Lapland Bunting at a sewage works just south of Peterborough. This isn't beyond the realms of possibility [...] though you need to get east to stand a good chance of seeing them wintering in England. This part of the country's water supply is controlled and managed by Anglian, which is ultimately owned by, among other concerns, The Canadian Pension Plan Investment Board. This means you would be watching a bird that breeds in a range encompassing the circumpolar tundra, wintering on a facility owned by a Canadian company. You are probably using Austrian or German optics. Welcome to the global edgelands.[9]

Edgelands and Wilderness

Returning to Glyn Maxwell, this early man of the green Savannah is deducing from observation. It is the poet as evolutionary psychologist asking, what are they looking at?

An open space (we can hunt) with trees (we can hide) whose branches spread out near the ground (we can escape) and bear fruit (we can eat). We see a river (we can drink, wash, eat) or path (we can travel) that winds away out of sight (we can learn), beyond the horizon (we can imagine). We see a few animals (we can eat more), we see changing clouds (rains will come again, we can tell one day from another) and all in all, we like what we see. What evolutionary psychologists – and I – believe is that aesthetic preferences, those things we find beautiful, originate not in what renders life delightful or even durable, but in what makes life *possible*.[10]

In Farley's vision, his 'aesthetic preferences' are the urban edgelands, a term he and his coauthor adopt from the geographer Marion Shoard. It plays host to a new theory of wilderness. We are a long way from Shakespeare's Forest of Arden or Wordsworth's Green-Head Ghyll. It is a different kind of solitude. For Farley and his collaborator, Michael Symmons Roberts, two poets growing up in urban Merseyside and Lancashire in the 1970s, the urban edgelands are the site of their awakenings to a new environment stretching out and across the margins of the edges of towns and cities. Their book, *Edgelands: Journeys into England's True Wilderness*, is an original vision that seeks to redefine our relationship to these in-between places and is central to the historical and cultural groundtruthing that poets contribute to the public imagination.

What exactly are edgelands? The 'elsewhere' of pastoral England is indeed just that; if it existed then our authors were not going to find it except in 'jigsaw puzzles', 'ladybird books' and the 'rolling hills of biscuit tin-lids'. The poets quickly stride in to a litany of new terms from *Drosscape*, Alan Berger's study of waste landscapes and urban sprawl in the United States. The signifiers of place in the unfurling urbanism of the late twentieth century shows the authors one thing: that 'language had obligingly proliferated':

Boomburb
citistate
datascape
dumpspace
enclaves
junkspace
landscape urbanism
limitless city
megalopolis
micropolis
midopolis
nerdistan
polycentric city
polynucleation
smart-growth

stimdross
technoburb
technopolis
transurbanism
urbalism[11]

These words are at odds with the traditional vocabulary of urban living. They speak of science-fiction dreams or the post-cityscapes of *Blade Runner* and *The Matrix*; even describing them one must yield to their power as signifiers of new kinds of compounded territories. To give a name to these places is the beginning of a process of discovery as all poets know, and their 'groundbreaking' book sets out what they see as a new idea of wilderness. It is a theme running through their poetry and one which links their work with the past as it is buried and re-discovered in these fringe environments.

Most of all the authors find beauty in the rusted neglect of peripheral zones, a world away from London and the metropoles of clinical cityscapes. Memories and sensations are galvanised through a post-industrial landscape of tunnels, railway backs, tower blocks, subways, ports, and warehouses, the places where we played out our dreams of the twentieth century and moulded the world urban. Farley and Symmons Roberts provide flashes of light that tantalise our imaginations, engorged in language, plumbed into the landscape to refresh our view of the human sweep.

The authors divide *Edgelands* into chapters dealing with an element of their vision. Already the contents page reads as a litany of the traces and capillaries of where global capitalism finds its beginnings and ends, from the drawing board to the scrapheap: Cars, Paths, Dens, Containers, Landfill, Water, Sewage, Wire, Gardens, Lofts, Canals, Bridges, Masts, Wasteland, Ruins, Woodlands, Venues, Mines, Power, Pallets, Hotels, Retail, Business, Ranges, Lights, Airports, Weather, and Piers. These places are epochal and 'since the last ice sheets retreated have found a way to live with each successive wave of new arrivals, places where the city's dirty secrets are laid bare, and successive human utilities scar the earth or stand cheek by jowl with one another'. The porous nature of edgelands – *where do they begin?* – suggest that these chapters run into one another framing a landscape that is anything but a clinical self-contained package. 'Edgelands aren't *sites*. They don't behave like castles or bird reserves or historic market towns. Nobody asks, *Are we there yet?*'[12]

With 'Cars', the authors are not interested in the glare and cut-glass sophistication of the car dealership, where customers parade the shiny new models, discuss APRs and hire purchase plans and raise eyebrows at the salesman's boastful pitch about miles-per-gallon. What they want to trace is the afterlife of cars. For this they must travel to the scrapyard:

These are the automotive equivalents of the Paris catacombs, mass graves in orderly array, but above ground, exposed to the elements. In these yards you find rusting car cadavers piled three, five, eight high [...] new cars are beautiful and we don't like to see them reduced to this by us, by those who should have taken better care of them.[13]

They even riff on the thought of the satnav as *memento mori*, as the driver reaches the scrapyard to kiss goodbye to his old motor, 'one final rhetorical flourish from the speech synthesiser's female voice: *you have reached your destination*'. It is what is returned to the earth, broken up for scrap and living out the days as totems of rust that ignites the authors' imagination and Ted Hughes' *Iron Man* is not far away. What takes root and survives the parcelling out of land on the city's edges is the opening of a vision of a new landscape on which our imprint is too large, cumbersome and unsightly for the inner city. It is a reconnective thesis out of which a poetry in celebration of territory is emerging.

Plants

There seems nothing Romantic about grass verges with their carbon-grey kerbs, or the trees and plants at lay-bys along the M1. As drivers speed by these pesticide-free borders one would be forgiven for not sparing them a thought. For Farley and Symmons Roberts however, these are the beds and boundaries of our edgelands, and as poets they have a keen sense of finding a history and a beauty in the flora of what jostles for space beside tarmac, railway and asphalt. 'Driving down the M1 today is to travel down a long historical garden, the product of competing landscape ideologies'.[14] The arteries of major and minor roads are contours for the poets' map-making. The grass verge acts as a silent border to the man-made world. Seen as it is from the window of a moving car or train window, a delicate counterpoint to this smoke-spluttering motorcade is the slow turning of the seasons in these places as hard to reach as a sea-cliff or moorline. The conditions for flowers and plants to flourish in edgelands are those of dereliction and neglect. Where nature rears its head is testament to the absence of a human footprint as the authors point out, 'well maintained public spaces, parks and playing fields and promenades are not edgelands. But with a little neglect and abandonment they can become edgelands'.[15]

Sean O'Brien's collection *November* opens with 'Fireweed', where the flower takes on a triffid-like potency evoking the ebb and flow of industrial land with a subdued celebratory tone. 'Fireweed' as it is commonly known is Rosebay Willowherb, a purple flower that tells its own story. It is a flower that quickly colonises scarred land and became famous in Edward Thomas' 'Adlestrop' to which Farley references in 'Google Earth' as a now 'dismantled barrow'.[16] The Willowherb sprang up along the borders of railway lines as the earth was dug up to carve out the railway cuttings in the 'age of the train'; here O'Brien pits the fireweed against his own vision of renewal and rebuilding of post-industrial towns and cities:

Look away just for a moment
then look back and see

> how the Fireweed's taking the strain.
> This song's in praise of strong neglect
>
> in the railway towns, in the silence
> after the age of the train.[17]

O'Brien's poem encapsulates that new silence of post-railway towns such as York, Derby, Crewe, Swindon and Peterborough. The Willowherb is silently thriving in these new landscapes and it is out of these roots that Farley and Symmons Roberts' edgelands grow. It may be sorrowful but the 'praise of strong neglect' is an optimism he shares with Farley and Symmons Roberts. Fireweed has a luscious purple colour that contrasts to the northern gloom of railway towns and it stands as testament to the renewal of nature, of the beauty that springs up from land left fallow. If left for long enough, the conditions for it to thrive can be seen as a positive force, a kind of opening up of the landscape as it transcends history to be viewed afresh.

Water

Edgelands are the sites of car-crushers, sewage works, waterworks and power stations. We cannot live without these places but we don't want to live with them. By contrast, the surveyed towns and cities are filled with 'cameras tilting like gargoyles from the roofs of every office or shop'. The city of today is mapped and monitored. It is now the edgelands that remain unknown and unmapped. It is not the glorious names of Lake Windermere, Coniston or Ullswater that appeared in the Romantic vision, it is a contemporary suburban sublimation, from source to sea: the unnamed, unchartered 'deep standing water [...] the riddle of depth [...]' seem to be hiding something, thoughts that lead us down, down'.

Farley's third collection, *Tramp in Flames*, includes 'The Westbourne at Sloane Square', about one of London's buried rivers; there is the memorialising poem of childhood, 'I Ran All the Way Home', where 'I remember dark-green seawater sloshing against Roman numerals and dock steps'.[18] Earlier, in *The Ice Age*, water is a central theme, as is the Mersey river from where Monkfish and Cod swim off the page as relics from the last ice age. What has been revealed in the slow turning of the epochs as 'the sea goes about its business'[19] is the making and death of landscapes. From the great fenlands that once covered East Anglia before the dredging of the nineteenth century, or the Mersey basin once home to smugglers and wading birds, poems such as 'The Sea in the Seventeenth Century' are acts of mind that connect water to the great history of colonisation, glacial retreat, to 'A pulsing, absolute state of affairs / where all our yesteryears go through the lives / we might still live'. This is water as power.

Compare this to 'Newts' from *The Dark Film* which sees him at 'the golf course pond where all ages collided' and that which as a boy staring into the 'element of newts: Knorr spring vegetable cold packet soup',[20] he conflates everyday urbane imagery and commodities with a keen sense of landing on where we are right now.

As a Liverpudlian, it's no surprise that the sea, fish, pond-life and stagnant water feature so heavily in his work. Farley's work leaves a watermark on the cultural history of his hometown.

In 'Civic', one of Farley's grand themes, low-lying hidden water plays host to his midnight escapade to the reservoir: 'I've read the reports / of city engineers, done my homework, / and move through the woods / warily [...] though I'm about as far / from another human being as it's possible to get here, / from our cities where you're never more than a few feet from a rat'.[21] He is again by the reed bed but this time without his recording equipment, something larger is urging him to the reservoir, a calling of some kind, a civic duty.

'Civic' is a long numerically organized poem of twenty-one seven-line stanzas. Once at the reservoir, the narrator invites us to taste the fresh water, 'the great nothing that comes before the pipes / pass on their trace of lead, before fonts / leech their peck of limestone / before public baths / annihilate with chlorine'. It's the unadulterated stuff, 'Manchester at source' that takes us out of the city and away to the edgelands. Civic suggests the poem is about responsibility, both social and political, and it surfaces at the characteristic turn when the author's voice leaps out to speak directly to the reader. We are already on stanza seventeen before his motives for his crepuscular plan are revealed:

In this poem disguised as a meditation on water

It's as good a time as any to tell you, reader
how I've driven up to this spot in a hire car
and stand at the water's edge
drawn by a keen sense
of civic duty: I plan to break
the great stillness and surface of this lake-
cum-reservoir by peeing quietly in to the supply

and no harm will come to anything or anyone.

We are deep in low-lying nocturnal Farley territory. With no effect from his civic act, it is an act that 'will only really occur in the mind's eye [...] I wasn't here'. The edgelands are only there because of cities, not in spite of them and so it is the city's throb in the distance that will engulf his act. He wants the traces of the edgelands to occur in his mind's eye whenever the city turns on its taps and 'mysteries of pipework' pull the water to its required destination. Farley wants a return to the source, to go straight for the inception of water in this long thought-sequence, as such the poem civically ties the narrator to a higher purpose: documenter of the rough origins of our daily hum, the unseen waters that lie a stone's throw from our urban centres.

To follow this vision to its conclusion, from pipework 'giving' to pipework 'taking-away', there's no wonder that sewage farms are of interest to Farley and Symmons Roberts; tracing the history of the sewage works reveals that even the language of waste has been sanitised over the last hundred years. 'Filth' was how the Victorians described waste; to imagine saying that now is to be crude about such a sensitive subject. Terms such as 'greywater' and 'blackwater' refer to the cleansing process of waste in the 'water-treatment plant'. The edgelands host these centres of waste and Farley and Symmons Roberts want us to see the collective city toilet in all its glory. It is for them almost an obligation to know where your waste goes as 'All of us are distantly connected and plumbed in to these lagoons and basins'.[22] Without knowledge of these places one cannot connect the urban with the natural, as to do so is to venture into the edgelands where a new topography awaits the city dweller unaccustomed to the raw workings of man-made culture.

'Cloaca Maxima' is a five-page sequence that pulls *The Dark Film* down to the depths of the ancient Roman sewer. The foundations for *The Dark Film* are found at the birth of western civilization.[23] It begins with a childhood memory of 'sewer jumping' where, 'there's a holding of the breath in a concrete outfall'. This frozen out moment is Farley's stop-clock for stepping sideways into history as the poem follows the lives of the enslaved; from the ones who built the great sewer of Rome in 600 BC to chain-gangs, 'nameless multitudes, the lost bones, / the leg-irons', and chimney sweeps fixed on the 'pinprick at the end of a carbon flue', all illuminated by Farley's light box in the dark underbelly of history's losers. There are 'workhouse children', 'cocklers', 'cotton pickers', 'galley rowers', 'railroad workers' and drainage diggers, 'Anacharsis Cloots – what's he doing here?' all doing the dirty work of history and erecting the lamina of the dark film. The final stanza showcases the poet's art of seeing in a final flourish of thought on the inception of his craft. The poem will take us back to 'The Power', to the 'greyscale empire of slate'. This is where the world reveals itself, and where the door to a vision of commemoration is opened:

> The millions of mixed shades
> are still running beneath our surfaces
> and visible to those who just step sideways /

Power

In their chapter on Power Stations, the huge elephantine cooling towers that dot the landscape of edgelands are totems to a mythic idea of progress. In *The Dark Film*'s 'Gas', it is the Iron cylinder's providing power to city homes that 'house the spite / and gloom of post-industrial towns'. In the poem Farley is 'seeing the country from a train' which allows him access to the city's side streets and underbelly. From within the arteries of cities, on public transport, he is following a thought through patterned speech, 'arriving anywhere', skipping across the stanzas is this all-encompassing, invisible element, 'whenever I do alight / each city reinventing itself / creaks like a warming glacier'. Railway cuttings in England snake between the back of glassworks, the edge of the shipping container yard, behind the industrial estates and builders' yards and office blocks that afford cheaper rent on the outskirts. Like O'Brien, the train is Farley's conduit for this behind-the-scenes view. The metaphor of the gasholders as 'housing the spite and gloom of post-industrial towns' is not a dismal portrayal of a stereotypical northern grittiness; the 'colourless, odourless leak' that seeps out in the poem is a grounding force of humility. In a world where we're coerced to 'enjoy' or 'have a nice day' the gloom represents a corrective to that nauseating positivity. Terry Eagleton's book *Across the Pond* illustrates this duality nicely. The staid British language has retained connection to the honesty of what it signifies. The US, in Eagleton's view, has lifted language away from any negativity and as such it is the language of ceaseless hope and optimism, one that can never settle on the truth of the matter as it is always en-route to something better: 'Any society that calls its prisons "correctional facilities" is excessively optimistic'.[24] It is a swift critique of the language of nature as it applies to man and his condition. Elsewhere he states: 'Those who have their sights fixed on earthly immortality are unable to live in the present, and so, ironically, have less to lose than those who can live in the here and now'. Language can be melancholy and honest, gloom is not doom, so when 'shoppers seethe and spend like mad. / Everybody wears a mask', for the poet this is a veil to stave off this gloom. 'Money, the old green-keeper / has brought a springy, turf-like step / to the pavements but can't deal with gas'.[25] Negativity won't wash in giddy consumer land and it is here used as a tonic to the airbrushed squeaky-clean world of consumer capitalism.

The metaphors for power or empowerment in the self-help industry are rife – *Power to You*™. What the authors imagine is the corrective power of metaphor and there is no better place for metaphor than edgelands. The authors playfully imagine the 'cooling towers'; we are here encroaching on the myth of the soul rising, places of empowerment for stressed-out executives. In their picture, the stressed-out executives are bussed out to the power station. Here they can:

> feel the force of the metaphors. The metaphors here could hardly be bettered. Stand in the shadow of the 'cooling towers'. Watch your anxieties turn to wisps of smoke and twist into the ether. Feel your pent up frustrations drawn out of you by this irresistible updraft. You are 'cooling', but you will not leave her empty. You are in a power station. Feel the force. Every minute you spend here you are more empowered.[26]

It is a whimsical idea, one which they are drawn to because the proliferation of the language of self-empowerment, yet it is not difficult to imagine this practice taking off as an expensive form of therapy. Living inside the metaphor is perhaps the only way to actively reconnect us to the power points of our own lives. By relocating our imaginations to the power-producing edgelands we are inserting language and the metaphors back into a causal relationship with ourselves and our urban environments. As with 'Civic', getting back to source is a crucial component of our civic duty: 'in one sense, all power stations are Cathedrals of the Electric Light and Kettle'.[27]

'Brent Crude' is *The Dark Film*'s sonnet and sonnets are the shape of oil barrels. The first line sees our poet imagining climbing in:

> Each one of us could fit inside a barrel,
> assume foetal positions, elbows in,
> suspended in the sweet and viscous black,
> to dream our dreams as protean as plastics, / [28]

The poem takes aim at the string or chain that leads from the barrel to the power. It is investigative language, a language that turns over every stone and takes us into the privatization of power utilities presided over by successive Prime ministers. The litany is the list: 'Heath, Wilson, Callaghan, Thatcher, Major', down the line of politicians as an identity parade of failure, those leaders who've succumbed to the ideological power of oil and fossil fuels. The oil embargoes of the early seventies, the pipelines and 'petropounds on stream and thick as blood', is a raw exposure of this elemental force of power. To be inside the barrel is to be inside its wall-to-wall power. It is to do agricultural work on the signifiers of oil as the sonnet continues, we're 'soundly sealed inside our private tar pits', and insulated from the effects of oil outside. The damning critique of 'peacetime sleep' is of that oft-used political phrase, 'in peacetime', yet one which in the context of our dependency on oil and the blood spilled in its name reveals the barefaced truth of the edifice of modern politics in thrall to black gold. The images of oil-slicks and spills from Milford Haven to Deepwater Horizon make their way into the close of the poem and it is Farley's beloved birds who are the ones who pay for our love affair with oil:

> / a colony
> of seabirds bottled up and stacked on ledges,
> a few waking to raise one useless wing
> or open beaks up wide in silent protest.

The closing poem in *The Dark Film* is the poet's dying wish. It is here where the topographies of metaphor reach their climax. 'The Circuit' is the governing presence of any electric appliance or power source. It is place where the stepping-up or stepping-down transformers distribute electricity across the country. The hum of the substation is his ideal resting place and it culminates *The Dark Film* that he has directed. It began with 'The Power' and the end is a return to the grid, to the great electric renewal. As each season turns he will forever be a part of the hum that flashes out from the edgelands whenever the light is switched on:

> I want to be laid to rest in a substation. /
> to be placed respectfully next to transformers.
>
> These will hum to me in the quiet after you've gone. [29]

The transformation of energy has altered the materiality of it before our eyes. It has altered our relationship to its proximity. *The Dark Film*'s elemental forces, Gas, Oil, Wind, Water and Power, are a source of deep reckoning for where we are right now. The opening up of energy, light and sustainability from the great trinity of the hearth where fire played many vital and visible roles – cooking, lighting, and heating - to the power station at the edgelands, this is poetry about loss and renewal at source and the human in between. The concreteness of the hearth has been replaced by abstracted forms of energy, and the substation internment that closes the collection is a folded note in a time capsule, the end credits of *The Dark Film*.

Acknowledgments

The Ice Age © Paul Farley, 2002; *Tramp in Flames* © Paul Farley, 2006; *The Dark Film* © Paul Farley, 2012. Reproduced with permission of Pan Macmillan via PLS Clear.

November © Sean O'Brien, 2011. Reproduced with permission of Pan Macmillan via PLS Clear.

On Poetry © Glyn Maxwell, 2012. Reprinted by permission of Oberon Books.

Edgelands: Journeys into England's True Wilderness © Michael Symmons Roberts and Paul Farley, 2012. Published by Jonathan Cape and reprinted by permission of The Random House Group Ltd.

Notes

1 Glyn Maxwell, *On Poetry*, (London: Oberon Masters, 2012), 9.
2 Ibid., 9.
3 Ted Hughes, cited in Keith Sagar, *The Art of Ted Hughes* (London: Cambridge University Press, 1975), 125.
4 The term 'edgelands' in the title of this paper is taken from the title of a collaborative book by two contemporary poets, Paul Farley and Michael Symmons Roberts. The former's poetry will be under discussion here to add texture and weight to the explication. Paul Farley & Michael Symmons Roberts, *Edgelands: Journeys into England's True Wilderness* (London: Vintage, 2012).
5 Ted Hughes, *Crow* (London: Faber & Faber, 1972), 29.
6 Paul Farley, 'The Big Hum' in *Tramp in Flames* (London: Picador, 2006), 47–50.
7 Rachel Carson's *Silent Spring* is widely regarded as the first text on what we understand today as environmentalism. Published in 1962 the book was responsible for the first ban on pesticide DDT a decade later in 1972. The title is inspired from a poem by John Keats, 'La belle Dame sans merci' in which appears the line 'The sedge is wither'd from the lake, and no birds sing'.
8 Paul Farley and Michael Symmons Roberts, *Edgelands: Journeys into England's True Wilderness* (London: Vintage, 2012), 89–90.
9 Ibid.
10 *On Poetry*, 10.
11 *Edgelands,* 3–4.
12 *Edgelands*, 185.
13 Ibid., 13.
14 Ibid., 99.

15 Ibid., 101.
16 Paul Farley, 'Google Earth' in *The Dark Film* (London: Picador, 2012), 16–17.
17 Sean O'Brien, 'Fireweed' in *November* (London: Picador, 2011), 1.
18 *Tramp in Flames*, 61, 65.
19 Paul Farley, 'The Sea in the Seventeenth Century' in *The Ice Age* (London: Picador, 2002), 29.
20 *The Dark Film*, 11.
21 *Tramp in Flames*,15–21.
22 *Edgelands*, 83.
23 *The Dark Film*, 49–53.
24 Terry Eagleton, *Across the Pond: An Englishman's View of America*, (New York: Norton, 2013) 102, 136.
25 *The Dark Film*, 24.
26 *Edgelands*, 186.
27 *Edgelands,* 188.
28 *The Dark Film*, 31.
29 *The Dark Film*, 55.

References

Eagleton, Terry. *Across the Pond: An Englishman's View of America*, New York: Norton, 2013.
Farley, Paul. *The Ice Age*, London: Picador, 2002.
Farley, Paul. *Tramp in Flames*, London: Picador, 2006.
Farley, Paul. *The Dark Film*, London: Picador, 2012.
Farley, Paul & Symmons Roberts, Michael. *Edgelands: Journeys into England's True Wilderness*, London: Vintage, 2012.
Hughes, Ted. *Crow*, London: Faber & Faber, 1972.
Maxwell, Glyn. *On Poetry*, London: Oberon Masters, 2012.
O'Brien, Sean. *November*, London: Picador, 2011.
Sagar, Keith. *The Art of Ted Hughes*, London: Cambridge University Press, 1975.

13 Know Food, Know Peace?

Community-Based Agriculture and the Practice of Non-Violence

Emily A. Holmes

> Willie was a peaceful person. He liked to be quiet and look at the clouds in the sky and listen to the birds. He liked the feel of the earth and the sight of little things growing. Willie would run his fingers through the dirt and smile and think, 'What more could a person want!'[1]

So begins an illustrated children's book, published in 1977, about one boy's love of gardening, beginning with the gift of a strawberry plant and growing, through hard work, into a bountiful harvest of assorted fruits, vegetables, and grains. Each new gardening success increases Willie's knowledge, happiness, and sense of belonging in the natural world. The book ends with a beautiful illustration of Willie peacefully dozing in the shade of a tree, dreaming of all that he has grown, and imagining his future as a farmer.[2]

Like Willie, respondents to a recent survey of urban community gardeners in Memphis, TN, confirmed the correlation between gardening and a sense of peace.[3] When asked how they measured the impact of their gardens in blighted, high-crime neighbourhoods, most gardeners did not speak in terms of nutrition or health. Instead they described building community, developing relationships, and creating an oasis of peace and beauty in the midst of impoverishment. One gardener said, 'I find peace when I'm in the garden. And I feel like it's a way to make a difference. And actually do something to fix something'. Another explained, 'For me, gardening is very peaceful. It's very peaceful for me. And very rewarding', while a third claimed, 'It's just good to be out with nature. And it's kinda peaceful and – spiritual, almost'.[4] In the view of the citizens doing the work of community gardening, these gardens have the power to beautify neighbourhoods, to displace criminals and drug-dealers, and to turn suspicious neighbours into friends. Gardens are sites and opportunities for peace in the middle of a city with a history of injustice, poverty, racism, and socioeconomic division. As one gardener explained,

> You could say, in a way, that [the garden] sort of brings light to the darkness. In this zip code, if you listen to the news, you listen to – you read the papers – all they talk about is the bad stuff that's coming from this area. What [the garden] does is that we are something *good*.[5]

Viewed in this light, community gardening is an expression of the intentional practice of non-violence, a way to address conflict by disarming it through the cultivation of beauty, relationships, and vegetables.[6]

This chapter addresses the possibility of community-based agriculture as a practice of peace and active non-violence. I use the term 'community-based agriculture' to include a variety of ways of growing food in and for local communities: in urban community gardens, on urban farms, and on small, biodiverse rural farms that supply food to their local community, through farmers markets, direct sales, or pre-paid community-supported agriculture (CSA) shares. What distinguishes these forms of growing food from conventional, industrial, or monocultural forms of agriculture is, first, a commitment to sustainable and organic – or chemical-free/natural – growing practices; and, second, a commitment to their local communities, whether it is their immediate neighbourhood or the larger rural-urban regions in which farmers grow and sell their produce. In other words, in community-based forms of agriculture, those growing the food share a commitment to the place in which they live; they know the land, they know the neighbourhood, and they know the people who consume their produce.[7] This commitment to a local place and a local people manifests in the desire not to harm either and, further, to identify the place of food production (garden or farm) as itself a gathering place for the community, a place of peace in high-crime or impoverished areas, as a 'light' in the 'darkness'.

Two recent books also directly link the concepts of peace and reconciliation with sustainable, community-based agriculture. In *Making Peace with the Earth* (2012), an expansion of her Sydney Peace Prize lecture of the same name, Vandana Shiva develops her critique of corporate globalization, industrial agriculture, and the exploitation of earth, water, seed, and people, particularly poor and indigenous women. Influenced by the Indian religious concept of *ahimsa*, Shiva proposes a positive vision of 'food peace' emerging from local, sustainable, and indigenous forms of agriculture rather than genetic engineering, monocultures, and growth economics. In *Making Peace with the Land* (2012), Fred Bahnson and Norman Wirzba argue from a Christian theological perspective for reconciliation with God's creation through local, sustainable forms of agriculture, including community gardens. Both books claim the title of 'Making Peace', and both propose sustainable, community-based agriculture as a way of enacting peace and reconciliation, both with land and with people. In what sense are these claims meaningful?

Each author offers a sharp critique of the violence and militarization of conventional agriculture; here I wish to develop and affirm this critique, while at the same time also cautioning against the dangers of idealizing or romanticizing community-based forms of agriculture. While sustainable practices of growing food indeed create the *possibility* for peace and reconciliation with the land, and within human and biotic communities, these are not a given. A facile opposition between two forms of agriculture and denial of the violence inherent in all forms of human sustenance impede the work of peace. This work must instead begin with the acknowledgment of human conflict and violence and its complicated history, both evolutionary and social, including the history of agricultural forms of oppression, which, in the U.S. context, includes the history of chattel slavery and share-cropping. Rather than seeing community-based forms of agriculture as a retreat from conflict, or an antidote to violence, or as an oasis of peace in the midst of destruction, here I argue that they can create peace only insofar as they provide opportunities to address conflict within human communities, as well as the violence between human and other species. That is, community-based forms of agriculture can function as sites of peace and non-violence only when we intentionally address (rather than retreat from) the various ways in which violence is manifest in communities, in growing food, and in eating. As an intentional practice of non-violence, community-based agriculture creates the *possibility* for reconciliation across racial, economic, and biotic boundaries when we actively acknowledge and confront our places of conflict and manifestations of violence.

The Violence of Industrial Agriculture

In their respective proposals for peace with the earth, both Shiva and Bahnson and Wirzba decry the violence carried out through industrial agriculture. The distinguishing characteristic of modern industrial agriculture, in contrast to earlier, pre-industrial forms, is its use of chemical inputs – artificial fertilizers, pesticides, and herbicides. Many of these originated in leftover war munitions. Michael Pollan tells the story of the industrialization of food beginning with 'the day in 1947 when the huge munitions plant at Muscle Shoals, Alabama, switched over to making chemical fertilizer'. He continues:

> After the war the government had found itself with a tremendous surplus of ammonium nitrate, the principal ingredient in the making of explosives. Ammonium nitrate also happens to be an excellent source of nitrogen for plants. ... [A]gronomists in the Department of Agriculture [suggested]: Spread the ammonium nitrate on farmland as fertilizer. The chemical fertilizer industry (along with that of pesticides, which are based on poison gases developed for the war) is the product of the government's effort to convert its war machine to peacetime purposes.[8]

In other words, 'Factories that produced poisons and explosives to kill people during the wars were transformed into factories producing agrichemicals after the wars'.[9] While the intent may have been peacetime conversion of wartime munitions – swords into ploughshares, so to speak – the close association of agrichemicals with violence can be seen wherever ammonium nitrate has been retooled back into weapons, from Oklahoma City to Afghanistan, or in accidents such as the deadly explosion in West, Texas, in 2013.[10] We might also mention in this regard the leak of toxic gas from the Union Carbide pesticide plant in Bhopal in 1984 that killed over 8,000 people. It's sometimes said that pesticides don't know when to stop killing.[11]

This post-war industrialized agriculture was exported to other countries through the Green Revolution of the 1960s. Norman Borlaug's Green Revolution increased grain production in developing countries and saved many (some say one billion people) from starvation through high-yield varieties of rice, wheat, and corn, but it also relied on monocultures rather than traditional polycultures, as well as synthetic fertilizers and pesticides, for its success. The use of these artificial inputs has had lasting negative effects on the quality of life in places such as the Punjab, where the soil and water show high levels of toxicity that correlate with high rates of cancer in the region.[12] As Vandana Shiva often says in her speeches, 'We're still eating the leftovers of World War II'.[13]

More recently, industrial farmers in America are exploring the use of drones to monitor fields, again revealing close ties between industrial agriculture and the weapons of war produced by the military-industrial complex.[14] Unmanned drone aircrafts allow farmers to own, operate, and monitor vast monocultures from a distance, without spending much time in the field. As one article reports, this technology allows farmers 'to survey crops, monitor for disease or precision-spray pesticides and fertilizers.... [T]he technology is a perfect fit for large-scale farms and vast rural areas where privacy and safety issues are less of a concern' than in populated urban areas.[15] The agricultural use of drones is another example of transforming technology developed for war into a different use: the war on pests, weeds, and soil.

But the warfare and violence of industrial agriculture extend beyond these obvious examples. In *Making Peace with the Earth*, Vandana Shiva describes three levels of violence in industrial agriculture and the larger global corporate economy of which it is a part,[16] the first of which is violence against the earth, and the resulting ecological crisis. Violence against the earth includes the use of artificial fertilizers, herbicides, and pesticides that poison the soil and water; topsoil depletion; the elimination of biodiversity through monocultures; the production of greenhouse gases that accelerate climate change; and genetic engineering. The second form of violence is perpetrated against people and results in poverty, hunger, and displacement. This form of violence is carried out through instruments such as coercive free trade treaties; the indebtedness of farmers who were promised high yields from the purchase of expensive genetically modified seeds and inputs and the consequent 200,000-plus farmer suicides of India;[17] biopiracy and the displacement of traditional farming practices; and widespread hunger and malnutrition.[18] Since many communities have been displaced by the effects of treaties such as the North American Free Trade Agreement (NAFTA),[19] and many migrants travel to provide agricultural labour, we can add to Shiva's list restrictive immigration policies as well as anti-immigrant sentiment, rhetoric, and even physical attacks.[20] The third form of violence is armed conflict and warfare waged over limited resources.[21] In a global economy and agricultural system that is dependent on non-renewable fossil fuels for energy, actual warfare – 'hotspots', militarization, invasion and occupation of other countries – is the inevitable result of efforts to privatize, commodify, and control finite resources such as oil.[22] When we eat the products of industrial agriculture, which are also the products of war, we participate in the violence of its production, and should not be surprised by its effects: a distorted food system that produces both obesity and malnutrition, excessive fossil fuel consumption, topsoil depletion, toxic runoff, greenhouse gases and climate change, as well as human and animal exploitation and suffering.

Making Peace with the Earth: Ahimsa

According to Shiva, these acts of violence against the Earth and its citizens begin in the human mind and in our misperception of ourselves, largely thanks to mechanistic science, as separate from the natural world rather than deeply connected with it and each other.[23] 'The violence of the mind', she writes, 'begins with fragmenting that which is whole, separating that which is connected, thus violating nature and the web of life'.[24] Seeing ourselves as separate from the earth leads to perpetual warfare through efforts to dominate and control, a kind of 'eco-apartheid' based on division. But this is an illusion, according to Shiva; we are not apart from nature, we are a part of it.[25] And because the problem of violence begins in our minds and our worldview, 'Making peace with Earth must [also] begin in our minds, by changing our paradigms and worldviews from those based on war with nature to those that recognize that we are a strand in the web of life. It involves', in her words, 'a shift from fragmentation and reductionism to interconnectedness and holistic thinking. It involves a shift from violence, rape, and torture as modes of knowing to non-violence and dialogue with the earth and all her beings'.[26]

Shiva briefly outlines this non-violent alternative to industrial agriculture as a way of 'making peace' with the Earth through sustainable organic farming; living within ecological limits; the recovery of the commons of air, soil, water, and seed; respect for indigenous knowledge systems and the knowledge of women; the production of more diverse and nutritious foods; and a new paradigm of living through Earth Democracy, as part of a wider Earth Community.[27] This way of living, and this non-violent way of farming, is rooted in the Indian religious concept of *ahimsa*, non-violence or non-harm. Ahimsa stems from the recognition that 'everything is connected, and life is relationship'.[28] Because we are part of the same web of life, harm to another is harm to oneself. For example, harm to the soil through use of chemical fertilizers and pesticides reverberates into harm to the human body. Thinking we can act at a distance or do violence to others without doing violence to ourselves is a delusion. Thus, making peace with the Earth, 'always an ethical and ecological imperative, … has now become a survival imperative for our species', an imperative which is also 'the broadest peace movement of our times'.[29]

Shiva's passionate critique of the violence of industrialized agriculture and the global corporate war against the earth is persuasive, and I share her fundamental conviction that life is relationship. The question, however, is whether non-violent farming of the type she describes is possible. Shiva sets up an opposition between two ways of thinking, the epistemology of warfare and control and the epistemology of embeddedness and relationship, and between two forms of agriculture, industrial or corporate monocultures and biodiverse, sustainable small farms. This oversimplification, including the image of standing at a precipice and having to make a choice,[30] may not serve us well in shifting our mental and agricultural paradigms. For instance, it does not account for violence that inevitably takes place on biodiverse, sustainable farms wherever different species compete for energy – whether squirrels are eating the tomatoes or rabbits discover the lettuce patch or uninvited seeds sprout in the rich, organic soil. From a farmer's or gardener's perspective, it is hard to see these other species as anything but 'pests', 'predators' and 'weeds', or to understand how we might make peace with them, when they are competing with us for the same food energy. And this is to say nothing of the violence against domesticated farm animals when those animals are slaughtered for food. Such animals are an essential part of the ecology of many biodiverse, sustainable farms, as a source of natural fertilizer and income for farmers. Although Shiva is right to argue for preservation of wild species, and that 'non-violent farming that protects species also helps us grow more food',[31] not every individual animal or plant of every species can or ought to be protected. Making peace with the earth is essential, but we may also have to make peace with the presence of violence in the production of our food. In other words, where *ahimsa* serves as a regulatory ideal for non-violent farming, that farming can only ever aim at the *reduction* of harm, and the lessening of conflict and suffering, rather than its elimination. To think otherwise is to engage in a dangerous oversimplification and romanticism that further separates us from the reality of our food production.

Making Peace with the Land: Reconciliation with Creation

In their co-written account of *Making Peace with the Land*, Bahnson and Wirzba echo Shiva's critique of the violence of industrial agriculture. Writing as Christian theologians, they argue for making peace with the land as an act of reconciliation with God's creation. Looking to the book of Genesis for their theological orientation, they suggest that God's vision for human beings within creation is *shalom*: the peace of right relationships among people, plants, animals, and the land. To that end, they argue for an inclusive understanding of salvation as the reconciliation of all creation in Christ.[32] To live according to the shalom of reconciled relationships means that 'We need to learn again how to live in the garden: not the Eden we've lost, but the garden of the New Jerusalem toward which we're bound'.[33] At times that means planting an actual garden in order to heal broken relationships and ease community tensions.

Bahnson and Wirzba describe human violence against the earth in terms of 'ecological amnesia' caused by both physical and existential separation from land and one another.[34] 'When we probe any community deeply', they write, 'we can find multiple sources of trouble that, under particular circumstances, might lead to a violent outcome. Most of our lands and communities bear the scars of racial and ethnic oppression, class antagonism, nomadic careerism, neighbourhood neglect and greedy ambition'.[35] They give the example of a small town in North Carolina that witnessed a brutal murder that may have been racially motivated. In response, townspeople came together in a vigil, black, white and Latino. One woman, moved by the vision of racial reconciliation, decided to donate five acres of her land to help feed the hungry. Community members organized to found Anathoth Community Garden, named from the book of the prophet Jeremiah, who was instructed to 'buy a field at Anathoth as a sign of hope that God would turn devastation into a peaceful living ... "Build houses and live in them; plant gardens and eat what they produce ... Seek the shalom of the city where I have sent you into exile, and pray to the Lord on its behalf, for in its welfare you will find your welfare" (Jer 29: 5, 7)'.[36]

The story of a community divided by race and class conflict coming together to grow food for the hungry is a powerful image of reconciliation. Importantly, this community garden emerges as an intentional response to violence in the community. As Bahnson and Wirzba write,

> The stories of Jeremiah's Anathoth field and Cedar Grove's Anathoth Community Garden help us see that peace and reconciliation, the mutual flourishing and convivial communality that Jewish people call *shalom*, is a deep and all-embracing reality. Rather than being simply the absence of violence, reconciliation takes us to a physical place – a plot of land – that puts down roots, produces food, provides stability and hospitality, fosters healthy relationships and inspires joy.[37]

They acknowledge that the community is not perfect; there are still tensions and divisions and disagreements over whether and how to fund the garden.[38] But the practice of gardening as a community, growing food and eating it together, creates the possibility of reconciliation or shalom, making peace with the land and with one another. In a claim that echoes Shiva, Bahnson and Wirzba describe the embeddedness of our lives in the larger web of life on earth: 'the most fundamental truth about our lives has not changed: our lives depend on countless seen and unseen, living and dead bodies that touch and nurture our own'.[39] This truth calls out for recognition and, where it has been broken or betrayed, for reconciliation.

Sites of Conflict

Even when founded as an intentional response to violence, however, community gardens themselves can frequently become sites of conflict, and at times the theological and spiritual vision of Bahnson and Wirzba's book overpowers the empirical reality of the challenges of gardening in community. Instead of solving social problems, community gardens can often ignite simmering racial and cultural tensions as well as socioeconomic resentments. The journal *Modern Farmer* has described community gardens across America as sites of theft, vandalism, drug use, race-based harassment and bullying, culture clashes, and even fistfights. Gardeners interviewed for the story note that the communal nature of a garden does not automatically make it a place of peace and reconciliation; conflict in gardens reflects the tensions of human communities.[40] One gardener claims, 'The garden is micro community living – heck, it is Syria, Iraq, USA, Russia – just in plots and plantings'.[41] While this might be something of an exaggeration, the conflicts and tensions are real.

Community gardens in my hometown of Memphis also reflect these tensions. One study suggested that community gardens have little impact on the neighbourhoods in which they are located, due to poor communication about their purpose.[42] While some studies have argued that community gardens are more about community than they are about gardening,[43] this means that gardens can actually magnify the social inequalities and power struggles of the community, particularly over decision making and control of limited resources. Some African-American neighbours see community gardening as primarily a 'white folk's project' that doesn't serve their interests, but instead reinforces white middle-class privilege.[44] Sexual harassment and gender-based discrimination are also unfortunately common in and around community gardens. As Vandana Shiva points out, most of the agricultural work in the world is done by women, and yet men frequently occupy positions of leadership in the environmental and food movements.[45] Instead of reconciling racial, class, and gender divisions, in these examples community gardens can amplify them.

However, just as gardening is a practice or 'form of attention that brings us into a sympathetic and nurturing relationship not only with pleasurable parts of our gardens ... but also with those elements that are less immediately attractive',[46] such as weeds, pests, and predators, it can also reveal the sources of conflict and tension within our communities, including power disparities, unequally distributed resources, and our own participation in systems of privilege and oppression. Growing food communally requires dedicated and intentional spiritual practice, the kind of self-awareness and self-discipline described by Martin Luther King, Jr., in his philosophy of non-violence.[47] Creating what he called 'the beloved community' does not come easily, and community gardens are like any other community in this regard. Reconciliation is never the total absence of conflict; rather it is the conscious effort to work through the problems of community-based agriculture as they arise.

Conclusion: Practices of Non-Violence, Gestures towards Peace

What, then, are the prospects for growing both food and peace, whether on small biodiverse farms or in urban community gardens? Community-based agriculture doesn't provide a simple alternative to the violence of industrial agriculture. In many ways, by bringing people closer to the sources of their food, it can heighten tension. The veil that typically separates the consumer from the production of commodities in global capitalism is lifted. Without the alienation, 'ecological amnesia',[48] or wilful 'ignorance'[49] encouraged by the industrial food system, eaters are forced to confront the reality of their food production. Should they visit a local farm to purchase humanely raised meat, they may be surprised to witness the reality of killing animals. Should they choose to grow their own food, perhaps in a local community garden, they may be shocked by acts of suspicion, greed, and theft. But any step that lessens the distance between the eater and the eaten seems to be a step in the right direction if it forces us to recognize the history of violence within our communities and the violence of our own eating.[50]

When we begin to pay attention, as Shiva suggests, to the production of our food and our embeddedness in the larger web of relationship that is life, we notice the inescapable violence of life's competition for food energy. When we attempt, as Bahnson and Wirzba suggest, to practice shalom and reconciliation with the land through community gardens, we notice how frequently the gardens themselves exacerbate tension within communities. This does not mean we should give up. But we do have to figure out how to address conflict and violence when it occurs,[51] and the solution will look different in different communities. For instance, as a response to theft, some 'gardens grow a certain amount of communal produce, free for the taking'.[52] Some gardens hold monthly meetings where neighbours can air their grievances with the opportunity for mediation and reconciliation.[53] Many small biodiverse farms that raise animals for meat allow and even encourage their customers to visit the farm and participate in the slaughter. Their abattoirs are outdoors and open-air, visible to those who purchase and consume the meat that is processed on site.[54] Shared meals are an important practice of communion, whether on farms or in gardens. Religious communities might further invoke ritual gestures of *confession* – of sin or guilt for participation in structural injustice and violence; of *remembrance* – memorializing the loss of life and its transformation into food for other lives; and of *thanksgiving* – expressing gratitude with humility for the sustenance that has been given. These gestures and rituals can help reconcile communities and help members come to terms with the violence of their eating.[55] Community-based agriculture can even become a kind of Voltairean garden in which to cultivate civic virtues, such as tolerance, justice, hospitality, and courage.[56] Once we recognize our interdependence with others through our food production, there are many opportunities for intentional practices of peace and reconciliation.

Sustainable agriculture and community gardening are not a simple antidote to personal and communal problems of violence, much less an idyllic retreat from the world. Nevertheless, these forms of food production can provide numerous occasions for reconciliation across racial, economic, and biotic boundaries through cultivation of practices and virtues that allow us to confront the problem of violence. Shared practices of growing food that are dedicated to self-awareness, justice, and sustainability can thereby create the conditions for the emergence of a positive vision of food peace.[57]

Notes

1   Myra McGee, *Willie's Garden* (Emmaus, PA: Rodale Press, 1977), 7–8.
2   Gardening often functions as a root metaphor for peace and non-violence; see, for example, 'Nonviolent seeds have power to change minds and hearts when the soil on which they're sown is fertile'. Gerard A. Vanderhaar, *Why Good People Do Bad Things* (Eugene, OR: Wipf & Stock, 2013), 131.
3   Kenneth S. Latta, 'A Community of Gardeners: Exploring GrowMemphis and the Experiences of Its Community Garden Leaders' (master's thesis, University of Memphis, 2014).
4   Latta, 'A Community of Gardeners', 15.
5   Latta, 'A Community of Gardeners', 12.
6   For the theory and practice of non-violence, see Maia Carter Hallward and Julie M. Norman, eds., *Understanding Nonviolence* (Malden, MA: Polity, 2015).
7   On localization and the significance of place, see Raymond De Young and Thomas Princen, eds., *The Localization Reader: Adapting to the Coming Downshift* (Cambridge, MA: MIT Press, 2012).
8   Michael Pollan, *The Omnivore's Dilemma* (New York: Penguin Books, 2006), 41.
9   Vandana Shiva, 'Making Peace with the Earth' (City of Sydney Peace Prize Lecture, 3 November 2010), 6. http://sydneypeacefoundation.org.au/peace-prize-recipients/2010-dr-vandana-shiva/.
10 Manny Fernandez and Steven Greenhouse, 'Texas Fertilizer Plant Fell Through Regulatory Cracks', *New York Times*, 24 April 2013, www.nytimes.com/2013/04/25/us/texas-fertilizer-plant-fell-through-cracks-of-regulatory-oversight.html.
11 Shiva, 'Making Peace', 7.
12 Balwant Garg, 'Uranium, Metals Make Punjab Toxic Hotspot', *The Times of India*, 15 June 2010, http://timesofindia.indiatimes.com/india/Uranium-metals-make-Punjab-toxichotspot/articleshow/6048431.cms#ixzz2jQljBGjs.
13 Cited in Pollan, *Omnivore's Dilemma*, 41.
14 Kelly Yamanouchi, 'Drones Tested to Help Georgia Farmers See Crops from Above', *The Atlanta Journal-Constitution*, 25 August 2013.
15 Gosia Wozniacka, 'Drones Show Promise as Farm Helpers', *The Commercial Appeal (Memphis, TN)*, 15 December 2013.
16 Vandana Shiva, *Making Peace with the Earth* (London: Pluto Press, 2013), 3–29.
17 Andrew Malone, 'The GM Genocide: Thousands of Indian Farmers Are Committing Suicide after Using Genetically Modified Crops', *The Daily Mail*, 2 November 2008, www.dailymail.co.uk/news/article-1082559/The-GM-genocide-Thousands-Indian-farmers-committing-suicide-using-genetically-modified-crops.html#ixzz31BOzAGA2.
18 See Shiva, *Making Peace*, 129–47.
19 On the effects of NAFTA, see Jennifer Ayres, *Good Food: Grounded Practical Theology* (Waco, TX: Baylor University Press, 2013).
20 Alan Rappeport, 'A Beating in Boston, Said to Be Inspired by Donald Trump's Immigrant Comments', *New York Times*, 20 August 2015, www.nytimes.com/politics/first-draft/2015/08/20/a-beating-in-boston-said-to-be-inspired-by-donald-trumps-immigrant-comments/.
21 Shiva, 'Making Peace', 13.
22 Shiva, *Making Peace*, 4.
23 Shiva, *Making Peace*, 11.
24 Shiva, 'Making Peace', 6. She continues, 'Mechanistic science also violates women and non-western societies and indigenous communities by denying them a status as knowing subjects'.
25 Shiva, *Making Peace*, 11.
26 Shiva, 'Making Peace', 6.
27 Shiva, *Making Peace*, 264–6. See also Vandana Shiva, *Earth Democracy: Justice, Sustainability, and Peace* (Boston: South End Press, 2005).

28 Shiva, *Making Peace*, 265.
29 Shiva, 'Making Peace', 11, 18.
30 Shiva, *Making Peace*, 264.
31 Shiva, 'Making Peace', 16.
32 Fred Bahnson and Norman Wirzba, *Making Peace with the Land: God's Call to Reconcile with Creation* (Madison, WI: InterVarsity Press, 2012), 24, 73–5.
33 Bahnson and Wirzba, *Making Peace*, 18.
34 Bahnson and Wirzba, *Making Peace*, 32–3.
35 Bahnson and Wirzba, *Making Peace*, 62.
36 Bahnson and Wirzba, *Making Peace*, 64–5.
37 Bahnson and Wirzba, *Making Peace*, 66.
38 See also Fred Bahnson's description of his experience as community garden leader in *Soil and Sacrament: A Spiritual Memoir of Food and Faith* (New York: Simon & Schuster, 2013).
39 Bahnson and Wirzba, *Making Peace*, 5.
40 Jesse Hirsch, 'Thievery, Fraud, Fistfights and Weed: The Other Side of Community Gardens', *Modern Farmer*, 6 December 2013, http://modernfarmer.com/2013/12/robbery-drugs-fistfights-dark-side-community-gardening/. Hirsch quotes Julie Beals, executive director of the Los Angeles Community Garden Council, who notes, 'People have this idea, because it's a "community" garden, you'll have a bunch of people sitting around holding hands, singing "Kumbaya", … Have you seen an actual community?' See also Colin Moynihan, 'Wary of a New Threat, Community Garden Activists in New York Look Back', *New York Times*, 15 February 2015, www.nytimes.com/2015/02/16/nyregion/wary-of-a-new-threat-community-garden-activists-in-new-york-look-back.html?_r=0.
41 Hirsch, 'Thievery, Fraud, Fistfights and Weed'.
42 Kevin M. Newton, 'Community Gardens and GrowMemphis' (unpublished paper, 12 December 2013), Microsoft Word.
43 Troy Glover, Kimberly Shinew, and Diana Parry, 'Association, Sociability, and Civic Culture: The Democratic Effect of Community Gardening', *Leisure Sciences* 27, no. 1 (2005): 75–92.
44 Kay Zagrodny, 'GrowMemphis Garden Leader Meetings Report' (unpublished paper, 12 December 2013), Microsoft Word. See also Troy D. Glover, 'Social Capital in the Lived Experiences of Community Gardeners', *Leisure Sciences* 26, no. 2 (2004): 143–62.
45 See Suzanne Goldenberg, 'Why Are So Many White Men Trying to Save the Planet without the Rest of Us?' *The Guardian*, 8 May 2014, www.theguardian.com/commentisfree/2014/may/08/white-men-environmental-movement-leadership.
46 Bahnson and Wirzba, *Making Peace*, 80.
47 See, for example, Martin Luther King, Jr., 'Letter from Birmingham City Jail', in *A Testament of Hope: The Essential Writings and Speeches of Martin Luther King, Jr.*, ed. James M. Washington (New York: HarperCollins, 2003), 289–302.
48 Bahnson and Wirzba, *Making Peace*, 28.
49 Wendell Berry, 'The Pleasures of Eating', in *Bringing It to the Table: On Farming and Food* (Berkeley, CA: Counterpoint, 2009), 229.
50 On ways to negotiate the violence of eating, see Norman Wirzba, *Food and Faith: A Theology of Eating* (Cambridge: Cambridge University Press, 2011), 110–43; and Michael Pollan, *Cooked: A Natural History of Transformation* (New York: Penguin Press, 2013), 25–121.
51 Christopher Peterson, Executive Director of GrowMemphis, suggests that 'What is promising about sustainable agriculture as a movement towards non-violence is precisely that we have to confront these realities head on…. We have to confront the fact that our sustenance means we participate in killing. Likewise, in the garden setting, once we have a place for [reconciliation] we can worsen the conflict if we don't use

it effectively. We have to make a choice to use the garden in that way'. Interview with author, January 21, 2014.
52 Hirsch, 'Thievery, Fraud'.
53 Hirsch, 'Thievery, Fraud': 'Each Los Angeles garden holds a monthly meeting, where LACGC members listen to people's complaints and attempt to mediate. These meetings get heated; yelling and screaming are common. Still, it's all part of the process. Beals believes it's all part of neighbors getting to know each other, learning to work side-by-side'.
54 See Michael Pollan's description of Polyface Farm in *Omnivore's Dilemma*, 226–38; and the website of my local farmers, Josephine and Randy Alexander, of Tubby Creek Farm in Ashland, MS: http://tubbycreekfarm.com/our-farming-philosophy.
55 See Bahnson and Wirzba, *Making Peace*, 125–34.
56 See Bahnson, *Soil and Sacrament*, 9.
57 I particularly wish to thank Christopher Peterson for his insight and reflections on an earlier version of this essay.

References

Alexander, Josephine, and Randy Alexander. 'Our Farming Philosophy'. Tubby Creek Farm, Ashland, MS. Accessed 4 May 2014. http://tubbycreekfarm.com/our-farming-philosophy.

Ayres, Jennifer. *Good Food: Grounded Practical Theology*. Waco, TX: Baylor University Press, 2013.

Bahnson, Fred. *Soil and Sacrament: A Spiritual Memoir of Food and Faith*. New York: Simon & Schuster, 2013.

Bahnson, Fred, and Norman Wirzba. *Making Peace with the Land: God's Call to Reconcile with Creation*. Madison, WI: InterVarsity Press, 2012.

Berry, Wendell. 'The Pleasures of Eating'. In *Bringing It to the Table: On Farming and Food*, 227–34. Berkeley, CA: Counterpoint, 2009.

De Young, Raymond, and Thomas Princen, eds. *The Localization Reader: Adapting to the Coming Downshift*. Cambridge, MA: MIT Press, 2012.

Fernandez, Manny, and Steven Greenhouse. 'Texas Fertilizer Plant Fell Through Regulatory Cracks'. *New York Times*. 24 April 2013. www.nytimes.com/2013/04/25/us/texas-fertilizer-plant-fell-through-cracks-of-regulatory-oversight.html.

Garg, Balwant. 'Uranium, Metals Make Punjab Toxic Hotspot'. *The Times of India*. 15 June 2010. http://timesofindia.indiatimes.com/india/Uranium-metals-make-Punjab-toxichotspot/articleshow/6048431.cms#ixzz2jQljBGjs.

Glover, Troy D. 'Social Capital in the Lived Experiences of Community Gardeners'. *Leisure Sciences* 26, no. 2 (2004): 143–62.

Glover, Troy, Kimberly Shinew, and Diana Parry. 'Association, Sociability, and Civic Culture: The Democratic Effect of Community Gardening'. *Leisure Sciences* 27, no. 1 (2005): 75–92.

Goldenberg, Suzanne. 'Why Are So Many White Men Trying to Save the Planet without the Rest of Us?' *The Guardian*. 8 May 2014. www.theguardian.com/commentisfree/2014/may/08/white-men-environmental-movement-leadership.

Hallward, Maia Carter, and Julie M. Norman, eds. *Understanding Nonviolence*. Malden, MA: Polity, 2015.

Hirsch, Jesse. 'Thievery, Fraud, Fistfights and Weed: The Other Side of Community Gardens'. *Modern Farmer*. 6 December 2013. http://modernfarmer.com/2013/12/robbery-drugs-fistfights-dark-side-community-gardening/.

King, Jr., Martin Luther. 'Letter from Birmingham City Jail'. In *A Testament of Hope: The Essential Writings and Speeches of Martin Luther King, Jr.*, edited by James M. Washington, 289–302. New York: HarperCollins, 2003.

Latta, Kenneth S. 'A Community of Gardeners: Exploring GrowMemphis and the Experiences of its Community Garden Leaders'. Master's Thesis, University of Memphis, 2014.

Malone, Andrew. 'The GM Genocide: Thousands of Indian Farmers Are Committing Suicide after Using Genetically Modified Crops'. *The Daily Mail.* 2 November 2008. www.dailymail.co.uk/news/article-1082559/The-GM-genocide-Thousands-Indian-farmers-committing-suicide-using-genetically-modified-crops.html#ixzz31BOzAGA2.

McGee, Myra. *Willie's Garden.* Emmaus, PA: Rodale Press, 1977.

Moynihan, Colin. 'Wary of a New Threat, Community Garden Activists in New York Look Back'. *New York Times.* 15 February 2015. http://www.nytimes.com/2015/02/16/nyregion/wary-of-a-new-threat-community-garden-activists-in-new-york-look-back.html?_r=0.

Newton, Kevin M. 'Community Gardens and GrowMemphis'. Unpublished paper, 12 December 2013. Microsoft Word.

Pollan, Michael. *Cooked: A Natural History of Transformation.* New York: Penguin Press, 2013.

Pollan, Michael. *The Omnivore's Dilemma: A Natural History of Four Meals.* New York: Penguin Books, 2006.

Rappeport, Alan. 'A Beating in Boston, Said to Be Inspired by Donald Trump's Immigrant Comments'. *New York Times.* 20 August 2015. www.nytimes.com/politics/first-draft/2015/08/20/a-beating-in-boston-said-to-be-inspired-by-donald-trumps-immigrant-comments/.

Shiva, Vandana. *Earth Democracy: Justice, Sustainability, and Peace.* Boston: South End Press, 2005.

Shiva, Vandana. 'Making Peace with the Earth'. City of Sydney Peace Prize Lecture. 3 November 2010. http://sydneypeacefoundation.org.au/peace-prize-recipients/2010-dr-vandana-shiva/.

Shiva, Vandana. *Making Peace with the Earth.* London, UK: Pluto Press, 2013.

Vanderhaar, Gerard A. *Why Good People Do Bad Things.* Eugene, OR: Wipf & Stock, 2013.

Wirzba, Norman. *Food and Faith: A Theology of Eating.* New York: Cambridge University Press, 2011.

Wozniacka, Gosia. 'Drones Show Promise as Farm Helpers'. *The Commercial Appeal (Memphis, TN).* 15 December 2013.

Yamanouchi, Kelly. 'Drones Tested to Help Georgia Farmers See Crops from Above'. *The Atlanta Journal-Constitution.* 25 August 2013.

Zagrodny, Kay. 'GrowMemphis Garden Leader Meetings Report'. Unpublished paper, 12 December 2013. Microsoft Word.

14 An Impossible Peace

The Aesthetic Disruptiveness of Climate Change

Paul Haught[1]

'It is a pity that there are so few such places left in the Appalachian forests, and that even these are now in peril. We should never forget what a good woods really looks like'.[2]

This essay interrogates the influence of the *concept* of anthropogenic climate change on aesthetic appreciation of place. Climate change – hereafter 'CC' – which is associated with broad trends in the warming of global atmospheric temperatures, is now forecast to have irreversible significant short- and long-term impacts on the structure, qualities, and even existence of all but the most remote terrestrial places. CC in this regard is the most prominent phenomenon associated with anthropogenic alteration of terrestrial ecological processes. It locks in the sense that we're in a major environmental crisis for the long haul. The particular question I'm chasing in this chapter asks what the significance is for aesthetic appreciation of place when aesthetic evaluators possess the CC concept. By 'possess', although environmental aesthetic evaluators are likely to vary in their particular beliefs about CC, I suggest that an evaluator is knowledgeable about CC insofar as her or his knowledge is generally consistent with the way CC is summarized in scientific consensus statements available to the general public.[3] With such a common sense criterion in mind, here is a concise rendering of what the concept is likely to entail:

- CC is a predicted measureable increase in average global temperatures resulting from a critical accumulation of greenhouse effect producing gases (especially CO_2);
- CC is anthropogenic;
- CC is mildly to massively disruptive to built places and ecosystems in the near term and long term (many scientists estimate impacts lasting a millennium or more);
- CC puts selection pressures on species not adapted to warmer average temperatures or ancillary climatic and ecological disruptions;
- CC has predictable overt (land loss) and uncertain but anticipated covert (microbiological) effects;
- CC is irreversible even if carbon pollution ceased today.

Collectively, these claims support a broader thesis that CC's disruptive effects are profound. Dale Jamieson has even gone as far as to claim that CC is not only ecologically damaging but alters the *meaning* of human life.[4] My thesis is not so bold, but if CC is so profoundly disruptive in the ways listed above, those effects ought to influence human aesthetic experiences of the natural world.

To determine the scope of that influence, my approach in this chapter is to urge reflection away from *nature* as an aesthetic object by pursuing a broader analysis of aesthetic appreciation as it relates to *places*. There is a descriptive and a normative rationale for this pursuit. Descriptively, I hold it as trivially true that agents experience nature aesthetically in acts of dwelling or moving through particular places. This is not to say that aesthetics precludes experiences of imaginary objects, and I am certainly not discounting the role of perspective in aesthetic appreciation. I am saying, however, that the primary milieu for *environmental* aesthetic appreciation is the local environment which gives rise to aesthetic experiences of the features of natural and artifactual objects within that environment. Less trivially, I am assuming for the purposes of this chapter that one can distinguish between naïve aesthetic experiences of environments and those experiences in which agents are responsive to the features of those environments as places. I make a detailed case for this distinction in the body of the chapter, but the difference may be expressed straightforwardly as follows. It is clearly possible, and I would assume commonplace, for people to appreciate landscapes, rivers, forest edges, plants, and insects without knowing much about what they are sensing. They are having aesthetic experiences, and they may even formulate judgments about those things. When those objects are experienced as or as part of places, however, the agent possesses a less naïve perspective. She or he has a perspective that is informed and regulated by the connotations carried by those places. Landscape becomes farmland or national park. The river has a name; it hosts a seaport at the city downstream. The forest edge occurs at the boundary of the athletic field. The tree was planted by the monastery. The insect is under the kitchen sink. In addition, as places, they create aesthetic expectations. These need not be monolithic. Farms and parks are dynamic places; they have seasons and storms. But those qualities belong to the set of anticipated conditions that agents know and apply – when they are conscious of place – in aesthetic appreciation.

There is a big question in aesthetics about how much information we ought to filter out of our sense field in order to have an appropriate aesthetic experience. That question is bigger than what I can address here. But what I suspect, and what I am urging, is that when and if knowledge of climate change is not filtered out as part of aesthetic appreciation, it ought to influence aesthetic judgments about the features of almost all terrestrial places. In so doing, it ought to carry connotations of disruption, change, novelty, and loss consistent with its scientifically measurable effects.

Two points of clarification are needed before proceeding into the body of the discussion. First, in writing about *aesthetic appreciation*, I am referring broadly to the many modes of interacting with environments – across the spectrum from the natural to the built – that induce aesthetic feelings and judgments. Aesthetic appreciation of place may entail feelings of aesthetic satisfaction or dissatisfaction, experiences that are personal and subjective – matters of taste; it may also involve more sophisticated consensus-seeking judgments in which the objective characteristics of a place or its features are conscientiously involved in ascriptions of aesthetic value. In the philosophical discourse of environmental aesthetics, an emphasis on place also engages a distinction between aesthetic values carried by human artifacts and those that are carried by the features of places whose origins are non-anthropogenic, or at least not overtly anthropogenic. As I discuss, one of the hallmarks of the climate change concept is that it troubles the distinctness of the artifactual and the non-anthropogenic. The scarlet tanager's song may be as beautiful as ever, but today I am hearing it outside of its historical range as the species adapts to anthropogenic disruptions to its habitat.[5] As blurred as the distinction may be and may continue to become, environmental aesthetics will typically hold open the possibility for discernment of the aesthetic values carried by the non-artifactual features of places. The tanager's song still belongs to it. Thus when I mention *environmental aesthetic values* I will be referring to these.

As a second point of clarification, in environmental aesthetics, there is also debate over the role of *concepts* in aesthetic appreciation of environments. Because agents can only understand anthropogenic climate change conceptually – agents experience its effects but never its totality – it is necessary to engage that debate here. Specifically, I inquire how an agent's possession of the concept anthropogenic climate change can be thought to disrupt – or not – aesthetic appreciation. As I argue, evaluator awareness of anthropogenic climate change affects aesthetic appreciation of place in at least three general ways:

1   Awareness of CC is awareness that all terrestrial places are – for all intents and purposes – already affected by anthropogenic impacts;
2   Awareness of CC is awareness that all terrestrial places – for all intents and purposes – are subject to uncertain but foreseeable threats of loss to environmental aesthetic value;
3   Following (1) and (2), awareness of CC poses a special challenge for environmental aesthetics wedded to a sense of naturalness, including positive aesthetics, which is the view that nature is essentially aesthetically good.[6]

In making these assertions, I am not claiming that CC precludes evaluators from having aesthetically satisfying encounters with place or encounters with place that give rise to ascriptions of environmental aesthetic value – even in a warmer and ecologically disrupted world. As uncertain as the effects of CC will be on particular places, places will continue to carry environmental aesthetic values. However, because the threat of lost value – including loss of aesthetic value – is relevant to the moral assessment of climate change, it may not be possible to isolate appreciation of a place's aesthetic values from moral beliefs and sentiments. For many, CC has a tragic profile. Emily Brady describes it as oscillating between sublimity and tragedy.[7] Although it is philosophically controversial to include moral beliefs in aesthetic appreciation, the moral weightiness of CC leads to a fourth general assertion for this essay:

4   For places defined by their tendency to convey environmental aesthetic values, the CC concept is especially disruptive to aesthetic appreciation.

This statement leaves the door open to the discovery of other aesthetic values in such places that are not closely linked to personal sentiment or moral and political beliefs, but it is necessary to assert insofar as many environmental aesthetic values are implicated in the histories and identities of particular places. At the conclusion of the essay, I describe a typology of places to illustrate especially how this fourth assertion might be realized in aesthetic appreciation of place.

The Place Concept and Environmental Aesthetics

In approaching this topic in terms of *place*, I am seeking a term that signifies both where and with what aesthetic appreciation within environments may occur. Although ecological science and natural history play significant roles in most accounts of environmental aesthetics, *place* is preferable over *ecosystem* as a term denoting the possibility of aesthetic engagement. While there are technical and non-technical senses of the term *ecosystem*, the breadth of connotations of *place* make it the more suitable term. I can experience the prairie aesthetically as place, but can I experience the prairie aesthetically as ecosystem? Perhaps, but I want to avoid claiming that such a scientifically informed perspective is always required for aesthetic appreciation to become non-naïve. In environmental aesthetics, many authors argue that scientific knowledge may *enhance* or otherwise contribute to aesthetic appreciation. Holmes Rolston, for instance, describes the impact of knowledge of the carbon cycle and awareness of 'deep time' on an evaluator's appreciation of forests.[8] But Rolston also shows how religion and culture are germane to forest aesthetics. The place-based approach I'm advocating likewise accommodates environmental aesthetic appreciation that is and ought to be informed at times by religious symbolism or cultural history, because these are important qualifications for the significance of places.[9] To confine aesthetic appreciation to a requirement of scientific knowledge places too artificial a limit on the myriad ways senses and cognition mingle in aesthetic engagement with place, and I follow Ronald Moore's analysis a little later on to support this claim.

   In writing about place I am also seeking a broader term than *natural environment*. In his own effort to define the context for environmental aesthetics, Allen Carlson settles on this term over *landscape* because 'it makes it explicit that it is an environment under consideration'.[10] For this type of environment to be appreciated aesthetically, it has to do more than reside in the background of our experiences. Rather, its aesthetically valuable features have to become prominent in some way. Thus for Carlson,

[Aesthetic appreciation] involves recognizing that nature is an environment and thus a setting within which we exist and that we normally experience with our complete range of senses as our unobtrusive background. But for our experience to be aesthetic, this unobtrusive background must be experienced as obtrusive foreground. The result is the experience of a 'blooming, buzzing confusion', which in order to be appreciated must be tempered by the common sense and scientific knowledge that we have discovered about the natural environment so experienced.[11]

Carlson's background/foreground distinction I submit also applies to aesthetic appreciation of *place*. The difference is that *natural environment* may too narrowly delimit the kinds of environments in which aesthetic appreciation of the natural features of place is possible and appropriate. Carlson suggests that it's possible to ignore the noise of distant traffic in the background in order to appreciate the sounds of cicadas in the foreground in their appropriate natural environmental setting.[12] However, this example, while it calls attention to a natural phenomenon, may indicate merely that the naturalness of the phenomenon – cicadas singing in tree – is pulled into focus. But that shouldn't mean that once foreground objects shift to the back, they then become insignificant for that particular instance of appreciation. We also have scientific knowledge of the processes that make it possible to design and engineer cars and roads. The physics and chemistry of the built environment are just as non-anthropogenic as the forces that compel cicadas to sing.

Of course, natural environments are indeed places. And when we recognize certain places as natural environments, they generate a set of expectations for evaluators to encounter as part of appreciating them aesthetically. Part of what is characteristic of natural environments is that they include place types – deserts, valleys, coral reefs, etc. – where the prominent features for aesthetic appreciation are not artifactual or at least obviously anthropogenic. But natural environments are not the only environments for which environmental aesthetics is possible or appropriate, and place is the term that does more work for accommodating the significance of our awareness of the dynamics of the more-than-human features of the environments with which we engage as dwelling or transient occupants.

Climate Change and Philosophy of Place

Even if one is sceptical of the consensus statements from the IPCC and AAAS reports I cited earlier, when over fifty-four percent of the world population reports very serious concern over global warming, it is clear that the CC concept is something many people possess.[13] And when they possess it, they are aware of the implications for CC to disrupt the phenomena they associate with particular places. Another implication of the CC concept is that CC is something for which humanity is collectively responsible. To the extent that this responsibility is for harms that have already occurred and harms that will continue to threaten human communities and ecological processes into the future, climate change has a recognizably *moral* connotation. This implication has special significance for environmental aesthetics which may demand distinctness between moral and aesthetic responses to place. If aesthetic appreciation is regulated by norms of disinterestedness or evaluator detachment, for instance, then appreciation should bracket out the influence of personal, moral or political beliefs. Interestingly, place-based environmental aesthetics may undermine the practicality of disinterestedness as a criterion for judgment. This is because places convey more than aesthetic values, and the aesthetic values may be intermingled with social and cultural ones. As Edward Casey observes in his rich and rewarding reflection on place, place always involves a mixture of the natural and the cultural: 'Implacement is an ongoing cultural process with an experimental edge'.[14] Moreover, a place is *a somewhere* to which human individuals and communities can have a commitment. One could say that places imply care. If so, then Marcia Eaton's advice is fitting for the approach described here. As she enjoins, aesthetics requires us to 'develop ways of using the delight that human beings take in flights of imagination, connect it to solid cognitive understanding of what makes for sustainable environments, and thus produce the kind of attitudes and preferences that will generate the kind of care we hope for'.[15] To this view I submit an emphasis on place in environmental aesthetics clarifies the appropriateness of including care within aesthetic appreciation. The moral connotations of CC only amplify this claim.

The temporality of place is also significant; places are dynamic and in flux – even without the impacts of CC. They exhibit countless characteristics over time. Places are often defined by cultural events or by their significance as conveyors of natural history. Many places bear names from these events just as they do for their aesthetic characteristics. Some places are wild places. Still others are developed places, places occupied by human communities, agricultural places, or places radically shaped by technological factors, all of which are marked by their temporality. As with the moral connotations of place, CC also augments awareness of the dynamism of place. This awareness in turn influences how we imagine ourselves adapting to CC. Although the aesthetic qualities of place may be fairly low on the list of priorities for planning how to adapt to CC, choices about those qualities is not a trivial matter. Among other things, the future places communities develop will reflect aesthetic choices on the part of those who inhabit them. Moreover, the places selected for protection or restoration necessarily will reflect choices to protect or restore environmental aesthetic values in addition to biodiversity or ecosystem integrity. If places have created expectations for aesthetic appreciation owing to their distance removed from humanity's footprint, CC signals a reversal of that pattern.

Concepts and Environmental Aesthetic Appreciation

If it is at all meaningful to suggest that the CC concept is disruptive to the aesthetic values carried by places, it is because it is relevant to the practice of aesthetic appreciation. That is, it would have to factor as a *concept* that influences personal taste and informs judgments about the presence of aesthetic values in particular places. In a relevant essay, Ronald Moore offers a constructive overview of what's at stake conceptually within environmental aesthetics. Moore's discussion starts with a question about aesthetic appreciation of facsimiles of natural objects, such as the glass flowers in Harvard University's Ware Collection of Glass Models of Plants. The issue for Moore is not the evaluator's confusion over the authenticity of the flower. Rather, the question is what is the role of understanding – whether x is a natural specimen or whether x is replica – in shaping aesthetic judgment. For Moore, that role hinges on whether one is a conceptualist or non-conceptualist about aesthetic appreciation. According to Moore, *conceptualists* insist that the objects of aesthetic appreciation must fall under certain categorial schemes. As he explains,

> Thus, the this-and-here item is made intelligible as an example of a given sort. It is by invoking the concept 'sonata' that a certain form of musical composition can be heard for what it *is*, as making sense and being good, bad, or indifferent, as having features that are standard for works of its type and allow us to become aware of the *Gestalt* it shares with other relevantly similar works.[16]

When conceptualism is applied to natural objects, the effect is similar. For the conceptualist, Moore explains, natural history and natural science become the primary means for providing criteria for natural aesthetic evaluation as the sources of 'the true and objective account of nature and its contents'.[17] By contrast, non-conceptualists contend that aesthetic experience of nature is a result of precognitive engagement with natural objects, 'a liberation of reflection from prior conceptual frameworks, so that imagination can gain ascendance over thought'.[18] As Moore acknowledges, both standpoints have much going for them. The conceptualist is able to capture the intuition that understanding – especially scientific knowledge – makes a difference in our aesthetic sensitivity to such phenomena as geological features, sexual dimorphism, rarity, or behaviour. Scientific understanding can even help an aesthetic evaluator overcome visceral repugnance at the features of natural objects, such as a decaying carcass or a violent act of predation. Conversely, non-conceptualists preserve the value of our immediate encounters with natural objects. Yet Moore also points out that as theories of aesthetic experience of nature, both standpoints are limited. Conceptualism leaves aesthetic evaluation too far removed from the qualities of natural objects that stimulate aesthetic experience in the first place, such as their particularity, or uniqueness in standing out against visual or auditory backgrounds. As Moore suggests, 'By being indelibly committed to the cognitive, the categorical, and the regular, science [for the conceptualist] provides no means of illuminating those aspects of our reflection on natural objects that is non-cognitive, particular, or anomalous'.[19] Non-conceptualism, however, invites its own risks of disconnection from nature. Citing Carlson, Moore notes that too much imaginative free play means that nature becomes mysterious, aloof, and alien. For Moore, 'It is a short step from declaring natural beauty ineffable to declaring it unintelligible'.[20]

Moore's own *syncretic* approach attempts to avoid surrendering aesthetic experience either wholly to the free play of the imagination or to the barren abstractions of concepts. It also offers a helpful way to think about the implications of the CC concept for environmental aesthetic appreciation. To limit the vices of conceptualism, Moore urges against over-ascribing scientific understanding to aesthetic evaluators: 'the perspective of science is not the perspective most people bring to the experience of nature, and it is rarely the source of the delight we experience when we enjoy natural beauty'.[21] Evaluators can appreciate environments aesthetically even without the aid of sophisticated concepts. That said, Moore also notes that imagination has to be guided by 'intelligent awareness'. Writing about the experience of observing a bald eagle flying over an urban environment, Moore explains,

> My awareness of background information about the eagle is not like the information about genre and type needed to locate a work of art in its niche and assess it, but more like information about the paint and canvas, or marble, or metal in the tuba, that are instrumental to the artistic production, yet not cognitive requisites for its appreciation.[22]

In other words, even if one lacks scientific understanding of the bald eagle's life cycle or rarity, one's aesthetic appreciation of the eagle is not obviously naïve.

Moore's syncretic approach is most liberal about aesthetic appreciation when he asserts that

> we have to regard the object as situated in a constellation of properties, some aesthetic, some scientific, some political and so on. And some of these properties attach to concepts and others don't. So the best we can do in responding to them is to use those parts of our intelligent awareness that suits each.[23]

One part of our intelligent awareness for Moore is the knowledge that humanity has contributed to the alteration of the meaning of *natural*. As he explains,

> we should admit that, in our modern world, most of what we want to call 'natural' is already, to some degree, human-made. We have carved out the areas we want to leave 'unspoiled', and we have reserved other areas for limited access with the idea that those who see them will get a sense of what nature is really like. Sunsets often look the way they do because of pollution we create. When a great glacier calves, and tons of ice plummet into the sea, part of the job was done by gravity and part by the heat we have been injecting into the atmosphere.... But there is no truly unspoiled world. And there is a natural world right there in the place they left. Clouds come everywhere, as do bugs and weeds.[24]

Noteworthy in this passage is Moore's casual employment of the CC concept in aesthetic appreciation of nature. Moore's injunction here is to set aside concerns about naturalness in order to take in events just as we encounter them. My own effort to shift the discussion of environmental aesthetics to aesthetics of place is sympathetic with this advice to the extent that one can be non-naïve in appreciating something aesthetically without also having to become a scientist or other kind of expert. However, if the constellation of properties of natural objects does include political, scientific, and aesthetic ones, then is it really reasonable to expect those properties not to play a prominent role in aesthetic appreciation? The calving glacier may be both aesthetically awesome and morally disquieting, but is my aesthetic appreciation cancelled, or less theoretically valid, if I don't filter out CC? And what if I know that the glacier is the reason I have travelled to this place because it is part of a protected place?

One way to respond to these concerns is to develop Moore's notion of 'intelligent awareness' more clearly as an aesthetically normative criterion for discernment of the role of the constellation of properties involved in aesthetic appreciation. Emily Brady does something like this in appropriating virtue language to restrict the flightiness of imagination in environmental aesthetics. She recommends that evaluators 'imagine well'. For Brady, this is a way of encouraging evaluators to become practiced at *disinterested* aesthetic engagement which is fundamentally non-practical and non-instrumental.[25] As I argued earlier, the disinterested aim of imaging well would be problematic for place-based aesthetics, which presumes an intermingling of the non-aesthetic and aesthetic values carried by places. Nonetheless, the idea that one could become practiced at discerning the role of concepts or imagination in one's aesthetic practice is not problematic. Thus it should be possible to acknowledge the influence of the CC concept on aesthetic appreciation both as one becomes intelligently aware of its activity and as one reflects on the immediate and imaginary factors that contribute to particular acts of appreciation. For both intelligent awareness and imagining well, appreciation becomes more careful, deliberate, and thorough. The evaluator is directed toward the production of an account of the experiences that induced the judgment, one that in its entirety includes the particular contributions of moral, aesthetic and other beliefs along with the contributions of the imagination.

If this modification of Moore's syncretic approach yields clarity on how the CC concept functions in aesthetic evaluation, it also sheds light on why the CC concept undermines the rhetorical force of environmental aesthetic views wedded to naturalness. Carlson's positive aesthetics is one such view. It is the view that nature is essentially aesthetically good. Science, particularly as the methodological commitment to correctness in describing and explaining phenomena, plays the key role in this awareness because it is one of our direct means of making the natural world intelligible. As Carlson explains,

> a more correct categorization in science is one that over time makes the natural world seem more intelligible, more comprehensible to those whose science it is. Our science appeals to certain kinds of qualities to accomplish this. These qualities are ones such as order, regularity, harmony, balance, tension, conflict,

resolution, and so forth. If our science did not discover, uncover, or create such qualities in the natural world and explain that world in terms of them, it would not accomplish its task of making it seem more intelligible to us; rather, it would leave the world incomprehensible, as any of the various world views which we regard as superstition seem to us to leave it. Moreover, these qualities which make the world seem comprehensible to us are also those which we find aesthetically good. Thus, when we experience them in the natural world or experience the natural world in terms of them, we find it aesthetically good.[26]

The CC concept does not disrupt the aesthetic goodness that occurs as the result of science's discovery of nature's intelligibility. It does, however, entail awareness of the uncertainty of the extent which nature's aesthetic goodness – particularly with respect to terrestrial and aquatic ecology – is now intermingled with humanity's contribution. This quality of the world that science has made more comprehensible to us does not make the aesthetic object obviously aesthetically good. To use an example from earlier, when the tanager signals its presence to rivals and mates, the song may still be beautiful and interesting. The fact that we hear it outside its historical range is scientifically explicable as well. It is found there, as it were, because of physical and environmental conditions that affected its migration. No damage has been done to our aesthetic appreciation of those physical, chemical, ecological, and biological conditions that render the bird's behaviour intelligible. And yet the bird is out of place.

Conclusion: Place Types in the Climate Change Epoch

The upshot of the preceding discussion is that the CC concept amplifies the aesthetically normative features of places. In closing, I wish to offer a partial typology of places to invite consideration of what that amplification looks like. One reason for differentiating places by type is to call attention to the normative pressures that places put on aesthetic appreciation by creating expectations for aesthetic experiences. Sometimes, moreover, these expectations occur as a result of human design; others are expectations derived from the non-anthropogenic features of those places. With respect to the latter, the CC concept may be strongly implicated in an awareness of vulnerability to loss of aesthetic value. For other places, the anticipated effects of CC might not involve loss of environmental aesthetic value at all. A consideration of place types also allows consideration of how place-derived aesthetic expectations may themselves evolve as sensitivities adjust to the features of place in a warming and warmer world.

1 Places valued for their uniqueness in support of wilderness values: national parks and protected wilderness areas.

   Historical fidelity is a key concept in debates about the goals and expectations of ecological restoration.[27] It refers to the aim of restoring a place to the set of qualities it possessed at a particular time or period of its existence. Many parks, conservation areas, and designated wilderness areas are valued because of their unique ecological properties. They also reflect human choices to protect and appreciate those values, often in the face of disruptive threats including tourism and recreation, biotic invasion, and acid rain. Historical fidelity has come under fire as a goal of restoration in large part because of CC. CC undermines the practicality of historical fidelity as a goal of restoration because it makes uncertain the sustainability of a place's historical values. CC implies that the wilderness and other environmental values they possess will be disrupted. In their place may appear other expressions of wilderness values, including aesthetic ones, but these will be marked by resistance to an uninvited human presence rather than as achieved as the aims of restoration or preservation.

2   Places valued as refuges from culture: sacred spaces and sanctuaries.

If the cherished features of a place stem from its apparent separation from other features of our lives, then it is difficult to imagine how these are not disrupted by CC. It stains the countryside with uncertainty: will the grove we planted be here next year, and will the cicadas return to sing in them? Will the beach have all but eroded away? Quiet places and places for refuge, contemplation, prayer, and awe will exist, but CC stands to alter the meaning of those activities.

3   Places that support ecologically significant values: biodiversity and endemism.

To the extent that these values are attached to particular organisms and ecosystems, they are arguably disrupted by the CC concept. Places that support species with high endemism, for instance, are especially vulnerable to new disturbance regimes. The CC concept magnifies the threat to loss of value carried by these places. Yet the CC concept might also induce wonder and curiosity about the future diversity of places. The wildness of a warmed world may be of our own making, but it is still a kind of wildness. Maybe we will be disturbed, concerned, or even unmoved by the characteristics of the species that adapt to the new conditions of places in a warmed world, but perhaps we will also have occasion to marvel at life's inventiveness in the face of anthropogenic climate dynamism.

4   Places that support disturbance regimes: alluvial flood plains, typhoon zones, volcanoes.

Many places are already characterized by their subjection to patterns of disruption. Yet CC implies that episodes of disruption will become more frequent, more powerful, or less predictable. By falling out of historical pattern, systems will lack the resilience to withstand floods, storm, tides, and fire. CC also poses unique threats to ocean systems as waters become increasingly acidic, further weakening their resilience. Their demise with all the values they carry seems imminent in many cases. What will be left in their place is too difficult to imagine. Awareness of imminent loss of value due to CC seems inextricable from aesthetic appreciation of many such places.

5 Home places: farms, towns, neighbourhoods, cities.

The aesthetics of built environments are already diverse and challenging, where aesthetic appreciation is rife with the influence of our technologies, our political life, and cultural imagination, not to mention the intentional aesthetic features of design. Such places, of course, support aesthetic appreciation of their non-designed qualities as well, including appreciation of features of the more-than-human world. The CC concept draws attention to the presence and dynamism of such features. It also invites consideration as to how the built environment may be designed to enhance the presence of those features.

6 Trammelled places: landfills, brownfields, firing ranges, and abandoned commercial zones.

Anyone who has enjoyed David Maisel's aerial photography is aware that aesthetic delight can be encountered in even the most disturbed and polluted environments.[28] Artists like Maisel prepare evaluators to appreciate the aesthetics of places that have lost the aesthetic characteristics of their natural histories. Maisel's imagery is made possible by the high altitude perspective he employs. The relative safety of distance obscures environmental aesthetic disvalues apparent to evaluators on the ground. If CC means that more and more places will become as inhospitable as the polluted lakes and fields in some of Maisel's photographs, perhaps that will make it more difficult to disentangle the values carried by places and our knowledge of what is happening to them from aesthetic appreciation.

Notes

1 Paul Haught wishes to thank Sergio Gallegos, Ned Hettinger, John Fisher, Blažz Mazi, and participants at the Poesis of Peace conference and at the Eleventh Meeting of the International Society for Environmental Ethics for comments on earlier versions of this essay.

2 Charles E. Little, 'A Few Good Woods', in *An Appalachian Tragedy: Air Pollution and Tree Death in the Eastern Forests of North America*, ed. Harvard Ayers, Jenny Hager, and Charles E. Little (San Francisco: Sierra Club Books, 1998), 115.

3 The United Nations Intergovernmental Panel on Climate Change (IPCC) has recently published its fifth report summarizing the latest findings by the climate science community. The tone of this document is dire, as it is for the much more concise position statement from the American Association for the Advancement of Science (AAAS). Both documents suggest that widespread and long-term effects of anthropogenic climate change are confirmed. Both documents contend these effects will persist for several centuries even if carbon dioxide emissions are radically curtailed. See Intergovernmental Panel on Climate Change, 'Summary for Policy Makers', in *Climate Change 2013: The Physical Science Basis. Contribution of Working Group I to the Fifth Assessment Report of the Intergovernmental Panel on Climate Change*, ed. Thomas F. Stocker et al.

(Cambridge: Cambridge University Press, 2013), 27; and American Association for the Advancement of Science, AAAS Climate Science Panel, *What We Know: The Reality, Risks and Response to Climate Change*, Washington, DC: American Association for the Advancement of Science, 2014.

4 Dale Jamieson, *Reason in a Dark Time: Why the Struggle against Climate Change Failed—and What It Means for Our Future* (London: Oxford University Press, 2014), Kindle edition, 3672.

5 I thank John Fisher for this example.

6 This is the view advanced by Allen Carlson in 'Nature and Positive Aesthetics', *Environmental Ethics* 6 (1984): 5–34.

7 Emily Brady, *The Sublime in Modern Philosophy* (Cambridge: Cambridge University Press, 2013), Kindle edition, 4270.

8 See Holmes Rolston III, 'Aesthetic Experience in Forests', in *The Aesthetics of Natural Environments*, ed. Allen Carlson and Arnold Berleant (Peterborough, ON: Broadview, 2004).

9 Rolston, 'Aesthetic Experience in Forests', 190.

10 Allen Carlson, 'Appreciation and the Natural Environment', in *The Aesthetics of Natural Environments*, ed. Allen Carlson and Arnold Berleant (Peterborough, ON: Broadview Press, 2004), 71.

11 Carlson, 'Appreciation and the Natural Environment', 72.

12 Carlson, 'Appreciation and the Natural Environment', 71.

13 Bruce Stokes, Richard Wike and Jill Carle, 'Global Concern about Climate Change, Broad Support for Limiting Emissions', *Pew Research Center: Numbers, Facts and Trends Shaping Your World; Global Attitudes and Trends*, 5 November 2015 (Washington, DC: Pew Research Center, 2015), www.pewglobal.org/2015/11/05/global-concern-about-climate-change-broad-support-for-limiting-emissions/.

14 Edward Casey, *Getting Back into Place: Toward a Renewed Understanding of the Place-World* (Bloomington: Indiana University Press, 1993), 31.

15 Marcia Muelder Eaton, 'Fact and Fiction in the Aesthetic Appreciation of Nature', in *The Aesthetics of Natural Environments*, ed. Allen Carlson and Arnold Berleant, (Peterborough, ON: Broadview Press, 2004), 180.

16 Ronald Moore, 'Appreciating Natural Beauty as Natural', in *The Aesthetics of Natural Environments*, ed. Allen Carlson and Arnold Berleant, (Peterborough, ON: Broadview Press, 2004), 220.

17 Moore, 'Appreciating Natural Beauty as Natural', 220. Moore names Allen Carlson and Marcia Eaton as leading conceptualists.

18 Moore, 'Appreciating Natural Beauty as Natural', 215–6. Moore's list of non-conceptualists includes Arnold Berleant, Emily Brady, and Noël Carroll.

19 Moore, 'Appreciating Natural Beauty as Natural', 224.

20 Moore, 'Appreciating Natural Beauty as Natural', 224.

21 Moore, 'Appreciating Natural Beauty as Natural', 226.

22 Moore, 'Appreciating Natural Beauty as Natural', 227.

23 Moore, 'Appreciating Natural Beauty as Natural', 227.

24 Moore, 'Appreciating Natural Beauty as Natural', 225–6.

25 Emily Brady, 'Imagination and the Aesthetic Appreciation of Nature', in *The Aesthetics of Natural Environments*, ed. Allen Carlson and Arnold Berleant, (Peterborough, ON: Broadview Press, 2004), 165.

26 Carlson, 'Nature and Positive Aesthetics', 29–30.

27 A nice collection of arguments on historical fidelity may be found in Allen Thompson and Jeremy Bendik-Keymer, eds., *Ethical Adaptation to Climate Change: Human Virtues of the Future* (Cambridge: MIT Press, 2012). See especially Ronald Sandler, 'Global Warming and Virtues of Ecological Restoration' and Eric Higgs, 'History, Novelty, and Virtue in Ecological Restoration'.

28 See David Maisel, *The Lake Project*, accessed 29 August 2015, www.davidmaisel.com/.

References

American Association for the Advancement of Science, AAAS Climate Science Panel. *What We Know: The Reality, Risks and Response to Climate Change*. Washington, DC: American Association for the Advancement of Science, 2014.

Brady, Emily. 'Imagination and the Aesthetic Appreciation of Nature'. In *The Aesthetics of Natural Environments*, edited by Allen Carlson and Arnold Berleant, 156–69. Peterborough, ON: Broadview, 2004.

Brady, Emily. *The Sublime in Modern Philosophy*. Cambridge: Cambridge University Press, 2013. Kindle edition.

Carlson, Allen. 'Appreciation and the Natural Environment'. In *The Aesthetics of Natural Environments*, edited by Allen Carlson and Arnold Berleant, 63–75. Peterborough, ON: Broadview, 2004.

Carlson, Allen. 'Nature and Positive Aesthetics'. *Environmental Ethics* 6 (1984): 5–34.

Casey, Edward. *Getting Back into Place: Toward a Renewed Understanding of the Place-World*. Bloomington: Indiana University Press, 1993.

Eaton, Marcia Muelder. 'Fact and Fiction in the Aesthetic Appreciation of Nature'. In *The Aesthetics of Natural Environments*, edited by Allen Carlson and Arnold Berleant, 170–81. Peterborough, ON: Broadview, 2004.

Higgs, Eric. 'History, Novelty, and Virtue in Ecological Restoration'. In *Ethical Adaptation to Climate Change: Human Virtues of the Future*, edited by Allen Thompson and Jeremy Bendik-Keymer, 81–102. Cambridge, MA: MIT Press, 2012.

Intergovernmental Panel on Climate Change. 'Summary for Policy Makers'. In *Climate Change 2013: The Physical Science Basis. Contribution of Working Group I to the Fifth Assessment Report of the Intergovernmental Panel on Climate Change*, edited by Thomas F. Stocker, Dahe Qin, Gian-Kasper Plattner, Melinda M.B. Tignor, Simon K. Allen, Judith Boschung, Alexander Nauels, Yu Xia, Vincent Bex and Pauline M. Midgley, 3–29. Cambridge: Cambridge University Press, 2013.

Jamieson, Dale. *Reason in a Dark Time: Why the Struggle against Climate Change Failed – and What It Means for Our Future*. Oxford: Oxford University Press, 2014. Kindle edition.

Little, Charles E. 'A Few Good Woods'. In *An Appalachian Tragedy: Air Pollution and Tree Death in the Eastern Forests of North America*, edited by Harvard Ayers, Jenny Hager and Charles E. Little, 115. San Francisco: Sierra Club Books, 1998.

Maisel, David. *The Lake Project*. Accessed 29 August 2015. www.davidmaisel.com.

Moore, Ronald. 'Appreciating Natural Beauty as Natural'. In *The Aesthetics of Natural Environments*, edited by Allen Carlson and Arnold Berleant, 214–31. Peterborough, ON: Broadview, 2004.

Rolston, Holmes, III. 'Aesthetic Experience in Forests'. In *The Aesthetics of Natural Environments*, edited by Allen Carlson and Arnold Berleant, 182–96. Peterborough, ON: Broadview, 2004.

Sandler, Ronald. 'Global Warming and Virtues of Ecological Restoration'. In *Ethical Adaptation to Climate Change: Human Virtues of the Future*, edited by Allen Thompson and Jeremy Bendik-Keymer, 63–80. Cambridge, MA: MIT Press, 2012.

Stokes, Bruce, Richard Wike and Jill Carle. 'Global Concern about Climate Change, Broad Support for Limiting Emissions'. *Pew Research Center: Numbers, Facts and Trends Shaping Your World; Global Attitudes and Trends*, 5 November 2015. Washington, DC: Pew Research Center, 2015. www.pewglobal.org/2015/11/05/global-concern-about-climate-change-broad-support-for-limiting-emissions/.

Thompson, Allen and Jeremy Bendik-Keymer, eds. *Ethical Adaptation to Climate Change: Human Virtues of the Future*. Cambridge, MA: MIT Press, 2012.

Index